LIBERTY

— and —

POWER

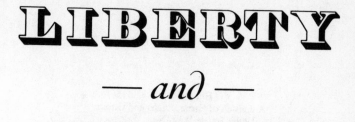

LIBERTY
— and —
POWER

*The Politics of
Jacksonian America*

HARRY L. WATSON

HILL AND WANG
Farrar, Straus and Giroux
NEW YORK

Hill and Wang
A division of Farrar, Straus and Giroux
19 Union Square West, New York 10003

Copyright © 1990 by Harry L. Watson
Distributed in Canada by Douglas & McIntyre Ltd.
Printed in the United States of America
Published in 1990 by Hill and Wang

Library of Congress Cataloging-in-Publication Data
Watson, Harry L.
Liberty and power: the politics of Jacksonian America / Harry L.
Watson ; Eric Foner, consulting editor. —1st ed.
Bibliography: p.
Includes index.
1. United States—Politics and government—1829–1837.   2. Jackson,
Andrew, 1767–1845.   I. Foner, Eric.   II. Title.
E381.W32   1990   973.5'6—dc20   89-7450

Paperback ISBN: 0-374-52196-4

Designed by Jack Harrison

19   20   18

For Adam and Hannah—
my two sturdy republicans

The spirit of improvement is abroad upon the earth. . . . While dwelling with pleasing satisfaction upon the superior excellence of our political institutions, let us not be unmindful that liberty is power; that the nation blessed with the largest portion of liberty must in proportion to its numbers be the most powerful nation upon earth, and that the tenure of power by man is, in the moral purposes of his Creator, upon condition that it shall be exercised to the ends of beneficence, to improve the condition of himself and his fellow-men. While foreign nations less blessed with that freedom which is power than ourselves are advancing with gigantic strides in the career of public improvement, were we to slumber in indolence or fold up our arms and proclaim to the world that we are palsied by the will of our constituents, would it not be to cast away the bounties of Providence and doom ourselves to perpetual inferiority?

PRESIDENT JOHN QUINCY ADAMS
First Annual Message, 1825

In my opinion liberty never was in greater danger; and such, I beleive [*sic*], to be the impression of the coolest and most considerate of our citizens. An issue has been fairly made, as it seems to me, between *power* and *liberty* and it must be determined in the next three years, whether the real governing principle in our political system be the power and patronage of the Executive, or the voice of the people.

VICE PRESIDENT JOHN C. CALHOUN
to General Andrew Jackson, June 4, 1826

Contents

Acknowledgments

My first thanks go to Arthur Wang and Eric Foner, who inspired me to undertake this book and gave me steady support and criticism while I worked on it. I hope the result has justified their expectations.

The Woodrow Wilson International Center for Scholars gave me an excellent head start by providing time and resources at the beginning. The University of North Carolina at Chapel Hill did the same at every stage. By the courtesy of Peter Braestrup and Timothy M. James of *The Wilson Quarterly* and Linda Blanken of *Humanities*, I was able to put my ideas together in useful preliminary fashion. I am sincerely grateful to all of these fine people and institutions.

Along the way, numerous friends have helped me with feedback. I would especially like to thank Mills Thornton, Dick McCormick, Marc Kruman, Sean Wilentz, Leon Fink, Alan Brinkley, and Catherine Clinton. Charles G. Sellers, Jr., and Robert V. Remini have likewise offered heartening encouragement. Long after I left their classrooms, I have continued to benefit from the wisdom of John L. Thomas and Robert H. Wiebe, the two outstanding teachers who first introduced me to the fascinations of the Age of Jackson. In addition to offering inspiration, Bob Wiebe read the penultimate draft and suggested invaluable improvements. If my friends and colleagues do not concur in everything I have said here, I hope it is because they taught me to follow a good example rather than duplicate it.

I owe a special thanks to Professor Catherine A. Maley of the Department of Romance Languages at the University of North Carolina at Chapel Hill. Not many Jacksonian historians are able to consider their subject from the perspective of contemporary France, but I got such an opportunity when Professor Maley invited my wife and me to serve as resident codirectors of the UNC Year at Montpellier. The year in Montpellier brought us many benefits, but I especially appreciate the time it gave me to finish this book. Moreover, while they did not contribute to the writing, the fifty-four students we accompanied to France were like our host country itself: lively, challenging, diverse, and a pleasure to know and learn from. I am also indebted to Dr. Eric E. Palo of the Circulation Department of Davis Library at UNC–CH, who gave me permission to keep library materials for an unusually long period while I was abroad.

Finally, I thank my wife and children. Margot B. Stein read the manuscript with her usual care and critical insight, but her contribution did not start or stop with that favor. Along with Adam and Hannah, she has given me my best lessons in Democratic liberty and Whig communalism.

Chapel Hill, June 1989
H.L.W.

LIBERTY
— and —
POWER

Introduction

IN THE FALL of 1834, a perceptive young Frenchman was visiting New York and witnessed an extraordinary parade. Michel Chevalier had come to the United States to study its system of railroads and canals for his government, but like many foreign visitors to the young country, he was also fascinated by its politics and culture. His visit coincided with the struggle of President Andrew Jackson against the Bank of the United States, headed by the Philadelphia patrician Nicholas Biddle. When the President's friends triumphed in the New York elections of 1834, Jackson's power over the Bank seemed assured, and the parade that Chevalier observed was a celebration of the Democratic Party's victory.

"The procession was nearly a mile long," Chevalier recalled later. "The democrats marched in good order to the glare of torches: the banners were more numerous than I had ever seen in any religious festival; all were in transparency on account of the darkness. On some were inscribed the names of the democratic societies or sections; *Democratic young men of the ninth* or *eleventh ward*; others bore imprecations against the Bank of the United States; *Nick Biddle* and *Old Nick* here figured largely." Other banners featured portraits of Washington, Jefferson, and Jackson himself, some depicting the President as a simple farmer and others showing him as a triumphant general. One marcher carried a live eagle mounted on a pole like a Roman standard. The stream of torchlit signs and faces stretched for as far as the eye could see, and it paused periodically to cheer the homes of Jacksonian leaders or to taunt the captains of the opposition with "three, six, or nine groans."

The visiting French official had never seen anything like this procession; the ordinary European was not even allowed to vote in Chevalier's day and popular demonstrations were regarded by the authorities as potentially seditious. Chevalier likened the parade to the popular religious processions of Catholic countries, but somehow even this comparison seemed inadequate. "These scenes belong to history," the awestruck foreigner concluded. "They are the episodes of a wondrous epic which will bequeath a lasting memory to posterity, that of the coming of democracy."

Other observers were far less favorably impressed. One of these was Philip Hone, Esq., a former mayor of New York and one of its principal merchants. Hone had built his fortune in the preindustrial mercantile economy, but he later invested in new ventures such as coal mines, railroads, canals, banks, and textile mills. Hone retired from business when he turned forty and spent his time in politics and public service and as a patron of theater, arts, and charities. His friends in New York's high society thought Hone worthy of an American title of nobility, but his enemies denounced him before the voters with the slogan "*Down with the aristocracy!*" If the torchlight parade was an emblem of the democratic future, Philip Hone was a symbol of New York's deferential past. Not surprisingly, he was prominent among the anti-Jacksonian leaders who were jeered on the evening of November 5, 1834.

Where the romantic Michel Chevalier had witnessed "a wondrous epic," Hone saw only the "revilings of a mob of midnight ruffians." For months he had been worried by outbreaks of rioting and what he felt were the efforts of Jacksonian leaders to array the poor against the rich, to overthrow natural social distinctions, and to put numbers over talent and property in the direction of the nation. The Democratic victory confirmed his worst anticipations. Blaming the problem on Jackson, Hone cried fervently, "Give us no more Tennessee Presidents!"

Different as they were from one another, Chevalier, Hone, and the crowd of triumphant Democrats had grasped an important truth. A profound transformation in politics was indeed sweeping the American Republic in the years when Andrew Jackson dominated its government. Michel Chevalier's description would prove to be prophetic. The intense political passions that he saw in the thousands of torchlit faces before him and the bumptious assertion of popular rights within government that he read in the vivid banners were injecting a new and more democratic strain into the fabric of American experience. By the Presidential election of 1840, scenes like the New York celebration of 1834 had become indispensable elements of every political contest, and a strident egalitarianism had become the staple of American political rhetoric. Though inequality never disappeared from Jacksonian America, the ethos embodied by the New York marchers became a new and permanent force to reckon with in the life of the United States.

The democratic changes recognized by Chevalier and Hone caught the attention of numerous other observers, among them Alexis de Tocqueville, a French aristocrat who toured the United States in 1831 and 1832 and published an account of what he found that became a classic of its kind. First appearing in 1835, Tocqueville's *Democracy in America* was an exhaustive analysis of social and civic equality in the young Republic that is still combed for its insights into American culture. For Tocqueville, the political parties that dominated American public life had little to recommend them. "All the domestic controversies of the Americans at first appear to be incomprehensible or puerile," he remarked, "and [a stranger] is at a loss whether to pity a people who take such arrant trifles in good earnest or to envy that happiness which enables a community to discuss them." Fundamentally, Tocqueville acknowledged, American political divisions expressed a clash between "aristocratic [and] democratic passions," but he could not take very seriously the specific policy differences that roused a cheering electorate and separated the friends of President Jackson from the supporters of the Bank of the United States.

This book will argue that Tocqueville erred in dismissing the importance of Jacksonian America's political parties. Though the dispute between "aristocratic [and] democratic passions" was real enough, Jacksonian politicians also carried on a serious policy debate about the future of the Republic and the nature of its society and economy. The raucous demonstration that thrilled Michel Chevalier and wakened Philip Hone drew its emotional energy from this fundamental debate.

America had known parties before, but the earlier competition between Federalists and Democratic-Republicans had been amateurish compared to the rivalry between well-established and increasingly sophisticated organizations that came to dominate virtually all aspects of American politics in the 1830s and 1840s. By 1840, party concerns affected the choice of almost every public official, from the President down to the lowliest fence viewer. Political leaders did their best to see that every public question was viewed through the lens of party rhetoric, and voter participation had roughly doubled. Perhaps most important, the Jacksonian Democrats were confronted by an opposition Whig Party that was almost as well organized as their own and nearly as skillful in the arts of popular electioneering. Passions as vehement as those witnessed by Chevalier were enlisted under Whig banners and thrown into clamorous conflict with the Democrats. The party combat that resulted was the single most important fact about American government for decades to come.

Even when the original Jacksonian party system collapsed, another one succeeded it. Political parties have been principal instruments of American governance ever since. Intensified public involvement in politics and the formation of enduring political parties in the government and in the electorate were the two most fundamental elements in the political changes of the Jacksonian era.

American public life had not always been based on these principles. For the Founding Fathers, "republicanism" meant that government rested on the sovereignty of the people and not on the privileges of kings and nobles, but it did not mean that the people would govern directly. Even Thomas Jefferson believed that republican government should remain in the hands of a "natural aristocracy." Distinguished by training, wealth, and family, only these gentlemen would possess the wisdom and virtue necessary to see the common good and act upon it. The task of ordinary voters was to recognize these sages, put them in office, and follow their capable directions. Republican government would thus have democratic features, but the possible excesses of direct democracy would be firmly limited by the power of a stable and enlightened gentry.

For almost a generation, the hopes of the Founding Fathers proved enduring. President followed President in well-appointed succession, with very little popular clamor to disturb the national equilibrium. In Congress and most of the states, political leaders and their followers identified themselves as Federalists or Democratic-Republicans, but while these parties attracted their passionate followers, party structures during the so-called first American party system were not regarded as permanent or beneficial and did not reach deeply into many sectors of the electorate. In many states, Presidential electors were chosen by the state legislatures, and local voters took no active role in the Presidential election at all. Elsewhere, state contests for governor or congressman frequently attracted more voters than the Presidential canvass.

When Democratic-Republican Thomas Jefferson defeated Federalist John Adams in an unusually stormy contest in 1800, many public leaders were frightened, but after a brief period of party tension the election was remembered as the final victory of republicanism over its enemies and not as the harbinger of things to come. The image of George Washington hovered over every President and served as the model of official conduct. Distant and heroic, a statesman and not a politician, the Father of His Country would never have given a stump speech or led a demonstration. His successors tried to cast themselves in the same image and hundreds of lesser representatives followed in their footsteps.

When the United States and Great Britain ratified the Treaty of Ghent and put an end to the War of 1812, a train of events was already in motion that would make the Republic of George Washington obsolete. For the first generation of its independence, the United States had been obsessed with preserving its republican experiment from the danger of internal collapse or foreign attack in the turmoil of the Napoleonic Wars. The year 1815, however, brought peace between the United States and Britain and between France and the European powers. This outcome left most Americans free to turn their attention to the resources of their own continent. Crossing the Appalachian Mountains in massive numbers, they quickly added several new states to the Union. New ideas and inventions in transportation and communication began a process of dramatic economic development. Immigration from Europe resumed, bringing large numbers of newcomers to the United States. An extensive revival of religion swept through Protestant America, intensifying popular piety and leading to a multitude of new religious institutions. Projects for social reform germinated in the new environment of religious benevolence and thousands longed for the imminent perfection of human society under God's guidance.

Suspicious of rapid change, the Founding Fathers had hoped that republican government would rest on a platform of social stability. After 1815, however, economic growth led to new demands on their government that the old structure could barely satisfy. As we will see, ambitious entrepreneurs pressed for government assistance to their projects, but the distribution of subsidies in the form of tariffs and corporate charters led to bitter charges of favoritism, corruption, and betrayal of republican principles. The factory system and its precursors created new social classes of wage earners and employers who found they did not share the common interests that republican theory promised them. An increase in ethnic and cultural diversity at a time of rapid geographical mobility threw strangers together who did not trust one another and frequently came into conflict. These developments led to political demands which no one had anticipated but which had to be addressed.

Most significantly for the long run, economic growth and westward expansion forced the United States to confront the divisive issue of Afro-American slavery. The new industrial economy in England and America had stimulated the growth of a vast Cotton Kingdom in the South. Instead of disappearing, as some had hoped, slavery expanded vigorously and the slaves frightened their masters with three major plotted or actual revolts between 1800 and 1831. Meanwhile, the religious revival stimulated antislavery sentiments in the North and a growing abolitionist movement met furious Southern hostility. The conflict between proslavery and antislavery forces brought out talk of secession in the Missouri crisis of 1820–21 and the nullification crisis of 1832–33 and posed a serious threat to American political stability.

In general terms, it was clear that the combined influence of social and economic change put strains on the older political framework that it could not accommodate. The slavery question was especially troubling to national politicians since it could not be evaded or compromised easily, but the debate over economic development was almost as divisive on the state and local levels. Simple appeals to republican virtue and the common good were no solution to political conflict in these areas, for no one agreed on what those things should mean in practice. The need for some means of resolving these controversies held out an incentive to political innovators who could piece together a more effective political order. Seizing their opportunities, an eager generation of politicians came forward and put together the structure of a second American party system.

As Philip Hone and his opponents both emphasized, President Andrew Jackson was a central figure in this process. Ironically, the seventh President never saw himself as an innovator, but as the restorer of an earlier standard of political service and integrity. On a day-to-day basis, Jackson did little of the humdrum work of party organization, leaving such tasks to his numerous lieutenants. But Jackson's role as the symbolic leader of American political transformation was unsurpassed. To his supporters, Andrew Jackson embodied all that was good and right about the American Republic. An average man by birth, he rose to lead the country by a combination of qualities that historian John William Ward has called "nature, providence, and will." That is to say, he defeated the nation's worst enemies and upheld its highest virtues by an extraordinary combination of natural ability, divine favor, and personal determination. To his enemies, Jackson was just the reverse, a vainglorious nobody without any qualifications for public office, a "military chieftain" who might overthrow the republic and establish a despotism in its place. For these Americans, only the outrages associated with "King Andrew I" could justify the organization of a political party to rival his own.

Instead of debating about slavery, therefore, most political activists of the 1830s and early 1840s were forced to argue about Andrew Jackson himself, a diverting but less explosive controversy. While they also continued to debate the question of economic development, they did so in a political and rhetorical framework that the President and his supporters had either created themselves or had shaped to their own advantage, using the political themes that had cropped up in hundreds of local disputes. Jackson's Administration was therefore the catalyst for a rapid transformation of American politics.

Jackson was also important because he directly addressed the issues that concerned his constituents in terms they could readily understand and spelled out the ideological basis for a new kind of republicanism. He was not a profound or original thinker, but he could express commonplace thoughts with vividness and conviction. His letters and state papers evoked a reverent memory of Washington and his heroic contemporaries, but did so in order to justify a significantly new set of policies and attitudes. More than any of his contemporaries, Jackson could express in his words and his life the linkages between the egalitarian ideology of his age and the near-sacred precepts of the Founding Fathers. The period of his leadership is justly known as the Age of Jackson, not only because he dominated its politics, but also because he dominated the thinking of both his friends and his enemies for most of the period between the end of the War of 1812 and the end of the Mexican War in 1848.

Jackson's message was couched in the popular language of republican political morality. Like his predecessors, the seventh President felt that a divine covenant imposed particular burdens upon the American people. In return for his special favor, God expected Americans "to preserve [liberty] for the benefit of the human race . . . and defend [it] until the end of time." While he warned his countrymen that "eternal vigilance . . . is the price of liberty," Jackson saw the greatest danger to liberty arising from inner decay rather than from external attack. "It is from within," he admonished, "among yourselves—from cupidity, from corruption, from disappointed ambition and inordinate thirst for power—that factions will be formed and liberty endangered." How could moral decay be prevented? Jackson's answer was plain: trust the majority of the people and all will be well. "Never for a moment believe," he insisted, "that the great body of the citizens . . . can deliberately intend to do wrong." Though parasitic minorities—those whom Jackson called "the predatory portion of the community"—might band together for selfish and corrupt purposes, Jackson believed that majorities would never do so. "If they have no higher or better motives to govern them," he reasoned, "they will at least perceive that their own interest requires them to be just to others, as they hope to receive justice at their hands."

For modern readers, Jackson's moralistic phrases tend to obscure the practical implications of what he was saying. In fact, the economic changes of his era generated numerous demands by minority "factions" for tariffs, subsidies, and other special privileges from the government. All the petitioners promised public benefits in return for their private advantages, but Jackson saw their efforts as "corruption" and he had them specifically in mind when he denounced the notion of special privilege. Even worse, in his view, were Northern and Southern agitators of the slavery question, who threatened to tear apart the federal union as they pressed their social theories upon the nation as a whole. Majority rule was thus no platitude in Jackson's day; it was advocated as a controversial alternative to contemporary movements that seemed to threaten the Union itself.

Unlike earlier Presidents, then, Jackson and his followers professed little faith in the benefits of a "natural aristocracy." Like all minorities, even these leaders could become corrupt, so the safest course was to treat all citizens exactly alike and allow the majority to rule. In an 1833 letter, Jackson had called "equality among the people in the rights conferred by government" the "great radical principal of freedom," and he came to view political equality as the cornerstone of the American Republic.

Jackson did not believe that equality could survive on words alone. It would need a determined and perpetual defense by a grand coalition of voters who had more to gain from equality than from legislative favoritism. Jackson thought this grand coalition had first taken shape in the days of Thomas Jefferson and that it had reassembled to save the Republic from corruption by placing himself in the White House. Originally known as the Democratic-Republican Party or sometimes just the Republican Party, this grand coalition was coming to be known in the 1830s as the Democratic Party. Though some of Thomas Jefferson's followers ended up as opponents of Andrew Jackson, Old Hickory continued to believe that he had only revived the Jeffersonian coalition and had not created anything truly new. It was thus one of Jackson's proudest achievements that he had "labored to reconstruct this great Party and bring the popular power to bear with full influence upon the Government, by securing its permanent ascendency." In Jackson's mind, the themes of equality, democracy, and party discipline were intimately bound together.

In Jackson's time and ever afterward, many other Americans have found this line of thinking ironic or even disgraceful. Republican virtue was indispensable, they agreed, but political parties had long been deeply suspect and thousands of Jackson's contemporaries still saw political partisanship as the antithesis of political morality. Jackson himself had expressed ideas of this kind earlier in his career. Writing to President-elect James Monroe in the fall of 1816, Jackson had declared that "now is the time to exterminate the *monster* called party spirit," and he urged the new Chief Executive to select for office "characters most conspicuous for their probity, virtue, capacity, and firmness, without regard to party." By the end of Jackson's Presidency some twenty years later, his opponents had come to wish that the old man had stuck by his earlier opinions. They not only disapproved of political parties in general, but viewed Jackson's own partisan conduct as a particularly deplorable example of the evils that political parties could lead to. When Jackson left office, Philip Hone confided to his diary that the President was a "terrible old man" whose Administration had been "the most disastrous in the annals of the country."

Somewhat unjustly, men such as Hone blamed Andrew Jackson for a wide variety of partisan abuses, including the "spoils system" of appointing officials on the basis of party ties rather than personal qualifications. Despite the President's insistence on the importance of political virtue, his enemies thought of him as opening the floodgates of corruption. Some versions of this judgment have persisted ever since, and Andrew Jackson has continued to be one of the most controversial U.S. Presidents.

Old Hickory's enemies quickly found that they could not oppose his party successfully without copying his tactics. By 1840 the Jacksonian Democrats were confronted by the Whigs, an organized opposition party. The Whigs were so successful in adapting to the new order that in 1840 they beat the Democrats at their own game and defeated President Martin Van Buren's bid for reelection with solid party organization and fervent charges that the New Yorker had become an "aristocrat." Replete with party nominating conventions, campaign songs, torchlight parades, and overblown electioneering rhetoric, the Presidential campaign in 1840 set the standard for all the elections to follow. Michel Chevalier's prediction had been correct: the parade he witnessed in 1834 had represented the future. The decorous but exclusive jousting of the gentry had disappeared and a more democratic politics had replaced it.

The democratic developments of the 1830s and 1840s did not change as many things as some supporters hoped and others feared. The party system did not pit monolithic blocs of rich and poor citizens against each other, for wealthy men led both parties and men of average means comprised the majority in both. Though economic differences between the parties were significant, they were also subtle and tended to vary by locality. Direct popular democracy, moreover, was never a reality in Jacksonian America. There was no burst of complete social or political equality then or later, and the new political institutions clearly led to a form of party elitism that could be as stultifying as the system it replaced. "Jacksonian democracy" did liberate ordinary white men from many of the deferential constraints of eighteenth-century political culture, and it gave their feelings and opinions a new respect in the public sphere. At the same time, the rise of new party institutions tended to channel popular democratic energies in conservative directions, giving recognition to popular feelings while blunting their potentially disruptive consequences. Even at its best, therefore, Jacksonian politics expressed a contradictory version of democracy.

At its worst, moreover, "Jacksonian democracy" was not democratic at all. When Old Hickory left office, almost 2.5 million black Americans were slaves. About 150 of these slaves were the personal property of Andrew Jackson, and the President had no sympathy whatsoever with contemporary efforts to free them. In almost every state, free blacks lacked the right to vote and suffered severe legal and informal restrictions on their other rights as well. Everywhere, North and South, blacks faced an implacable racial prejudice from whites. American Indians confronted a similar hostility, and the President made it his special mission to remove the Eastern Indians from their tribal lands. White men gained rights in Jacksonian America, but men of color lost them. Many historians would argue that these two processes were deeply intertwined, as white men used racist assumptions about the proper qualifications for citizenship to justify their own aspirations and deny those of nonwhite Americans.

Jacksonian equality did not apply to women, either. In every state, women were denied the right to vote and hold office. Married women could not own property or sign contracts because the law submerged their identities in the persons of their husbands. Divorce was almost impossible, especially for wives. Women were routinely barred from higher education and most responsible professions. Disseminated from pulpits and ladies' magazines, a cloying sentimentality ruled that the "true woman's" place was confined to her home and her church. Early American feminists struggled against this treatment, but they received derisive dismissal from the friends of Andrew Jackson.

The appeal of Jacksonian ideology was nevertheless contagious and appealed to those who enjoyed the least of its rewards. When feminists looked for an issue that would most effectively dramatize their demand for full gender equality, they met at the first women's rights convention in 1848 and called for the right to vote exactly as their brothers did. When blacks protested their condition in antebellum America, they called for the abolition of slavery in the South and the extension of political rights to free blacks in the North. When the Cherokee Indians fought back against expulsion from their ancient territories, they adopted a written republican constitution and began to conduct themselves like other American politicians. Nothing testifies so effectively to the strength of Jacksonian ideals as their power to inspire their victims as well as their beneficiaries.

The era of Jacksonian politics thus brought new ideas and enduring institutions to the United States. President Jackson thought of himself as reestablishing an older standard of perfection, but the means he used to return to the past brought irreversible changes. Early in his second term, Jackson wrote: "If only I can restore to our institutions their primitive simplicity and purity, can only succeed in banishing those extraneous corrupting influences which tend to fasten monopoly and aristocracy on the constitution and to make the Government an engine of oppression to the people instead of the agent of their will, I may then look back to the honors conferred upon me, with feelings of just pride—with the consciousness that they have not been bestowed altogether in vain." Despite the President's longing to reclaim the "primitive . . . purity" of the Founding Fathers, the party structures and egalitarian rhetoric that he and his supporters introduced were very different from the intentions of George Washington and could not have been possible were it not for the fact that Washington's America was disappearing rapidly in the 1820s and 1830s.

The Age of Jackson was also the age of steam and iron, an age of complex developments in the economy and larger society. Many Americans looked upon these changes optimistically, confident that new technology and a new society would bring wealth to all and fulfillment of republican ambitions. Others were not so sure and wondered how their own liberties would survive in a world overshadowed by the power of distant institutions and monopolies. Competing visions of the future jostled uneasily in Jacksonian America. Citizens were acutely aware that government could lend a decisive hand to the forces of change, or it could try its best to reverse the tide, and every election became an urgent referendum on the character of the future. "Jacksonian democracy" and the political party system it inspired grew up in this atmosphere of social and economic confrontation.

— 1 —

The Great Body of the People

A TRAVELER in 1815 who looked for the farthest western settlement of the United States of America might well have set his sights on the Boon's (or Boone's) Lick country of north central Missouri. Daniel Boone, the celebrated pioneer of Kentucky, had given his name to the place near the end of his life, when he and his sons had come there to make salt. Boone had found rich, rolling prairie, interspersed with numerous streams and fine stands of timber. Game abounded for the hunter and fertile bottomlands promised ample harvests from cornfields and vegetable gardens. Following the War of 1812, settlers "came like an avalanche," recalled John Mason Peck, a frontier Baptist missionary. "Caravan after caravan passed over the prairies of Illinois, crossing the 'great river' at St. Louis, all bound to the Boone's Lick."

In the early years of Boon's Lick, the male settlers dressed in skins and ate with their hunting knives. Their wives and children did without schools and churches and comfortable society while the energies of everyone were thrown into the task of erecting log cabins, clearing fields, and creating a new community. "The men were all heroes and the women heroines," marveled one chronicler, foreshadowing a long future tradition of popular admiration. "They are robust, frank, and daring," wrote another observer. "Taught by the hardships . . . to depend . . . upon their own individual exertions . . . , they . . . feel true independence flowing from a conviction that their own physical exertions are equal to every call." Poised between the Indian cultures farther west and the jaded civilization of the Atlantic seaboard, the pioneers of Boon's Lick were acting out a recurrent national dream of heroic experience and frontier valor.

A thousand miles to the east, the world of Manhattan Island was very different. New York City did not extend north of Fourteenth Street in 1815, but 100,000 people packed its teeming wards, making it the largest city in America. A forest of masts lined the wharves; ships of every flag brought the commodities of Europe, Asia, and Latin America to trade for the cotton, tobacco, and foodstuffs of the United States. Banks and merchants' counting-houses crowded Wall Street and Pearl Street; warehouses bulged with goods; and thousands of wagoners, porters, and stevedores jostled in the streets as they tugged and hauled the commerce of a continent. Inside the shops that lined the less prestigious streets, skilled artisans plied their trades, carefully fashioning by hand both the articles of everyday consumption and the luxuries demanded by opulence. New York was a city of paupers, laborers, artisans, and merchants; it was the scene of intense activity, soaring hopes, sturdy pride, and desperate misery. Like Boon's Lick, New York was a frontier, for it lay on the edge of an immense expansion of commerce and manufacturing that would transform the daily lives of millions. This frontier would bring America to a very different future from the vision of simple independence envisioned by Missouri pioneers.

Between the extremes represented by New York and Boon's Lick, the American traveler of 1815 would have found a large and diverse country. The nation's territory stretched from the Atlantic coast to the crest of the Rocky Mountains and from the Great Lakes to the Gulf of Mexico. It stretched even farther after 1819, when Florida was acquired from Spain. There were 8.4 million Americans in 1815, and their numbers were growing rapidly; by 1840, the population would more than double, to 17.4 million. About 15 percent of that total were black slaves who were concentrated in the most fertile and accessible farming regions of the South. White Americans comprised a variety of ethnic groups, including Germans in Pennsylvania and Dutch in New York, Scotch-Irish everywhere in the backcountry, and English along the seacoast. Beginning in the 1830s, large numbers of Irish immigrants began arriving in the Eastern ports and took laboring jobs in cities and construction projects. Many of these new settlers were Roman Catholics, but most Americans were Protestant. Despite the growth of New York and the other northeastern cities, most Americans still lived on the farm. Only 7.2 percent of the population lived in towns or cities of more than 2,500 persons.

Many rural Americans in 1815 followed a basic pattern of life that had not changed dramatically since the early days of colonization. Most heads of household owned a farm of 50 to 200 acres or soon expected to acquire one. Their tools were heavy and crude, and most families concentrated on raising food for themselves and their animals. They devoted a smaller portion of their time to preparing a small surplus to exchange for goods that they could not make. Trade often consisted of barter, either with village storekeepers and artisans or with the merchants of a more distant town. At all times, land and the independence it provided were the central features of the rural family's life.

In the more recently settled portions of the United States, this pattern persisted undisturbed in the first decades of the nineteenth century, but demographic pressures were subverting it in some older sections of the East. By the early nineteenth century, many New England farms had become too small for parents to divide among their heirs, and a new generation of young people had appeared who could not look forward to a landed inheritance. Casting about for alternatives, they sought out urban opportunities or looked for fresh lands to the west. Not everyone succeeded in the search for a personal "competence," and a permanent population of landless laborers now found themselves working as hired help on the farms of others or as unskilled operatives in the early factory system. As the Age of Jackson dawned, in other words, growth was accompanied by serious and increasing social and economic inequality.

The farmer who wished to protect his independence in this environment faced increasing pressure to make fewer acres more productive. Agricultural reformers increasingly urged farmers to put aside old-fashioned notions of self-sufficiency, to farm scientifically, and to devote their energies to large-scale production of cash crops for sale in urban or international markets. Prosperous farmers in the most fertile sections of the Northeast embraced this advice, using tenants and hired hands to produce wheat, wool,

fruit, vegetables, or dairy products for city customers. These farmers had adopted a system of capitalist agriculture, but many ordinary husbandmen were suspicious of such practices. Those who
gambled on the new methods could lose their farms if short-term
profits were insufficient to cover their newly acquired debts. Even
when an individual farmer preferred subsistence methods, he could
be forced to change along with his neighbors if their transition to
a cash economy left him without partners for the more traditional
forms of exchange. The movement to a new farm economy was
therefore slow. One historian has estimated that no more than 20
percent of farm products were sold off the farm in 1820 and the
amount did not reach 40 percent until 1870. In time, however, the
pressure grew to adopt new methods, as marginal farmers failed
and the survivors faced the choice of changing or going under.

Every rural community also held a variety of artisans whose
skills enabled them to specialize as blacksmiths, wheelwrights, tai-
lors, shoemakers, carpenters, and so forth. Farmers also needed
water-powered mills for grinding grain, sawing logs, and "fulling"
homespun cloth before it was made into clothing. Small towns
were home for rural doctors, lawyers, teachers, and ministers.
Storekeepers in these villages supplied country people with essential items such as iron, salt, and gunpowder that could not be made
locally, and also stocked items such as sugar, coffee, tea, and fancy
fabrics that could add variety to the drabness of homegrown subsistence. Stores like these were the centers of a growing cash economy that would eventually replace the practices of self-sufficiency,
but the extent of the market economy should not be overestimated
for the decades just preceding Jackson's Presidency. Outside the
major cities, storekeepers accepted "cash or country produce" for
their goods and even rural tradesmen did their business on the
basis of local bartering. Artisans, merchants, and professionals
frequently combined their occupations with farming, so that it is
sometimes difficult to see where the commercial economy began
and self-sufficient agriculture left off.

The Southern plantation was the great exception to the general
rule of mostly noncommercial farming. Most Southern farms produced enough food for their inhabitants, but ever since tobacco
had saved the English colony at Jamestown, Southern planters had
depended on market crops such as tobacco, rice, sugar, and, increasingly, cotton. The most successful Southern farmers used

black slaves to cultivate their cash crops, and blacks outnumbered whites by as much as nine or ten to one in the most fertile regions of the slaveholding states. The wealthiest whites owned hundreds of bondsmen, but half the masters owned five slaves or fewer, while two thirds of white families owned none. In the areas where transportation was poor and cash crops were unprofitable, slaves were rare and the nonslaveholding white farmers lived in a manner roughly similar to that of their counterparts in the North.

Southern exports created the demand for a thriving shipping industry based in the Northern port cities. Northern banks and mercantile houses did good business by financing and marketing the annual cotton crop. Profits from the cotton trade fueled the growth of the national economy and laid the basis for the industrial expansion that was beginning to occur in well-favored areas of the North. Unlike most nonslaveholders, Southern planters were deeply enmeshed in a world of credit transactions and complex international trade.

Southern slaves did every kind of labor, from the crafting of fine furniture to the managing of other slaves, but most of them did house and field work on small-to-medium-sized plantations. They usually worked from dawn to dark, six days a week, and longer during harvest and on special occasions. Field hands usually got a rest for a couple of hours in the hottest part of the day during summer and all slaves normally enjoyed a week's holiday between Christmas and New Year's Day. Otherwise they were kept busy plowing, planting, hoeing, harvesting, and preparing the fields for the next season's crop. Slaves were valuable property; masters whose fields were losing fertility could earn important extra income by the regular sale of surplus slaves to the labor-hungry regions of the Southern cotton frontier. Even masters who preferred not to sell their human chattels sometimes had no choice when forced to settle a debt or liquidate an estate. Every slave faced the possibility of being sold, and the separation from family and friends that often resulted was one of the heaviest burdens slaves were forced to bear.

The pain that slavery caused was obvious to most detached observers of the South's "peculiar institution," but Southern whites defended the system by arguing that blacks were an inferior race, fit for nothing else, and indifferent to the trauma that enslavement would inflict on a white person. They even argued that slavery made Southern society superior to the North's, by freeing ordinary whites from the necessity of menial labor and raising all whites to the position of true social and political equality that they deserved, as freeborn Americans. Masters liked to think of themselves as decent people whose power was based on justice and morality, so they often thought of their chattels as children and preferred to manage them by offering rewards for good service and threatening the withdrawal of privileges from slackers. Ultimately, however, the master's authority rested on force, and the whip was an indispensable element in efficient plantation management. "Thirty-nine lashes on the bare back, well laid on," was an all too familiar entry in plantation and court records throughout the slaveholding states.

Slaves defended themselves against the dehumanizing effects of bondage by a variety of means. Slaves protested their condition by breaking tools, feigning sickness, and running away. Slaves had virtually no rights of any kind and their marriages were not recognized by the law, but most slaves lived in family groups and relied on one another for emotional support under severe oppression. They drew on a rich Afro-American cultural heritage and their own variant of Protestant religion as sources of solace, solidarity, and release. When these forms of resistance seemed insufficient, there was always the possibility of revolt. Major slave conspiracies were crushed in Richmond in 1801 and in Charleston in 1822, and terrifying rumors of small-scale uprisings periodically swept through the white communities of the South. Finally, in 1831, a violent plot was actually put into effect, as Nat Turner and a small group of fellow slaves swept through the countryside of Southampton County, Virginia, killing some fifty-seven white men, women, and children before succumbing to an overwhelming counterforce. Whites retaliated with a bloodbath in which a hundred or so blacks were summarily murdered, but the horror of slave rebellion remained an ever-present source of Southern white anxiety.

The dynamics of slave society changed considerably in the aftermath of the War of 1812. Before 1815, powerful Indian tribes had blocked white expansion into the Old Southwest, the territory now comprising the states of Alabama and Mississippi. This territory contained the finest cotton soils in the world, and Andrew Jackson's victories over the Creeks and their British allies had opened it to American settlement. The restoration of trade with Europe gave an immense boost to the price of cotton, and British buyers were soon paying 25 or 30 cents a pound, double the wartime level. A thirst for Deep South lands struck the worn-out plantation districts of the Upper South like an epidemic. *"The Alabama Feaver* rages here with great violence," wrote one North Carolina planter in 1817, "and has *carried off* vast numbers of our Citizens."

Thronging the southwestern land offices, eager planters and speculators drove the price of cotton lands high above the official minimum price of $2.00 per acre, to $4.00 or as much as $25.00 an acre. Even the minimum price was more than many squatters could pay, and only the presence of U.S. marshals prevented the outbreak of violence between the district land officers and the poor white families who had settled on choice tracts in the absence of legal title. Left with no recourse, the squatters departed to the cheaper and less fertile districts of north Alabama and the Mississippi hill country and nursed their grievances against the "aristocrats" who had seized the jewels of the emergent Cotton Kingdom. Savoring their success, however, the lucky purchasers quickly brought in thousands of slaves from Virginia and the Carolinas and put them to work transforming forest and canebrake into cotton fields. In 1810, the U.S. Census found 40,000 people in the territory that became Alabama and Mississippi, not counting Indians. Ten years later, the two states together held 132,000 white inhabitants and 118,000 slaves. The land that would later become the Confederate States of America was beginning to fill out its boundaries.

The boom in southwest cotton lands would not have been possible without a series of prior changes in the international textile industry. Beginning in the eighteenth century, British inventors had developed new and faster machines for twisting cotton fiber into yarn and, later, for weaving it into cloth. These new inventions lowered the price of cotton cloth and contributed to a dramatic increase in demand for raw cotton. In 1793, after Eli Whitney invented the cotton gin, large-scale cultivation of the staple became practical and the industry began to grow rapidly. The once-languishing Southern economy began to revive as planters shifted to cotton culture, and the institution of slavery got a new lease on life. American trade with Britain halted in the years prior to and during the War of 1812, but capitalists in the Northern states took advantage of the lull to strengthen the infant textile industry of

New England. When peace came and victory over the Indians opened up the southwestern frontier, the "Alabama Feaver" swept the South.

The early Industrial Revolution had far-reaching implications for the South, but the impact of new technology was not limited to the cotton states. The quickening pace of business activity in the early nineteenth century created a demand for new and faster means of transporting goods throughout the United States, where the common roads were so bad in 1815 that it cost as much to ship a ton of freight across the Atlantic Ocean as to haul the same cargo across thirty miles of inland highway. A U.S. Senate committee reported angrily that "a coal mine may exist in the United States not more than ten miles from valuable ores of iron and other materials, and both of them be useless until a canal is established between them, as the price of land carriage is too great to be borne by either." Subsistence farmers could get along easily enough with the existing system, since they hauled relatively little and traveled only when there was nothing else to do, but the men who wished to tap new streams of wealth needed something better. Outside the cotton South, therefore, the new economy touched Americans most directly through the promotion of improved transportation.

Early experiments with paved turnpikes had little success because travelers found ways of circumventing the tollgates. Water transportation was preferable, and shippers were very interested when Robert Fulton succeeded in taking the first practical steamboat up the Hudson River in 1807. Steamboats were quickly adapted to the western rivers as well, and the stern-wheeler loaded with cotton bales became a familiar sight on the Mississippi and other Southern waterways. Oceangoing steamers followed the development of rivercraft, and soon the science of steam navigation had revolutionized the process of getting from one place to another.

Steamboats could not go where rivers did not run, and many ambitious promoters thought that canal construction was the answer. Canals had long been used in Britain to transport coal and grain; Americans had experimented with them as early as the 1790s. The canal movement got its greatest boost, however, when the state of New York followed the leadership of Governor DeWitt Clinton and began the construction of the great Erie Canal from the Hudson River at Albany to the waters of Lake Erie at the village of Buffalo. The canal was a tremendous technical and financial gamble. It would traverse 363 miles of wilderness and no one could be sure how much it would cost, but Clinton was positive that the technical problems could be solved.

Fortunately for canal supporters, DeWitt Clinton was right. Beginning on July 4, 1817, the vast construction project inched west along the Mohawk Valley. The first portion was opened in 1819, and revenue exceeded all previous expectations. Construction was completed in 1825 and crowned by a ceremony in which Clinton emptied a barrel of water from Lake Erie into the harbor of New York City. The Erie Canal created a water highway from the Great Lakes to the Atlantic and opened the vast interior of the North American continent to commercial exploitation. Later, a network of feeder canals would bring commercial opportunities to the remotest corners of the Empire State.

Other states hastened to copy New York's example, for the merchants of rival cities were hardly resigned to the commercial supremacy of Manhattan. A mania for canals briefly gripped politicians and businessmen in Pennsylvania, Ohio, Indiana, and elsewhere, leading states and private companies to build over three thousand miles of canal between 1816 and 1840, at a cost of $125 million. Unfortunately for New York's rivals, the Erie Canal's imitators never matched the revenues of the original. Overextended states were almost bankrupted by the indebtedness incurred in canal building, and others were severely frightened by close brushes with financial calamity. Canal building virtually halted after a serious recession began in 1837, but the search for cheap transportation did not.

The ideal solution had appeared in the late 1820s. Mineowners had already introduced the idea of cars rolling on tracks to carry ore, and engineers had devised many new uses for the steam engine. When the tracks were taken out of the mines and a steam engine was harnessed to pull cars along them, the railroad was born. The first working locomotive appeared in England in 1825, and Americans were quick to see its possibilities. Railroads could be built almost anywhere. They did not need a large supply of water and they did not freeze in the winter. American cities that lacked the geographical basis for a canal system quickly adopted railroads as a substitute. Baltimore merchants began construction of the Baltimore & Ohio Railroad in 1828; Charleston completed a line in 1833 that connected it with the Savannah River valley. Boston was not far behind, and soon there were railroad schemes afoot in virtually every state. By 1840 railroad mileage slightly exceeded the length of the canal system and by 1850 more than doubled it.

Until the development of the automobile in the twentieth century, no form of transportation caught the imagination of the American people like the railroad. Michel Chevalier captured their feelings vividly. "The American has a perfect passion for railroads," the French visitor noted. "He loves them . . . as a lover loves his mistress." Americans not only appreciated the railroad's practical advantages, Chevalier wrote, but "their supreme happiness consists in that speed which annihilates time and space." Sober American businessmen competed furiously for railroad stock, railroad charters, and railroad rights-of-way. By 1860 a basic railroad network overlay most of the country east of the Mississippi.

Historians have used the term "transportation revolution" to describe the introduction of new technology for moving things and people and to emphasize its profound impact on American society. During the antebellum years, America became a highly mobile nation. Historians who have studied the population of Boston between 1830 and 1860 have found that the majority of household heads left the city between one census year and the next. In any given year, almost one Bostonian in three changed address within the city. Similar figures appear in studies of other towns. Some rural neighborhoods were just as unstable. Alexis de Tocqueville quickly observed that the earliest migrants to the western frontier were often emigrants from states that were still not a generation old. "These men had left their first fatherland to better themselves," he concluded in 1835. "They leave the second to do better still; they find prosperity almost everywhere, but not happiness. For them desire for well-being has become a restless, burning passion which increases with satisfaction. . . . To start with, emigration was a necessity for them; now it is a sort of gamble, and they enjoy the sensations as much as the profit."

The technological changes that revolutionized American transportation had a similar impact on communications. The number of post offices increased from three thousand in 1815 to over eight thousand in 1830. As steamboat and railroad schedules became more reliable, mail moved as rapidly as people and goods, and the price of a long-distance letter dropped from twenty-five cents in 1816 to three cents in 1851. Oceangoing steam packets brought news about foreign prices and business conditions more rapidly than ever, integrating the United States yet more fully into the international economy.

Improved communications quickly affected the popular press. The United States had the highest per capita newspaper circulation in the world; almost every village turned out a four-page weekly sheet of advertisements, political commentary, and reprinted news reports. But a newspaper cost the workingman six cents a copy, or about a week's wages for an annual subscription, until the introduction of the rotary steam press in 1830. Soon afterward, the "penny press" hit the streets of America's largest cities, offering juicy stories of mayhem and scandal for only one cent a copy. Imitating the scandal sheets, serious journalist Horace Greeley followed up with the *New York Tribune* in 1841, providing sophisticated news coverage for the same low price. Within two months, eleven thousand New York readers were buying the *Tribune*'s daily edition, while a weekly version later sent Greeley's views across the nation. Other journalists were quick to imitate Greeley's success, so that soon America faced an information explosion. The same technology also made it possible to flood the mails with religious tracts, political broadsides, abolitionist propaganda, or testimonials to patent medicine. Anyone with a message and modest capital could now bypass established local leaders and address himself directly to the ordinary reader. The Communications Revolution was giving birth to popular mass culture.

Canals, railroads, and newspapers intensified the transformation of the American countryside. The "prices current" column of every weekly journal linked the average farmer or planter to market conditions in his favorite faraway port. Commercial farming became more feasible for those who had the capital and the inclination to risk it. Machine-made goods became less expensive and many farmers proved willing to buy what the storekeeper had to offer. Within twenty-five years of the opening of the Erie Canal, the home manufacture of woolens had collapsed in the counties immediately adjacent to it, as farm families put aside their looms and spinning wheels and sampled the products of the early textile industry. Their purchases required cash, and Mohawk and Gen-

esee Valley farmers began to specialize in raising wheat for sale
to the flour millers of Rochester instead of insisting on the virtues
of homespun cloth. A similar process led Henry David Thoreau's
neighbors in Concord, Massachusetts, to throw themselves into
the production of milk and vegetables for the nearby Boston market, much to that philosopher's disgust. Similar opportunities appeared in other rural neighborhoods with easy access to rivers,
canals, or railroads.

Some historians have begun to describe the diverse economic
changes in American life after 1815 as a "Market Revolution," for
these changes included much more than new developments in
transportation and communication. The farmer who began to reduce production of food crops for his family in favor of staples he
could sell was following the signals of a new international market,
not simply responding to the availability of transportation. So was
the manufacturer who replaced skilled workers with a new machine, or a merchant who changed his traditional way of doing
business to attract new customers. These numerous shifts in daily
life were influenced by the new technology of transportation and
communication, but not limited to them. At bottom, they depended on actions, taken voluntarily or under duress, by millions
of economic actors who began to live their lives according to the
shifting signals of prices, hoping always to maximize profit in an
economy based on buying and selling. The Market Revolution was
not the birth of capitalism itself—that had happened much earlier—but it did intensify the impact of capitalism on the lives of
ordinary Americans.

The effects of the Market Revolution were far from uniform.
Economic historians have estimated that the opportunities generated by canals did not extend more than forty miles on either
side of their banks, leaving large numbers of Americans outside
the range of their influence. Even when transportation was available, it did not benefit everyone. Subsistence farmers who did not
succeed at the risky game of commercial agriculture could lose
their farms and family independence, even while more fortunate
players were riding the wave of success. As a result, the competing
pulls of relative self-sufficiency and wholesale commitment to the
market remained a source of tension in rural life throughout the
antebellum period.

The allure of the Market Revolution was especially powerful in the cities and towns of Jacksonian America. Foreign travelers observed a quickening of business enterprise almost everywhere they visited. The Englishwoman Frances Trollope lived in Cincinnati from 1828 to 1830 and felt repelled because "every bee in the hive is actively employed in search of that honey of Hybla, vulgarly called money; neither art, science, learning, nor pleasure can seduce them from its pursuit." Michel Chevalier noted the same thing on his travels, though he liked America much more than Mrs. Trollope did. "Nowhere in the world is everybody so regularly and continually busy as in Pittsburgh," he marveled. "I do not believe there is on the face of the earth, including the United States, . . . a single town in which the idea of amusement so seldom enters the heads of the inhabitants. . . ." Hezekiah Niles, the editor of *Niles' Weekly Register*, the era's most popular weekly magazine, captured the same spirit in a famous phrase when he spoke of "the almost *universal ambition to get forward*" that gripped America in 1815. Niles's comment had little meaning for traditional farmers and artisans, but it was particularly true of the urban and middle-class citizens who subscribed to his publication.

The stepped-up pace of urban America had a special impact on the manufacturing sector of the economy, particularly among the masters, journeymen, and apprentices who had fashioned the ordinary articles of daily use in the late eighteenth and early nineteenth centuries, before the full onset of the Transportation Revolution. Traditionally, the typical artisan or "mechanic" learned his trade as an apprentice, bound while a teenager to serve an established master in exchange for his maintenance and training. After a term of years, the apprentice became a journeyman, free to seek employment from any master and paid in wages by the day or by the piece. Apprentices and journeymen frequently boarded with their master's family, worshipping with him in family prayer, and subject to his authority as head of the household. The typical journeyman hoped to save his wages and purchase his own shop someday in order to set up as a master in his own right. Not all of them did so, but those who succeeded stood as credible models of self-improvement for every aspiring apprentice. Because they were essential to the larger life of the community yet followed no one's orders, master mechanics enjoyed substantial respect in their towns and considered a substantial role in urban politics as no more than their due.

Close personal ties between master and apprentice were a model for social relations throughout the preindustrial city. Even when they did not share one roof, rich, poor, and middling Americans frequently shared the same neighborhoods. The homes of the wealthy fronted on the main streets while the tenements of the poor were tucked into alleys behind them. Master mechanics and merchant princes spoke frequently of their moral obligations to their dependents and expected a respectful deference to their claims for social, political, and moral leadership. Physical proximity did not take the sting out of poverty and it subjected the poor to continual surveillance from their "betters," but it also emphasized the personal dimension of economic and social power.

New means of transportation and new sources of credit disrupted these older relationships and opened new opportunities for ambitious masters and middlemen. Instead of waiting to make a new suit or a pair of shoes for each customer who ordered one, well-connected individuals could buy large quantities of cloth or leather on credit and arrange for production of consumer goods in bulk. Instead of depending on one master craftsman, for example, who measured the customer, cut the materials, and stitched them together, the capitalist could insist on standard sizes, break up each job into its component tasks, and assign each to a different, poorly skilled worker, none of whom could demand the high wages of a master tailor or shoemaker. Long before the invention of the sewing machine, mass-produced garments or shoes could be shipped to distant consumers—Western farmers, urban laborers, or Southern slaves—much more cheaply and profitably than the old master craftsman could have done on an individual basis. The practice was called domestic production or the putting-out system because the work was "put out" to employees who worked in their homes and were paid by the piece. The system was first devised for textiles, clothing, and shoes, but consumer goods of all descriptions were being produced in urban garrets and beside rural firesides throughout the Jacksonian North. Business would never be the same.

The implications were serious for workers. In the eighteenth century, master mechanics controlled their trades and even the humblest apprentice could hope to own his own shop someday. The new system brought increased productivity but concentrated power and profits into fewer hands. The greatest share went to the capitalists who owned the raw materials and controlled access to markets. Competition with the larger firms put the little shops out of business, and thousands of independent artisans became permanent wage earners instead. The ordinary journeyman was increasingly stripped of his skill, his independence, and his standing in the community. It was a bitter pill for many.

In the textile industry, early factory owners carried new production methods a step further. In 1813, a group of wealthy investors known as the Boston Associates started a new mill at Waltham, Massachusetts, which combined the spinning, weaving, and finishing of cloth in the same operation. The new company also benefited from unified marketing procedures, heavy capitalization, and skilled professional management. The Boston Associates soon built more mills at Lowell in 1822 and Chicopee in 1823, and there they perfected another feature that made their experiment quite famous. Instead of depending on local families, the management recruited young women from all over New England to serve as the new labor force. The "Lowell girls," as they were called, lived under strict moral supervision in company-owned boardinghouses and received relatively high wages for an average of seventy-three hours of labor per week. Standards of education and culture were high, for somehow the women found time to attend lectures and church activities and to produce a polished literary magazine, *The Lowell Offering*. The typical female operative stayed at Lowell for several years, tried to save some money, and then returned home to marry or to take up some other occupation. The pressure of business conditions eventually brought wage cuts and industrial strife to Lowell, but during the 1820s and 1830s the village was the center of American textile production and inspired other groups of manufacturers to adapt their business to integrated machine production. The factory system was still in its infancy as late as 1850, but to many observers, Lowell's success implied that a disciplined industrial labor system could be the logical culmination of economic change in Jacksonian America.

While social and economic change was thrusting some downward into the ranks of a new class of permanent wage laborers, the same process was elevating other citizens. In addition to the wealth earned for its owners, every new mill created opportunities for time clerks, bookkeepers, foremen, superintendents, engineers, and other management personnel. The same was true for every

railroad company, canal company, bank, insurance firm, or mercantile house that flourished in the new commercial environment.
These prosperous townsmen wanted the services of doctors, lawyers, ministers, editors, and schoolteachers. Urban growth in the
early nineteenth century thus laid the basis of a solid middle class.

The middle- and upper-class citizens of commercial and manufacturing towns began to conduct themselves differently from their
eighteenth-century predecessors, breaking the personal ties that
had once bound them to their subordinates. After the onset of the
factory era, "hands" never lived with their "bosses." In the extreme cases, the wealthiest inhabitants of New York, Philadelphia,
and Boston formed rigidly exclusive castes who worked, lived,
married, partied, and prayed only among themselves. Even in
smaller towns, business- and working-class families began to cluster
in different neighborhoods. Employers' households grew smaller
as boarders left and the husband, wife, and children began to live
by themselves with no more than one or two personal servants.
While eighteenth-century craftsmen had frequently lived above
their shops, home and workplace began to diverge in the nineteenth century. Workplaces took on the specialized character of
offices, mills, or stores, while dwelling houses became exclusively
residential. More than his eighteenth-century grandfather, the
nineteenth-century middle-class husband left his home for work in
the morning, entrusting his children to the exclusive care of their
mother. A familiar pattern of family structure began to emerge,
with fathers increasingly identified as the sole breadwinners, while
women were more and more limited to the joys and frustrations
of motherhood. It was a transition that brought tension to everyone, men, women, and children alike.

Most contemporary observers seemed to think that the economic
changes that were reshaping the families and the social structure
of early antebellum America brought greater opportunities to the
average citizen and a greater degree of economic and political
equality to the nation as a whole. Alexis de Tocqueville put this
view in classic form in the opening passages of *Democracy in America*. "No novelty in the United States," he mused, "struck me
more vividly during my stay there than the equality of conditions.
. . . The influence of this fact extends far beyond political mores
and laws, exercising dominion over civil society as much as over
the government; it creates opinions, gives birth to feelings, suggests

customs, and modifies whatever it does not create." Tocqueville also thought that fortunes were impermanent in America; that "most rich men were born poor," that "wealth circulates there with incredible rapidity, and . . . that two successive generations seldom enjoy its favors."

Though Tocqueville was a close observer of American society, historians who have compiled evidence on the amounts of wealth actually owned by Americans at the time of his visit have not been able to prove his impressions about the distribution of wealth in the country. The United States was not a strictly egalitarian society in the antebellum period; foreign observers invariably noted that blacks had no equal standing in white society; neither did women or Indians or the truly destitute. Within the large but privileged order of white males, some were immensely rich, others were desperately poor, and most were scattered at every level in between. Some inequality was generated by the simple fact that older men had accumulated more property than youths, but economic change itself had generated new sources of wealth that were not shared equally by all Americans.

A careful reading of Tocqueville's writings suggests, however, that he did not truly mean that all white Americans had equal amounts of property when he wrote that "the social state of the Americans is eminently democratic." He seems to have meant that most white Americans enjoyed an adequate standard of living and a roughly equal status in the public eye, at least in comparison to the society he knew in France. Tocqueville emphasized that a certain mediocrity of culture, tastes, and opinion seemed universal among Americans. He laid great stress on the fact that a certain level of education was widely available in America but that true intellectuals were scarce. Wealth in America could not put on a face of public arrogance, and poverty did not require a posture of cringing deference. Instead, all white male Americans demanded and got a certain rough equality in personal respect from the other citizens of the republic. In almost every cultural respect, Tocqueville found that a "middling standard" prevailed in America. He realized acutely that American political culture and the spread of almost universal white male suffrage put distinct checks on American government that no other contemporary government experienced. Indeed, one of the greatest political challenges faced by men of property in Jacksonian America was their desire to secure legal and governmental power without violating this widespread sense of general civic equality. As Tocqueville would explain in his classic writings, it was a challenge that exercised their fullest political ingenuity.

Social historians will continue to debate the intricate questions of whether Americans were experiencing more or less equality in wealth, income, and standard of living during this period, and whether the industrializing economy offered them more or less opportunity to rise in the social scale by hard work and their own efforts. What seems beyond doubt is that the Market Revolution made getting a living an increasingly complicated and uncertain affair in the years after 1815. The changes that cleared the path to middle-class respectability for some opened a trapdoor into poverty and dependency for others. Anxious citizens could not always predict which fate would be theirs, and their worried uncertainty would have significant implications for politics in Andrew Jackson's America.

Participation in politics was the birthright of all white men in America, a precious corollary of the Revolutionary ideology that set America apart from virtually all contemporary European societies. When political issues were presented to the voters in ways that touched the problems of everyday experience, they were very eager to exercise their political privileges and claim the dignity and respect that belonged to active members of the civic community. Politics was the arena where divergent values and interests confronted one another and demanded resolution; it became the focal point for the principal tensions of the Jacksonian era.

Politics was very directly related to the practical process of economic change. Many states, like New York, took the lead in financing systems of transportation, or "internal improvements." The federal government was also solicited for contributions to internal improvements, for investors knew that private savings were rarely sufficient to fund the mammoth construction projects they desired. The federal government was also asked to establish a protective tariff, or prohibitive tax, on imports that would protect American manufacturers from better-established foreign competitors. The new companies also wanted corporate charters that would limit the liability of the stockholders. They called for patent protection and tax advantages, monopoly privileges and subsidized credit, government contracts and a thousand other forms of assistance that only a government could offer. They argued, often persuasively, that a strong and modern economy was in the national interest, even a military necessity, and that the public must support projects that the private sector could not accomplish alone. Other Americans retorted that economic change was none of the government's business, that "improvements" lined the pockets of a few more than they benefited the many, and that business forces were undermining the social and economic equality essential to a genuine republican society. Because the citizens could vote on such things, the question of economic development became an urgent political issue.

The political controversy over economic development came to focus most acutely on the issue of money—the currency that Americans passed from hand to hand—and the banks, the institutions that issued, collected, and dispersed it. The spread of commercial activity after 1815 brought more and more farmers, artisans, and professionals into the world of monetary exchange. As true commerce replaced barter, Jacksonian Americans learned that money could hardly be taken for granted, that its influence over society was far from neutral, and that power over money could be used to remake the social and economic landscape in previously unimagined ways. In particular, the value and supply of money could be manipulated in order to stimulate economic growth or to slow it down, to encourage a broad distribution of the benefits of economic change or to concentrate economic power more tightly. The currency question therefore became one of the most troubling political controversies of Jacksonian America, as Andrew Jackson led a successful crusade to destroy the Bank of the United States (the nation's largest bank), to suppress the most commonly used forms of paper money, and to establish a national currency composed of gold and silver coins.

Money in the antebellum United States consisted of paper currency and specie, or gold and silver coins. Issued by the federal government and foreign nations, specie was valued for certain purposes but was also scarce and cumbersome to use. Most daily transactions were conducted with paper money, which was issued not by the government but by commercial banks. The banks were therefore central institutions of the new economy, and it is important to understand something of how they worked.

A bank originated with a group of potential investors who applied to their state legislature for a charter, a document establishing them as a corporate body and limiting each shareholder's personal liability for the debts of the corporation. Widely available today, incorporation was a rare privilege in the 1820s and 1830s, supposedly bestowed by state legislatures on companies with a special public service function. Railroad and canal companies were frequent recipients of corporate privileges, and banks argued successfully for the same status because they supplied the currency that the community relied upon. In practice, political favoritism and inside connections were often key determinants of who received a valuable corporate charter.

Once they were incorporated, shareholders paid in their capital, preferably in specie. Under the lax standards of the day, however, purchasers frequently gave personal IOUs for stock, offering nothing more than the stock itself as collateral. Once a specified portion of the stock was paid for, the bank elected officers and opened for business. Ordinarily, loans were made to borrowers for renewable periods of sixty to ninety days, and profits accrued from the interest on these loans. The typical customer was a merchant who borrowed money to purchase goods in a distant city and repaid the loan when the goods were sold, but renewable notes could also be used to purchase land, slaves, equipment, or any other investment. The banks made their loans by issuing their own notes, which were paper certificates supposedly convertible to specie on demand and which therefore passed as money. The borrower spent his notes for goods and services, and the notes began to circulate in the community.

There was no specific limit to the volume of loans that a bank could make, and it was expected that bankers would lend out far more notes than they could ever redeem in specie at any one time. As long as the ratio between the specie in the bank's vaults and the volume of its notes in circulation did not become excessive, the bank was usually sound, but the temptation to lend extensively and to profit from the resulting interest sometimes led bankers into perilous financial waters. When too many loans were made and too many notes were issued, business temporarily boomed under the generous supply of money and prices tended to rise. Inflation could be followed by severe deflation, however, and then the economy settled into depression.

The greatest fault of the paper money system was this tendency to instability. The value of each bank's notes depended on its reputation for sound management, so each bank's notes circulated at a discount that varied according to time, place, and circumstance. Even the best-informed merchant could not always be sure of the value of the money he held. The ordinary citizen who lacked the privilege of inside information might be forced to accept, in exchange for his crops or his labor, money that later turned out to be worthless. Matters became worse in a panic, when noteholders lost all confidence that the banks could redeem their notes and converged on banks to demand specie. When that happened, even the soundest banks quickly exhausted their reserves of coin and "suspended specie payments." In other words, they simply refused to pay specie in exchange for their notes. The notes then depreciated while specie gained in value. Wages and prices collapsed and the commercial economy suffered. Eventually, when prices had fallen far enough and coin had regained a tempting level of buying power, hoarders released their gold and silver back into circulation and the banks could afford to "resume specie payments."

The threat of panic became real in 1819, 1837, and 1839. During these episodes, no one could be sure when or whether a given bank would return to normal operations. Uncertainty about the value of bank notes became even more acute and the danger of getting caught with worthless paper was even more serious than usual. While the banks refused to honor their obligations to pay specie, they were very strict on those who owed them money, because the banks' own creditors were being stringent. With the commodity prices depressed, however, debtors had little means of repaying their loans and frequently lost their property to the banks. Many borrowers therefore suspected that the panics were simply cooked up by the banks as pretexts to seize the farms and shops of honest citizens. Some bankers were indeed dishonest, but personal immorality was not at the root of the problem. The alternating rhythm of boom and bust was an inevitable feature of the early capitalist economy, but the nature of the business cycle was not widely understood and there was widespread confusion about the remedy for the recurring pattern of monetary instability.

One possible source of relief was the Bank of the United States, chartered by Congress in 1816 for a twenty-year period. The B.U.S., as it was called, had a capital of $35 million and was the largest bank in the country. The U.S. government had purchased one fifth of its stock and appointed one fifth of its directors. The B.U.S. received a monopoly of the government's banking business and its notes were receivable for federal taxes. It had paid a premium of $1.5 million for these privileges and was expected in return to provide a stable national currency. An earlier Bank of the United States had been allowed to go out of existence in 1811 amid doubts about its constitutionality, but fiscal confusion in the War of 1812 convinced congressional leaders that a large national institution was necessary to provide financial services to the government and to discipline the inflationary tendencies of the smaller and more numerous state banks. In 1819, the Supreme Court under Chief Justice John Marshall ruled in favor of the Bank's constitutionality in the case of *McCulloch* v. *Maryland*, and strengthened its legal position in the 1824 case of *Osborn* v. *Bank of the United States*. As the economy continued to grow, the established position of the mammoth institution on Philadelphia's Chestnut Street seemed secure. Properly managed, a bank so large should have been able to pressure the smaller state banks to maintain adequate specie reserves and avoid the worst excesses of inflation, panic, and depression. Beginning in the 1820s, the B.U.S. did start to exercise some central control over the state banks and the national economy, but in its early years it simply operated as any big bank might, primarily concerned with earning large profits for its shareholders. The Bank's performance was particularly disappointing during the Panic of 1819.

The Atlantic economy had done quite well after 1815. European nations traded eagerly in the aftermath of the Napoleonic wars, while cheap land, easy credit, and high prices for farm products stimulated an American land boom that state banks happily fueled with generous issues of notes. The bubble broke when the B.U.S. made a sudden demand for specie that the state banks could not easily meet. Alarmed for the liquidity of his own institution, Langdon Cheves, the new president of the B.U.S., continued to insist on payment, exhausting the meager reserves of the state banks and forcing a general suspension of specie payments outside New England. More flexible management would have helped matters, but a parallel credit shortage had seized Europe as well, so hard times were inevitable in any case. By 1819 prosperity had turned into depression.

The impact of the panic varied with the extent of an area's or an individual's involvement in the market economy. Isolated farming regions were affected but little, while the cities suffered more heavily. Estimates of joblessness varied from 40,000 to 60,000 to 100,000, but there is no way to verify these guesses. At a time when most free Americans were self-employed on their own farms, unemployment figures could be misleading, but the impact of the depression was nonetheless severe. Americans had been pleased to enjoy the benefits of expanding commercial society, but now they were stunned to learn of its costs. The air was soon filled with cries for political remedies for the depressed economy.

President James Monroe permitted easier credit terms for purchasers of public lands, but took no other action. In the states, proposals for relief soon flooded the legislatures. "Stay laws" to prevent the collection of debts until business conditions improved were proposed in many statehouses and passed in Illinois, Indiana, Tennessee, Kentucky, and Missouri. Most of these states also founded publicly owned banks that were required to lend small sums to hard-pressed debtors. Creditors were then required to accept these notes or face the cancellation of their debts. When the Supreme Court of Kentucky invalidated such a relief program, the legislature abolished the court and appointed another that would be more responsive to public opinion. The resulting squabble between Old Court and New Court parties dominated Kentucky politics for several years thereafter. Eastern states were more resistant to public pressure, but the demands of injured citizens were serious in every part of the country.

In the midst of this controversy and distress, the Bank of the United States sat safe and sound, rescued from possible insolvency by the drastic policies of Langdon Cheves. As one critic later noted sourly, "the Bank was saved but the people were ruined." Though Cheves was replaced in 1823 by Nicholas Biddle, the B.U.S. continued to carry a heavy legacy of blame for what had happened. Senator Thomas Hart Benton of Missouri spoke for many enemies of the Bank when he assured the Senate that "I know towns, yea, cities . . . , where this bank already appears as an engrossing proprietor. All the flourishing cities of the West are mortgaged to this money power. . . . They are in the jaws of the monster! A lump of butter in the mouth of a dog! One gulp, one swallow, and all is gone!" Nicholas Biddle, the new president of the B.U.S., concluded that in the future the Bank must be managed with greater vision and finesse, but men like Benton would not be satisfied by Biddle's assurances. They suspected that any mammoth private institution would act the same way in a crisis, and decided that the Bank was inimical to popular liberty and prosperity. The collision between these two points of view would color American politics for the next three decades.

As the nation's largest bank, the B.U.S. symbolized the dramatic changes that were rebuilding the American economy and altering the meaning of independence in the lives of ordinary citizens. For Americans who supported those changes, the Bank was a legal and necessary bulwark of an orderly credit-based economy. For Americans who opposed those changes, the Bank was far more sinister. Because the Bank was a creation of the federal government, moreover, it depended on political support for its existence. When disagreement about the future of the American economy led to political disagreement during Andrew Jackson's Presidency, the friends of banking, both at the state level and at that of the B.U.S., faced serious public challenge. In fact, the related questions of banking and the economy became central to the political conflicts of the era.

As the War of 1812 receded into memory in the 1820s, ordinary Americans were experiencing a profound set of changes. In the Eastern cities and their hinterlands, where economic development had gone the furthest, modern middle and working classes were beginning to take shape. On the frontier, pioneer adventurers sought to re-create the experience of personal liberty and opportunity that seemed increasingly elusive in the older states. In the South, masters, slaves, and yeomen struggled with the contradictions of a system that seemed indispensable to whites but increasingly anachronistic and cruel in a world based on economic freedom and legal equality. In settled rural regions, where the events of frontier and seaport seemed equally remote, puzzled citizens studied the news of a changing world and wondered if they should welcome new developments or resist them.

Americans met the challenges of the Market Revolution with apprehension and enthusiasm, but almost never with indifference. Among adult white males, who constituted the civic community, most responded with a heightened political interest, both because the government was deeply involved in the changes affecting them and because the still-recent experience of the American Revolution seemed to teach that political engagement was the right of all citizens and their proper response to community crisis. The Panic of 1819 was a painful blow, but it seemed to reinforce the lesson that the problems of a free society were ultimately political and must be addressed by political means.

Republican Theory
and Practice

AMERICANS of the early nineteenth century were enormously proud of their country and especially of their government. Unlike the European powers, the United States lacked such signs of national greatness as glittering cities, fabled ruins, or a polished literary culture. It boasted instead of popular self-government. Though the reality of self-government was ordinarily more limited than the rhetorical claims that were made for it, American politics was indeed unusually democratic for the age. At a time when representative institutions were struggling in Latin America, limited in Britain, and severely restricted on the Continent, the citizens of the United States enjoyed political and civil rights for the most part unavailable elsewhere.

Highly conscious of their achievements and their good fortune, Americans loudly proclaimed the superiority of their system and brashly invited the rest of the world to copy it. In his inaugural address in 1817, President James Monroe reflected a common, though immodest, sentiment when he urged his countrymen to remember "how near our Government has approached to perfection; that in respect to it we have no essential improvement to make; [and] that the great object is to preserve it in the essential principles and features which characterize it." Foreigners found this attitude maddeningly smug, but they could hardly escape the universal celebration of what Monroe grandly described as "the

principles of our republican Government." A good deal of insecurity lay behind this ceaseless bragging, but it accurately reflected
the importance that Americans attributed to politics.

Americans called their system of government "republican" to
contrast it to the aristocratic or monarchical governments that
dominated Europe. At the simplest level, a republic was a country
without a king, a nobility, or a system of hereditary legal privileges.
In a republic, citizens were equal before the law and governed
themselves through representative institutions. With a few excep-
tions, white men of the early nineteenth century assumed that
women, children, and men of color could not qualify as full-fledged
republican citizens, but the principle of equality between white
men made political rights more widespread in the United States
than in any major country in Europe.

Republicanism had deep intellectual roots, with important
sources in English opposition politics of the eighteenth century,
radical movements of the seventeenth century, Renaissance political theory, and the classical traditions of Greece and Rome. Most
recently, Americans traced republicanism to the outcome of their
own Revolution and glorified its success as the turning point of
world history. As one typical Fourth of July orator put it in 1832,
"the independence of the United States of America is not only a
marked epoch in the course of time, but it is the end from which
the new order of things is to be reckoned. It is the dividing point
in the history of mankind; it is the moment of the political regen-
eration of the world."

In describing the benefits of republican government, Americans
usually began with "liberty." In a typical tribute made in 1828,
Edward Everett, a future U.S. senator from Massachusetts, hailed
"the History of Liberty" as "the real history of man." As a concept,
liberty was so important and self-evident that Americans rarely
stopped to define it. At the very least, liberty implied that no white
man would be subject to the arbitrary rule of another and that the
community of white men might rule themselves by means of majority rule. The champions of liberty, spelling out their views in
thousands of patriotic addresses, sermons, essays, and stump
speeches, also used the term broadly to embrace other benefits of
a free society: freedom of the individual to improve himself, both
morally and materially; freedom from an established religion; freedom from a legally privileged aristocracy; freedom of expression

as defined by the federal and state constitutions. Most American spokesmen also added that liberty was not the same as "license," or the absence of all personal or social restraints. A cautious member of the Massachusetts constitutional convention of 1820–21 contrasted "a spirit of universal or unlimited liberty" with "the spirit of limited liberty; of reciprocal control," and other republican advocates would have agreed with him, at least in principle. Under a system of "constitutional" or "balanced" liberty, the rights of minorities would be as safe as those of the majority. Lawyers and politicians often differed, however, on how balances or limits ought to be applied to popular liberty. They often warned that liberty was fragile and easily endangered; if carried too far, efforts to protect liberty by limiting it could snuff it out instead.

In particular, good republicans feared "power," liberty's tyrannical opposite. If liberty was the promise of self-control in self-governing communities, power was the threat of control by others. Power was a terrible attribute of governments and private authorities that constantly sought to restrict what it did not control. The eighteenth-century English radicals John Trenchard and Thomas Gordon had expressed the relationship between liberty and power very eloquently in their well-read pamphlet series *Cato's Letters*, and Americans continued to heed their warnings in the early nineteenth century. "Liberty chastises and shortens power," "Cato" had warned, "therefore power would extinguish liberty, and consequently liberty has too much cause to be exceeding jealous and always upon her defense." Continuing to elaborate on the same classic themes, many American spokesmen put the eternal warfare between liberty and power at the center of their national history. "The love of liberty . . . grew with the growth, and strengthened with the strength, of the Colonies," a Virginia reformer declared to his state's constitutional convention in 1829. "It declared war, at last, not only against the *power* of the *King*, but against the *privilege* of the Noble, and laid the deep foundations of our Republic on *the sovereignty of the people* and *the equality of men*." Inspired by such sentiments, some Americans of the early nineteenth century sought to expand the sphere of liberty still further. At the very least, all agreed, the encroachment of power upon liberty must be resisted, lest power's pernicious appetites grow stronger.

The continual warfare between liberty and power made some

republicans seem unduly suspicious, even paranoid. The exceptionally cautious could sense a threat to liberty in the most innocent or practical developments: a reform in voting requirements, for example, or a plan for public education. Nevertheless, when liberty was protected by the proper balances, Americans described its effects as downright utopian. A South Carolina clergyman summed up a widespread optimism in 1825, when he pointed proudly to "the present flourishing state of our country, where liberty is happily blended with Government and Laws, where Agriculture, Commerce, and the Arts are making daily advances in improvement, where science is cultivated with care and success, and where religion . . . diffuses [its] benign influences through our widely extended country, among men of every rank and character."

To preserve the precarious balance between liberty and power, republicans laid heavy emphasis on what they called "virtue." A key republican concept, the idea of public virtue meant more than simple honesty; it implied a civic-minded willingness to set aside private interests for the sake of the common good. If citizens used their liberty to advance themselves ruthlessly at everyone else's expense, no one's liberty would be secure. President Andrew Jackson explained why in his Farewell Address of 1837. "No free government can stand without virtue in the people and a lofty spirit of patriotism," he declared. "If the sordid feelings of mere selfishness shall usurp the place which ought to be filled by public spirit, the legislation of Congress will soon be converted into a scramble for personal and sectional advantages," and the resulting discord could tear apart the Union. Republican theorists therefore hoped that virtuous citizens would remember that everyone's private interests would benefit in the long run if the common good came first. History seemed to teach that the Greek and Roman republics had fallen when their citizens lost their sense of virtue, and thoughtful Americans feared the same outcome for their own fragile venture in self-government. They accordingly looked upon virtue as the moral cement of republican society and sought to preserve it at all costs.

Like liberty itself, republican virtue was a very delicate quality that could survive only under special historical circumstances. It flourished in a middling state of civilization, when men were cultured enough to understand morality and reason, but not so sophisticated that luxury, commerce, and exploitation had enabled the few to corrupt or dominate the many. Americans identified themselves with just such a middling state, just as they associated the Indians with savagery and their British contemporaries with excessive refinement. They used the word "corruption" to refer to the changes that could drag a nation from a pure and virtuous stage of cultivation to the state of decay when republicanism became impossible. As such, corruption could refer to specific misdeeds such as bribery, but its widest meaning applied to the social, economic, and moral changes that could undermine the basis of republican society.

Republicans thus identified corruption with social change, particularly those changes which might diminish the liberty of the individual freeholder. As heirs of the European Enlightenment, republicans saw links between men's moral states and their material circumstances and took it for granted that liberty and virtue required a favorable social and economic environment. Every theory of republicanism also implied a theory of political economy, though republicans differed over what this should be. According to Thomas Jefferson, for example, liberty could flourish only in an agricultural society where small proprietors tilled their own fields and formed the bulk of the body politic. "Those who labor in the earth are the chosen people of God, if ever he had a chosen people," Jefferson declared, "whose breasts he has made his peculiar deposit for substantial and genuine virtue." By the same token, he insisted, the proportion of nonagricultural workers in a nation "is a good-enough barometer whereby to measure its degree of corruption," for wage earners were controlled by their employers and lacked the independence that true virtue required. "Dependance begets subservience and venality," he wrote, "suffocates the germ of virtue, and prepares fit tools for the designs of ambition." Spelling out beliefs that would continue to resonate powerfully in the minds of Andrew Jackson's followers, the Virginia philosopher thus explained that republicanism depended on agriculture. "While we have land to labor then," he concluded, "let us never wish to see our citizens occupied at a work-bench, or twirling a distaff. . . . The mobs of great cities add just so much to the support of pure government, as sores do to the strength of the human body."

Not all republicans shared Jefferson's views of the ideal society, but they did tend to agree that republicanism must rest on an appropriate material foundation. "By hammer and hand, all arts do stand," proclaimed the banners of America's urban artisans, and the port cities of the young republic sustained large populations of skilled craft workers who insisted that their work was just as essential to republican society as farming. Other republican thinkers made room for an even larger cast of ideal citizens. Alexander Hamilton designed his economic program for the early federal government to appeal to the interests of merchants, creditors, and investors, arguing candidly that the Republic could never thrive without the friendship of commercial interests. Hamilton's vision would have particular relevance for the future opponents of Andrew Jackson. The seeds for future bitter quarrels were thus hidden in these various contrasting formulas for the political economy of an ideal republic.

Concerns over the corrupting effects of social change persisted long after the Revolutionary era and suffused political thinking in the years after the War of 1812. In the New York constitutional convention of 1821, Chancellor James Kent mournfully predicted that social change would almost certainly corrupt the nation's primitive simplicity. "We are no longer to remain plain and simple republics of farmers," he warned. "We are fast becoming a great nation, with great commerce, manufactures, population, wealth, luxuries, and with the vices and miseries that they engender." With no hope of halting this process of decay, the judge advocated a state senate based on landed property as a permanent check on the dangerous power of propertyless urban masses. Less conservative republicans saw greater dangers to liberty and virtue in different quarters, but they still worried constantly that social corruption could undermine the material basis for free government.

Republicanism in the young United States was therefore more than an abstract preference for popular government and a dislike of kings and nobles. It also included a disposition to see politics as a struggle between good and evil, expressed as the eternal warfare between liberty and power, virtue and corruption. It did not imply a tolerance for many and varied interests, each contending with the other for a place in the sun. Instead, when republicans of that era quarreled with one another, they tended to regard their opponents as enemies of liberty itself, not as rival interests having equal claims to public favor.

Distrust of contending interests fed republican suspicion of political organization and partisanship. In a pure republic, they believed, honest purposes would be honestly and independently pursued; only corrupt intentions would require an individual to scheme with others and to subordinate his personal judgment to the dictation of a political organization. Early American republicans used the terms "party" and "faction" almost interchangeably. If they no longer believed that organized political opposition was semitreasonous by definition, they uniformly regretted the appearance of political parties as a sign of republican degeneration. A profound antiparty spirit pervaded American politics at the outset and remained powerful through the Presidency of James Monroe.

Americans would eventually come to see their government as an arena for routine competition and compromise of contending interests, a political model that scholars call the "liberal" state. In this view, political parties would be accepted as normal. Though James Madison and others in the early national period had already begun to move toward a liberal theory of politics, such ideas were not fully elaborated or widely understood in the early nineteenth century. While republican politicians claimed to put a high value on conciliation and the common good, prevailing political attitudes tended to make compromise very difficult, if not impossible. Since each participant in a quarrel tended to view the interests of his constituents or himself as essential to the common good and those of his opponents as subversive of liberty itself, polemical controversies were frequent and vociferous.

The appeal of republican ideas spread far beyond the circle of an educated elite. Ordinary free Americans were conscious that republicanism offered them dignity denied elsewhere, and responded to public appeals that drew on this widespread conviction. No public figure spoke to the patriotism of ordinary citizens more eloquently than Major General Andrew Jackson, commander of the Tennessee state militia and eager proponent of war against Great Britain and her Indian allies. Calling for volunteers in 1812, Jackson summoned republican passions to address the central question of American national identity. "Who are we?" he asked his troops in an address that richly evoked the popular basis for American nationalism. "Are we the titled slaves of George the third? the military conscripts of Napolon the great? or the frozen peasants of the Rusian Czar? No," he thundered. "We are the free born sons of america; the citizens of the only republick now existing in the world; and the only people on earth who possess rights, liberties, and property which the[y] dare call their own." Having distinguished Americans from all other peoples in the world, Jackson went on to propound the purposes of the war. "We are going to fight for the reestablishment of our national character," he explained, "misunderstood and vilified at home and abroad." The General mentioned impressment, free trade, and the conquest of Canada, but the emotional thrust of his message bore on the rights of free Americans, whom Jackson described as *"a free people compelled to reclaim by the power of their arms the right which god has bestowed upon them, and which an infatuated King has said they shall not enjoy."* The substance of the dispute mattered less to Jackson than the act of trespass and the impossibility of submission for a truly free people. In his eyes, the scruffiest frontiersman in Tennessee was better than all the "titled Slaves of George the third," and that belief gave the American Republic a central place in world history. Americans would long remember and celebrate Jackson's personal achievements in the ensuing conflict, but he won his widest following by combining his military talents with an appeal to a popular republican culture.

Republicanism could grasp the popular imagination so vividly because it was not an abstraction for the typical American freeholder. At the practical level, such a man could identify liberty as the independence he enjoyed as the owner of a farm or shop. Power, by contrast, was the total authority that a master could exercise over his dependents, whether they were slaves, servants, women, or children. Starting with a few simple principles, political theorists could develop some very sophisticated implications of republicanism, but political thinkers kept in touch with their followers because liberty had a concrete personal meaning.

As Americans' personal experiences changed, so too did their concept of liberty. In the time of the American Revolution, for example, citizens had accepted fundamental laws severely limiting the power of the popular will. State constitutions frequently established elaborate gradations of political rights and privileges, with a relatively open franchise for some offices, a stricter set of requirements to vote for others, and still higher requirements for holding office. Many officials were chosen by legislatures rather than voters, and legislative seats were frequently monopolized by older and wealthier sections of each state. Governors exercised few powers and judges were carefully protected from political pressure. Tolerable at first, unequal restrictions on majority rule seemed less and less republican in the early nineteenth century. By the 1820s, "equality" was joining liberty as a central aspect of republicanism in the minds of many citizens.

A series of state constitutional amendments reflected these changing popular notions. Maryland took the lead in 1802 by extending the right to vote to all white men who met a residency requirement. South Carolina followed ten years later, and suffrage extension became commonplace in the 1810s and 1820s. Because the federal constitution ties voting eligibility in congressional elections to the requirements for voting for members of the most numerous house of a state's legislature, moreover, changes in the right to vote spilled over from state to federal politics.

Advocates of a wider franchise attacked some fundamental notions of eighteenth-century republicanism, including the belief that landed proprietors held a greater stake in society than others and should thus enjoy greater rights to protect what they owned. Did not the Declaration of Independence proclaim the equality of all men? "It is consequently a tyranny to endow one class of men with privileges which are denied to another," a Virginia essayist maintained. "It is erecting a landed aristocracy, ugly and deformed, in the sacred temple dedicated to freedom and the rights of man." In a rapidly changing economic environment, it was hard for conservatives to convince others that one form of property was more influential than another in persuading an owner to defend free government. Even impoverished laborers would support the state if it respected their fundamental equality. In the words of an 1829 petition from the landless citizens of Richmond, Virginia, "virtue [and] intelligence are not among the products of the soil. Attachment to property, often a sordid sentiment, is not to be confounded with the sacred flame of patriotism."

By the same logic, voters should have more control over branches of government that had once been shielded from the pressure of public opinion. State leaders who expanded the right to vote in the 1810s and 1820s also moved to increase the number of elective offices in state government, to streamline executive branches of government, to bring courts more closely under democratic control, and to equalize representation in the legislatures.

If one white man was as good as another, then simple majority rule would be a safer source of virtue and a more reliable guide to the common good than the paternal benevolence of a few well-trained and high-minded gentlemen. Reform did not supplant republicanism in American political thinking, but significantly shifted its emphasis toward majoritarian democracy.

Changes in political rights brought gradual but permanent shifts in the tone of republican politics. Colonial leaders had counted on a deft combination of coercion with "deference," or the voluntary submission of the middling and lower classes, to guarantee the position of a social, economic, and political elite. As the suffrage broadened and electioneering tactics grew more popular, successful individuals won their struggles for higher local status, but automatic respect for social and political superiors declined as well. Officeholders were still likely to be wealthier and better educated than ordinary voters, but they could no longer count on automatic deference after trading public insults with their peers or rubbing elbows with their inferiors. Eager for political success, ambitious members of the gentry descended on taverns and militia musters to flatter and wheedle for the vote of the common man. "How contemptible and degrading it is to see gentlemen assembling at such places," complained a North Carolina editor in 1820, "treating, fawning and courting, nay *soliciting* the suffrage of men to *honor* them with a seat in the Legislative Councils of the State." For statesmen of the old school, such subservience to the popular will seemed to corrupt the tenets of republicanism itself. "Gracious God!" the editor exclaimed. "If this is independence, save us, we beseech thee, from participating in the blessings it imparts." Despite such complaints, the democratization of American politics would continue to accelerate in the coming decades.

Significantly, as free white men moved to claim equal rights of citizenship, the prospect of equality seemed to slip even further from free blacks and women. Though blacks had never been fully equal in Revolutionary America, the concept of a gradation of rights and privileges could give some citizenship rights to the black man who satisfied the same property requirements as whites. States as different as New York and North Carolina had thus offered a limited franchise to "all men" who met certain broad qualifications, and free black inhabitants of both states used these provisions to claim the right to vote. Some women were likewise enfranchised by a New Jersey constitution that gave the ballot to property-owning "persons" rather than to "men," and other state constitutions were similarly vague. The question of black and woman suffrage in post-Revolutionary America needs further study, but it is clear that the same reformers who extended suffrage and other rights to all white men began to close the opportunities for blacks and women left open by previous generations of lawmakers.

When wealth and status no longer distinguished between those who were full members of the republican community and those who were not, republicans looked for other means to mark these differences. Enfranchised citizens defined who they *were* by emphasizing who they were *not*. An endless catalogue of hostile or dismissive stereotypes thus ascribed traits to blacks and women diametrically opposite to those that qualified white men for the rights of citizenship. If white male citizens wished to think of themselves as intelligent, hardworking, thrifty, self-controlled, and civic-minded, they described blacks as stupid, lazy, sensual, improvident, drunken, licentious, and otherwise unqualified for the privileges of democratic self-government. Women were likewise described as weak, submissive, trusting, and preoccupied by domestic concerns. Though they might be morally superior to men in some respects, they did not have the aggressive qualities necessary for a proper defense of liberty from power, or the broad civic awareness needed for genuine public virtue. A delegate to the New York constitutional convention of 1821 expressed a common view of blacks, but he might just as well have been speaking of women. "They are a peculiar people," the gentleman reflected, "incapable, in my judgment, of exercising [the right to vote] with any sort of discretion, prudence or independence. They have no just conceptions of civil liberty. They know not how to appreciate it, and are consequently indifferent to its preservation." Accepting this reasoning, the convention abolished the property-holding requirement that had previously limited voting among whites, but retained a stiff requirement for voting by free blacks. The delegates did not consider the possibility of women's suffrage at all, but lumped women together with children, convicts, and the mentally disabled to prove that the principle of political equality had "obvious" natural limits.

Throughout the Union, states that had once maintained a complex gradation of political rights based on economic class moved in the 1820s and 1830s to impose a radical legal dichotomy based on race and sex. Those who "passed the test" were increasingly regarded as politically equal in every respect, while those who "failed" were stripped of every legal basis for political participation. Free blacks lost the right to vote in Maryland in 1810, in New York in 1821, in Tennessee in 1834, and in North Carolina in 1835, while New Jersey women were disenfranchised in 1807. In the "Age of Egalitarianism," all white men would be equal, at least in theory, but no one else would be the equal of a white man.

The new emphasis on racial distinctions had implications for slaves as well as for free blacks. Blacks were utterly different from whites, slaveholding theorists argued, and totally incapable of freedom. God had undoubtedly created them for servitude, to allow all whites to escape menial duties and assume the equality they naturally deserved. "Break down slavery," warned Congressman Henry A. Wise of Virginia, "and you would with the same blow destroy the great Democratic principle of equality among men." In the eyes of many white Southerners, slaveholding states were the only genuine republics.

The logic of racial exclusion could extend beyond political rights to the basic right of habitation. In the cases of both Indians and blacks, the very idea of free, nonwhite people living side by side with white Americans seemed to inspire white fantasies of race war or annihilation. Most of the Southern states passed laws expelling newly emancipated slaves from their borders, while most frontier states banned the entry of free blacks. White observers often assumed that the end of slavery would bring on a bloodbath, and called for the colonization of freed blacks in Africa as the only safe policy of emancipation. Alternatively, whites argued that freedom itself was fatal to blacks, and sought to prove that mortality, insanity, and mental retardation increased among free blacks in direct proportion to the victims' distance from slavery.

Despite plain evidence to the contrary, it was also frequently asserted that the Indians were dying out. As U.S. Secretary of State Henry Clay confided to a fellow Cabinet officer in 1825, "it was impossible to civilize Indians. . . . It was not in their nature. . . . They were destined to extinction, and, although he would never use or countenance inhumanity towards them, he did not think them, as a race, worth preserving." Other white observers declared that removal of the remaining Eastern Indians to the area beyond the Mississippi was the only way to save these people from extinction, ignoring the fact that the Cherokees, Creeks, and other neighboring tribes were numerous and flourishing. Later, in the 1840s, the advocates of American expansion into Mexico and other Latin American countries likewise predicted that Hispanic peoples would miraculously disappear as Anglo-Americans moved to the west and south. As one such advocate wrote after visiting California in 1842, Mexicans were "an imbecile, pusillanimous race of men, and unfit to control the destinies of that beautiful country. [They] must fade away [before] the mingling of different branches of the Caucasian family of the States." In each case, the prediction that nonwhites would or ought to disappear was clearly based on white longing rather than reality. Not content to establish a free and equal community of citizens by excluding nonwhites from the circle of political equality, many whites hoped to expel them from the landscape itself.

Joined by historian George M. Fredrickson, sociologist Pierre L. van den Berghe has applied the term "*Herrenvolk* ('master race') democracy" to societies such as the Old South, where the oppression of one group is used to establish and defend a system of egalitarianism among those who oppress them. In a diminished but significant form, the term also applies to the antebellum North, where the unequal condition of blacks and Indians was routinely cited to justify the superior position of white Americans. In both sections, white men used the lines of race and sex to create a fraternity of equals, though they did not succeed in suppressing all sources of difference or debate within their ranks.

Certain strains in Protestant religion were the most important sources of dissent from popular republican assumptions that defined human worth on the basis of race and sex. Since the days of the earliest Puritan settlements, devout Americans, especially in New England and the areas affected by New England migration, had thought themselves burdened with a special mission, a unique "errand," to proclaim God's truth in the wilderness. For pious Protestants, the American Revolution had been a consummation and a spur to this mission, reaffirming the rights and the obligations of self-government for God's people. For these citizens, the Republic would flourish only to the degree that it was dedicated to sacred purposes. President John Quincy Adams of Massachusetts reiterated this old Puritan tradition when he reminded Congress in 1825 "that the tenure of power by man is, in the moral purposes of his Creator, upon condition that it shall be exercised to the ends of beneficence, to improve the condition of himself and his fellow-men." Carrying this line of thinking a step further, many concluded that the good citizen was not only a white man, but a committed Christian as well. Carrying their ideals to the public sphere, these Christians came to hope that the new Republic would grow in moral perfection, just as others hoped to improve in secular liberty. The numbers of such reformers would expand dramatically in the years after 1815, fed by an extraordinary growth in religious commitment known as the Second Great Awakening. The results of this religious movement would have profound implications for the future of Jacksonian politics.

Though Protestant ministers and their flocks had embraced the American Revolution, they worried in the post-Revolutionary generation about the apparent spread of religious skepticism, French revolutionary extremism, decaying moral standards, and apathy among the faithful who remained in the pews. After a decade or more of proselytizing on the frontier and elsewhere, their work bore its first conspicuous fruits in 1801, with a huge camp meeting in Cane Ridge, Kentucky, which inspired dozens of imitations across the South and West. Throngs of listeners fell under the spell of evangelists who preached in teams around the clock, driving "convicted" sinners to tears, shouts, and fits of unconsciousness before their confidence gradually grew in the possibility of personal forgiveness and salvation. Subsequent revivals were somewhat more sedate, but the spirit of religious renewal flourished in them all. Known as the Second Great Awakening to distinguish it from a similar episode in the mid-eighteenth century, the revival movement brought dramatic increases in church membership, particularly in the Baptist, Methodist, Presbyterian, and allied denominations.

After cresting in the South, the revival movement spread to the towns along the Erie Canal in the 1820s and then east and south into New York City and the interior of New England. Some Protestants were largely immune to the evangelical spirit, particularly in denominations like the Lutherans or the Episcopalians who cherished a traditional liturgy and a strong identification with the European past. The small but rapidly growing number of Roman Catholics in America were likewise untouched by revivalism and were often the targets of evangelical hostility. Considerable numbers of nominal Protestants in America never felt the grip of evangelical conviction. Nevertheless, evangelical Protestantism suffused most areas of the United States in the ensuing years. In the North, it found its warmest support among middle-class New Englanders and in the areas outside New England where they had settled. The canal district of western New York was ignited so often by religious enthusiasm that it became known as the Burnt-Over District.

An essential aspect of the Second Great Awakening in the North was an enhanced popular belief in the perfectibility of human beings, with the remembered ideals of the orderly New England village being taken as the model of perfection. Converts began by reforming their own lives and frequently renounced strong drink, idle amusements, Sunday games, and careless work habits. They urged others to take the same steps in order to rededicate families, communities, states, and the nation itself to spiritual as well as worldly progress. Many employers clearly hoped that evangelical virtues would produce a sober, industrious, and contented work force, but the moral sincerity of their crusade was also very obvious. Ministers warned that America stood at a historic crossroads: one path led to national and worldwide salvation; the other, to a world maddened by greed, infidelity, and debauchery. It was in the power of living Americans to choose which path would be taken. Businessmen and other middle-class Americans felt that the choice was theirs to make.

Evangelical Protestants therefore bent their considerable energies to a variety of programs to spread the gospel message. The American Bible Society sought to put the Scriptures in every home. The American Sunday School Union tried to educate the laboring children of the poor. Missionaries left for Asia, for the western states, for the slums of New York and Philadelphia. Support for them came from wealthy philanthropists as well as from sewing circles and mite societies in every community. "Disinterested benevolence" soon reached from the victims of sin to unfortunates of all kinds, and efforts were made to alleviate the condition of the blind, the deaf, the insane, and the destitute. Penitentiaries, asylums, and poorhouses were all founded with the common purpose of reclaiming social, physical, or moral defectives by housing them in salutary environments and encouraging the divinely inspired processes of self-improvement. Exhorters were dispatched to uplift sailors, prostitutes, drunkards, Indians, immigrants, anyone who seemed to deviate from the ideals of evangelical piety, industry, and sobriety.

Eventually, the evangelical movement confronted secular politics, when active ministers and laymen began to demand that the government stop the transportation of the mail on Sunday, in recognition of the Christian Sabbath. Further political involvement would follow when Andrew Jackson's government sought to deal harshly with Indians (many of whom were evangelical converts) or to challenge the interests of Christian businessmen whose profits supported a variety of benevolent enterprises. Though the evangelical movement was frequently intolerant of nonevangelical preferences, it also expressed the highest humanitarian ideals of the age.

The evangelical vision quickly collided with the institution of slavery. Brutality to slaves was an outrage to the Northern evangelical conscience, just as forced labor was an affront to the ethos of an emerging wage labor economy. Reformers expanded on a preexisting eighteenth-century antislavery tradition and urged slaveholders to abandon the sin of bondage just as they urged alcoholics to abandon the sin of drink.

Southern slaveholders were instantly hostile to the new abolitionist movement and did everything in their power to suppress it. They found support from Southern evangelical ministers, who had wrestled with the question of slavery in earlier years, but could not overcome the proslavery convictions of white church members or their own misgivings about the social consequences of abolition. Unlike their Northern counterparts, Southern white clergymen had come to view slavery as a providential institution for the conversion of the African race and the creation of a superior Christian civilization led by the master class. They increasingly rejected the notion that personal salvation obliged Christians to work for earthly reform of any kind, with the exception of the temperance cause. The evangelical impulse in the North and the South thus pointed in opposite directions and fueled a tendency to sectional confrontation as the antebellum period continued.

Despite the potential for moral conflict, sectional disputes seemed unlikely in 1815, for America's secular concerns seemed far more pressing. The gathering movement for political equality and democracy brought more and more Americans into the circle of political power, but it did not lead to increased harmony within the civic community. Though Americans hoped for a season of fruitful domestic tranquillity, the years after 1815 saw a steady rise in political friction and turbulence that the republican tradition alone could not pacify.

Before the War of 1812, federal politics had revolved around a conflict between the Federalist and the Democratic-Republican (or simply "Republican") "parties." Though not as entrenched or well organized as later parties, the Republicans and Federalists of the first American party system had recruited rival blocs of voters and leaders around an ongoing set of policy disputes. The Republican followers of Virginia's Thomas Jefferson believed that a simple farming economy would be most beneficial to the Republic. Inspired by Alexander Hamilton of New York, Jefferson's Federalist rivals maintained that a weak agrarian Republic could never survive in a world of rival empires, so the federal government must do everything possible to encourage commerce and manufacturing. Federalists also took a dim view of popular political participation, with a tendency to oppose what the youthful Daniel Webster mocked as "the dirt and mire of uncontrolled democracy." Federalists likewise favored a "broad construction" of the Constitution, since the document's literal wording offered meager authorization for their legislative program. Republicans, by contrast, were usually more sympathetic to popular democracy and resisted the Federalist program by insisting on "strict construction" of the Constitution. They denounced proposals for federal subsidies to banking, commerce, or manufacturing as unconstitutional, arguing that such Federalist policies were not only unwise, but also illegal, since the Constitution gave no explicit authorization for them. In the nonpartisan sense, both Hamiltonians and Jeffersonians were actually "republican," since both partook of the earlier political tradition of the Revolution, but the Jeffersonians fought a largely successful battle to associate the older doctrines of "republicanism" with the platform of their own "Republican" organization.

The Federalist Party was the biggest loser of the War of 1812. Federalists had voted against the declaration of war and had continued to harass the war effort in the states they controlled. After the war's triumphant conclusion, Federalists were remembered as unfaithful to the Republic in its hour of need, and their party's support fell rapidly. A Federalist candidate won some votes in the Presidential election of 1816 and the party hung on in Massachusetts, Delaware, and certain other localities for about another decade, but Federalism was clearly finished as a force in national politics.

As Federalism declined, a large but unstable alliance of Republicans took over public life. Their titular leader was President James Monroe of Virginia, a trusted but colorless associate of Madison and Jefferson who won the Presidency in 1816 as a final representative of the Revolutionary leadership. He was reelected in 1820 with only one dissenting vote in the Electoral College. Opposed to party divisions but suspicious of a Federalist resurgence, Monroe adopted a policy of "amalgamation" to bring all Americans into the Republican fold. He distributed patronage cautiously, eventually allowing some Federalists to return to appointive office, and he almost always spoke in the blandest platitudes possible, hoping to create a broad-based national consensus. Hoping in turn that the decline of active partisanship would eventually lead to the rehabilitation of Federalist men and measures, a New England editor hailed Monroe's Presidency as an "Era of Good Feelings," and the name has stuck ever since, despite the record of personal discord and factional rivalry that increased as the Administration grew older.

The desire for national consensus opened the way for a paradoxical change in Republican public policy. Federalists had long defended such Hamiltonian measures as a national bank, a protective tariff, and a national transportation program, but Republicans had opposed these proposals as unconstitutional and tending to a dangerous consolidation of power over liberty. Not only would they damage the immediate interests of farmers and planters, they could undermine the agrarian, egalitarian economy that supposedly sustained republicanism itself. At the same time, James Madison and other moderate Republicans had long believed that some commerce, especially the export of farm surpluses, was needed to reward the toil of America's rural population. In part, the War of 1812 had been fought to protect this commerce. For similar reasons, handicraft manufacturing was considered necessary for American survival, so long as urban development did not hinder prosperity of the farm. Wartime experience had strengthened these convictions among Republicans and persuaded many doubters that certain measures of political centralization and economic development were essential for American national security. With the larger, "aristocratic" designs of Federalists discredited, Republican politicians felt more latitude in adopting specific Federalist programs that would further these moderate Republican goals. Beginning in the congressional session of 1816, therefore, support for nationalist policies flourished, particularly among "War Hawk" Republicans such as Henry Clay of Kentucky and John C. Calhoun of South Carolina, younger leaders who had strongly supported a militant policy against Great Britain.

In particular, these Republicans found that the lack of manufacturing facilities had been a serious disadvantage to America's military effort. Industries had sprung up under wartime pressures, however, and the return of British trade was threatening to wipe out these new and struggling enterprises. To preserve this infant national resource, Republicans from the South, West, and Middle Atlantic states joined together in 1816 to pass the nation's first protective tariff.

They founded a national bank for similar reasons. The first Bank of the United States had gone out of existence in 1811, but wartime experience persuaded a majority of Republicans to suspend their constitutional scruples and establish a second Bank of the United States in 1816. Fixing his eyes on the $1.5 million "bonus" that the Bank's stockholders paid to the government in return for its charter, young South Carolina Congressman John C. Calhoun introduced a "Bonus Bill" that allocated the money for a national system of internal improvements. "Let us conquer space!" he challenged his colleagues, only to be rebuffed when President Madison's constitutional scruples impelled him to veto the measure at the close of his term in office. Republican friends of internal improvements continued to seek a formula for successful federal subsidies, but they also pursued their projects avidly in the various state legislatures.

The privilege of incorporation was one of the most valuable forms of assistance they could obtain from the states. Corporate status for a company gave businessmen the opportunity to invest in risky enterprises without endangering their uninvested personal assets. Unlike partners in a business, the stockholders of a corporation were not liable for the corporation's debts, beyond the limits of their own investments. Corporations were legal "persons" with the right to do business, hold property, and conduct lawsuits. In the early years, many corporations also received monopoly rights over a certain line of business or exemption from taxation or other special privileges, a further advantage to the stockholders.

Often, some of the capital for these early corporations came from the state itself, with governments buying shares along with private individuals. Legislators justified the mixture of public and private enterprise on the ground that the corporation was prepared to meet a pressing public need that could not be met in any other way, but that private capital was insufficient for the purpose. Legislators also hoped that profits from lucrative enterprises would reduce the burdens on ordinary taxpayers. Railroads, banks, and canal companies were frequent recipients of corporate privileges in the Jacksonian era, and critics often charged that political favoritism and inside connections were the key determinants of who received their benefits.

Though most public subsidies of internal improvements took place at the state level, the federal government was also involved in the process. Lighthouses and other harbor improvements had long been objects of federal spending, and public land sales had been used to finance road construction in Ohio and neighboring territories since 1802. By 1818 this policy had led to the opening of the National Road from Cumberland, Maryland, to Wheeling, now in West Virginia, on the Ohio River. In 1825 President Monroe approved a federal purchase of stock in the Chesapeake and Ohio Canal Company, and similar "subscriptions" multiplied rapidly in the subsequent Adams Administration.

Not all Republicans were satisfied by their party's embrace of internal improvements and other Hamiltonian measures. Conservative Republican thinkers, especially those from the declining plantation areas of the Upper South, had long been suspicious of any deviation from strict constructionism. Led by such men as John Randolph and John Taylor of Virginia and Nathaniel Macon of North Carolina, these men called themselves "Old Republicans" and urged their countrymen to remember that wealth and growth could be fatal signs of corruption rather than of national improvement. They argued in Congress and in the columns of newspapers such as the Richmond *Enquirer* that the tariff, bank, and internal improvements measures would stimulate commercial interests unduly, undermine agriculture, centralize power in the federal government, and violate the Constitution.

Fears for the future of slavery lay at the heart of the Old Republicans' concern. "If Congress can make canals," warned Nathaniel Macon, "they can with more propriety emancipate." Broad construction of the Constitution would create the constitutional authority for an attack on slavery, while legal privileges for commercial and manufacturing interests would create a society in the North with the material incentive and moral inclination to undertake such a mission. The future would vindicate Macon's foresight, but the Old Republicans' warnings were widely ignored in the booming years of the early postwar period.

Old Republicans won certain converts to their views. Moved by strict constructionist arguments, President Madison had vetoed a proposal for a federal system of internal improvements in 1816, and President Monroe seemed sympathetic to their principles. Faced with opposition, some advocates of federal aid favored a constitutional amendment to clarify the situation. Others warned that the effort to obtain an amendment would be difficult and vulnerable to defeat. They also refused to surrender to the argument that federal action must always be hamstrung by the narrowest possible reading of the Constitution.

Beneath the legalistic dispute, an undercurrent of fear and suspicion flowed against the superficial consensus in favor of rapid economic development. Since before the days of Jefferson, political theorists had argued that a republican government could exist only in a society marked by a widespread and roughly equal diffusion of private property, where no citizens could be forced to submit to the arbitrary domination of others. For some Americans, government aid to internal improvements and the other features of the Market Revolution threatened to alter the delicate social and economic balance that had so far staved off corruption, by creating huge private fortunes, large cities filled with penniless laborers, and mammoth corporations lacking all human sympathy and conscience. Opponents also grumbled that internal improvements would cost too much, that citizens should not be taxed for enterprises which could not benefit everyone equally, and even that the whole idea of "improving" God's creation was impious.

Some of the best-known dissents from the gospel of economic development came from the authors and poets who fashioned the classic works of nineteenth-century American literature. In their varying ways, such writers as James Fenimore Cooper, Ralph Waldo Emerson, Henry David Thoreau, and Herman Melville all raised searching questions about the social and moral costs of the departure from America's traditional way of life. One of the sharpest of such critiques came from Jacksonian Democrat Nathaniel Hawthorne, who in 1843 published "The Celestial Railroad," a satiric parody of the classic Christian allegory *Pilgrim's Progress*. In John Bunyan's original story, a solitary pilgrim named Christian toiled on foot from the City of Destruction to the Celestial City, patiently seeking salvation by God's help despite endless temptations and obstacles. In Hawthorne's version, a modern traveler was delighted to find that Christian's archaic footpath had been superseded by a railroad, though its engine looked "more like a sort of mechanical demon that would hurry us to the infernal regions than a laudable contrivance for smoothing our way to the Celestial City." By the end of the journey, these suspicions were confirmed. Though promoted as a mechanical savior, the diabolical invention proved no substitute for Christian's old-fashioned piety and treacherously delivered its idle and heedless passengers to the gates of hell.

Hawthorne's worries about the moral course of a materialistic society beguiled by seemingly miraculous technology were repeated in various ways by other contemporary authors and occasionally in popular political discourse. An electioneering ballad from North Carolina, for example, denounced internal improvements, scientific agriculture, and political corruption in verses that appealed to a variety of conservative sentiments. Speaking of pro-improvement candidates in the state elections of 1826, "Voice of the Illiterate" warned citizens to keep them out of the legislature.

> So therefore let it be our care,
> To keep these men away from there,
> Who build their castles in the air,
> Who dream they can vast things perform
> And in a breath God's works reform.
> [*But to*] us send such men as will

Cut no canals through vale nor hill,
Till the ground the good old way,
And let the funds in the Treasury stay.

Compatible sentiments cropped up in private communications. Alfred Balch, one of President Jackson's numerous correspondents from Tennessee, urged the President to reject the policy of federal aid to internal improvements on the ground that it would lead to the destruction of the states and the corruption of the republic. "When the day arrives that shall see our citizens paying tolls at turnpike gates and on canals for the benefit of the national Treasury," Balch predicted, "when the time arrives that Members of Congress shall be scuffling for a division of the spoil to be gathered from the Treasury of the General Govt. in order to sustain their own popularity and that of some corrupt administration, the *sovereignty* of the States will be but a shadow—a mere name." New York editor and Democratic ideologue John L. O'Sullivan likewise reminded his readers that the "sallow complexions, emaciated forms, and stooping shoulders" of New England mill workers proved that it was "almost a crime against society to divert human industry from the fields and the forests to iron forges and cotton factories." Compared to the optimistic promises of the supporters of internal improvements, such sentiments did not dominate the written record, yet they were clearly present in the public mind and gave a distinct ambivalence to the surface tone of public boosterism in the age of the Market Revolution.

Though concerns over rapid development were rarely voiced in the Era of Good Feelings, politicians found tranquillity in the states just as elusive as they did in the national arena. As quarrels over suffrage and representation demonstrated, social and economic controversies repeatedly fractured the republican consensus, while personal rivalries and jealous factionalism rent the fabric of political harmony. In most states, a handful of surviving Federalists struggled to maintain an alliance with one or more factions of Republicans. In Pennsylvania, for example, the "New School" Republicans sought state support for banks, tariffs, and internal improvements, while their "Old School" opponents resisted them, sometimes in association with Federalists and sometimes not. Local resentments undercut any attempt to create consistent divisions over these issues, as country voters opposed the influence of town politicians, Eastern leaders condescended to the West, and Pittsburgh quarreled with Philadelphia. In New York, Governor DeWitt Clinton put together a personal following based on patronage and family connections and sought to beat down all opposition as he dreamed of running for the Presidency. Opposing Clinton, a motley collection of factions—sporting exotic names such as Bucktails and Martling men, Burrites and Federalists—jostled with one another as they sought to topple the man New Yorkers called the "Magnus Apollo." In Virginia, by contrast, politics continued as a gentleman's game, with stiff property requirements for voting and low voter turnout at elections. Old Dominion insiders put together the "Richmond Junto" of politicians, led by Thomas Ritchie, editor of the Richmond *Enquirer*. Mainly depending on the arts of conciliation and persuasion to keep a coalition of conservative planters at peace with one another, Ritchie and his Old Republican colleagues controlled the party caucus in the state legislature and usually arranged the choice of governor and other leading state officials.

Farther south, politics was more divisive, but still infused with personal rivalries between competing leaders of the gentry as much as with consistent differences of principle or social base. In Georgia, the planters of the rice coast and the interior cotton country had created a state faction to protest a massive land grab by outside speculators in the first decade of the century. Maintaining their cohesion, this coalition of planter-lawyers fought with a more backwoods-oriented group. Class rivalries were very evident in the tone of Georgia politics, but rarely led to concrete differences in public policy. Likewise in Tennessee, a faction of planters, merchants, and land speculators dominated state politics, but they fought for power with a more roughhewn set of frontiersmen. Alabama was similarly divided between an intermarried group of transplanted Georgia gentry who dominated the fertile Black Belt and an opposing cluster of settlers in the small-farm country of the Tennessee Valley to the north. Rivalry between plantation districts and backcountry districts gave Deep South politics a more overt basis in social conflict than elsewhere, but rival groups in most states sought the symbols of popular approval more than they used state power to advance one set of class interests over another.

The factional bickering and personal aggrandizement typical of state politics in the Era of Good Feelings were precisely the evils that classical theorists had warned were fatal flaws in a republic. Factionalism seemed to reveal that politicians had become more interested in their own welfare than in the public good, a condition synonymous with corruption. Many thoughtful state leaders were disturbed by the seemingly aimless system of backbiting and intrigue that was taking the place of what they remembered as a more principled struggle between Republicans and Federalists. Following conventional wisdom, most such leaders searched for some means to unite Americans behind a widely accepted vision of the public good. Unfortunately, the irrepressible ambitions of individuals and the increasing social and economic diversity of the country combined to make this search fruitless.

For some New York politicians, however, the search for unanimity became so hopeless that they came to question the assumptions that inspired it. Instead of searching for selfless consensus, these Republican activists devised a means to combine personal advancement with pure republican principles by promoting political conflict. They called themselves the "Bucktail" faction of the New York Republican Party, and their leader was a dapper country lawyer named Martin Van Buren.

Van Buren's origins were in many ways typical of the men who came to dominate the politics of his era. Unlike the heroes of the Revolution, he did not start out with the trappings of gentry status—his father was a barely solvent tavern keeper in Kinderhook, New York, and his formal education ended after several terms in the village academy. Friendly relatives, amiable manners, and the increasing fluidity of American society enabled Van Buren to find a place in an attorney's office, where he read law and copied documents. Admitted to the bar in 1803, he began to practice in the county courts of his birthplace.

Though heavily pressured to join the local Federalist establishment, Van Buren clung to his father's Jeffersonian principles and became active in Republican politics. Offended by his stubbornness, the wealthy men of the neighborhood took their legal business elsewhere, and Van Buren's clients became the small farmers of the area whose land titles were under assault from the manorial landlords who dominated the Hudson Valley. "For my business," Van Buren later recalled, "I was to a marked extent indebted to the publick at large, having received but little from the mercantile interest or from Corporations, and none from the great landed aristocracies of the country." As he started his law practice, Van Buren also embarked on a political career that would make him President in 1837 and architect of a second American party system, as well as a classic prototype for the self-made American as professional politician.

New York politics in Van Buren's youth was dominated by bitter rivalry between Federalists and several factions of Republicans. The Federalist Party in the state had been led by Alexander Hamilton, and Van Buren always believed that "the object of its original establishment" was "to combat the democratic spirit of the country . . . , an object which it has pursued with unflagging diligence, by whatever name it may have been designated." Throwing himself into the Republican opposition, Van Buren quickly learned that party unity was the only weapon that could defeat the antidemocratic purposes of the Federalists. Other Republicans were not so perceptive and fought with each other incessantly. Hunger for office was so intense that individual Republicans were not above collaboration with the Federalist enemy in order to gain a personal advantage. Adhering to what he firmly believed was a principled position, Van Buren set his face staunchly against such behavior and made strict party loyalty the basis of his political creed, as he rose from volunteer party activist to "surrogate," or probate officer, of Columbia County, to state senator in 1812.

Short in stature and elegant in dress, Van Buren never overcame a feeling of inferiority about his origins. He compensated by rigid self-control, unfailing courtesy to friend and foe alike, a surefooted gift for intrigue, and skillful evasiveness on controversial issues. Enemies belittled him with such nicknames as the "Little Magician" and the "Red Fox of Kinderhook," but they could not diminish his increasing stature in the world of New York politics.

The opposing political style was represented by DeWitt Clinton, mayor of New York City and a man who stood for everything Van Buren could never be. Tall and imposing where the Magician was slight, Clinton belonged to a patrician family. He entered politics as the nephew and protégé of George Clinton, Revolutionary governor of New York who from 1805 to 1812 served as Vice President of the United States under Presidents Jefferson and Madison. Cultivating the scientific and literary pursuits of a gentleman amateur, DeWitt Clinton turned his greatest energies to the creation of a family-based political machine. "Why is Pierre C. Van Wyck Re-

corder of the City of New York," demanded Clinton's enemies in
1811, "[as well as] Commissioner in Bankruptcy, and why is his
brother Notary Public?" Back came the angry answer, "Because
his mother is the sister of Pierre Van Cortlandt, who married the
daughter of George Clinton, who is the brother of James Clinton
who is father of DeWitt Clinton." Fully in the spirit of eighteenth-
century politics in England and the colonies, Clinton's blatant
nepotism seeming increasingly improper in the more egalitarian
atmosphere of the nineteenth century.

Respected more than he was liked, Clinton won his greatest
public admiration as the father of the Erie Canal. As one of his
followers brusquely told him, "the charge of a cold repulsive
manner is not the most trifling charge, that your political enemies
have brought against you—you have not the jovial, social, Dem-
ocratical-Republican-how-do-you-do Suavity" of a truly popular
politician.

In Van Buren's eyes, however, Clinton's greatest sin was per-
verting the Republican Party of New York to private and selfish
purposes. Not only had the "Magnus Apollo" once made a secret
deal with Federalists to split the national Republican Party and
advance his own Presidential ambitions, he had lied to Van Buren
to conceal these tactics. Disgusted, Van Buren cut all his ties to
Clinton. Joining with like-minded friends in 1813, he helped to
establish a newspaper, the Albany *Argus*, dedicated to strictness
in Republican Party regularity. As Van Buren and his associates
guided New York through the War of 1812, they came to realize
that their own political futures and the well-being of the state
depended on the complete overthrow of DeWitt Clinton and his
principles.

Acquiring the name "Bucktails" from the emblem they wore to
party meetings in their hat brims, Van Buren and his friends began
by discarding the antiparty rhetoric that was so typical of most
Republicans of the postwar period. Parties were inevitable, the
Argus declared, and mankind has always been divided between
the parties of the few and of the many. Looking back on the
political scene as it had existed in the Era of Good Feelings, Van
Buren later spoke of the period in the direst terms. "In place of
two great parties arrayed against each other in a fair and open
contest for the establishment of the principles in the administration
of Government which they respectively believed most conducive

to the public interest, the country was overrun with personal factions. These having few higher motives for the selection of their candidates or stronger incentives to action than individual preferences or antipathies, moved the bitter waters of political agitation to their lowest depths."

The Bucktails insisted that a correct political party should be a democratic body organized at the grass roots. Ward committees should send delegates to county conventions, which would in turn send delegates to a state convention. Candidates for office should be selected by these conventions, and every participant in the process was morally bound to support the nominees selected by the party. Any deviation on the basis of personal likes or dislikes would be ruthlessly punished by stripping dissidents of official patronage and expelling them from the councils of the party. Once in office, party representatives were strictly bound by the decisions of the party caucus, even if that meant violating personal convictions or the desires of the voters.

The one thing missing from the Bucktails' program was a consistent and principled set of state policies. Emphasizing patronage and party discipline, they concentrated on the dead issue of Federalist elitism and evaded the substantive questions of their own times. As good Republicans, for example, the Bucktails were ostensibly opposed to the overwhelming power of banking institutions, but bankers who endorsed the Bucktail faction had no trouble getting what they needed from the legislature. The Bucktails' opponents later made considerable political capital by pointing to the cozy relationships that had developed between favored businessmen and the political leadership of Republican New York. Under Van Buren's leadership, the strength of the Republican Party became synonymous with republicanism itself, and party loyalty alone became the test of the common good.

Bucktails justified their rigid demand for party loyalty by explaining that the only alternative to party discipline was party disunity and the ultimate return of Federalism. As Bucktail lieutenant Silas Wright proclaimed, members were "safe if they face the enemy, but the first man we see *step to the rear*, we *cut down*." Fellow loyalist William L. Marcy later horrified the U.S. Senate when he candidly avowed the Bucktail dogma that government jobs were like the spoils of war, and that they saw "nothing wrong in the rule that to the victor belong the spoils of the enemy."

Marcy's phrase endured, and high-minded reformers ever since have deplored the influence of the "spoils system" in American politics. Ignoring such protests, however, the Bucktails propounded these principles endlessly from party platforms, from the pages of the Albany *Argus*, and from a large network of subordinate papers around the state. By following their precepts rigorously, Van Buren and his followers put the Clintonians to rout and in 1820 made themselves the masters of New York. To crown their success, they elected Van Buren to the U.S. Senate and he left for Washington, destined to repeat there what he had earlier accomplished in Albany. In his absence, he left behind a tightly knit alliance of Bucktail party leaders who soon became known as the Albany Regency.

Arriving in Washington, Van Buren found the capital in disarray. Though President Monroe had longed for national unity, the federal government was riven by the same forces of economic conflict and personal ambition that disrupted the politics of the states. The question of who would succeed Monroe was already splitting the government into feuding camps. The Panic of 1819 had overthrown postwar prosperity and restrictive measures by the new Bank of the United States seemed to make matters worse, casting grave doubts on the Republican decision to discard ideology and embrace this controversial Federalist nostrum. More seriously, the decline of interparty conflict had created a situation in which Republicans felt free to quarrel among themselves about the country's most deeply divisive social issue—the institution of slavery. Suddenly, with little prior warning, the controversy burst on Congress with the clangor of what the aging Thomas Jefferson called "a firebell in the night."

When the territory of Missouri applied for statehood in 1819, Representative James Tallmadge of New York, a Clintonian, asked Congress to prohibit the further importation of slaves into the territory and to require the eventual elimination of slavery there as a condition for admission to the Union. His proposal threw the House into an uproar. Republicans who had thought themselves united by a common love of liberty and a broad desire for national improvement suddenly found themselves divided by the institution of human bondage. In the angry speeches that followed, Northern congressmen pointed to the Declaration of Independence as the embodiment of republican principles. As a congressman from Massachusetts put it, slavery violated the right to liberty and the pursuit of happiness, so "the attempt to extend slavery to the new States, is in direct violation of the clause [in the U.S. Constitution] which guarantees a republican form of government to all the States." Infuriated slaveholders shot back that the immortal principles of the Declaration did not apply to black people, only to whites. Some of them went further and dismissed the phrase "all men are created equal" as meaningless—"a fanfaronade of metaphysical abstractions," as Old Republican John Randolph later put it. An attempt by Congress to interfere with the freedom of Missouri to continue slavery was a violation of white rights and states' rights. If Congress could restrict slavery in Missouri, what could stop it from attacking slavery anywhere? One Georgia congressman roared that Tallmadge "had kindled a fire which all the waters of the ocean cannot put out, which seas of blood can only extinguish."

The New Yorker's amendment passed the House on a strictly sectional vote, only to die in the Senate, where the balance of free states and slave states gave a veto to the South. The significance of this sectional balance of power would grow in the years to come, but in the meantime, numerous congressmen felt that the immediate controversy should be compromised. In March of 1820, at the urging of Henry Clay, the Senate agreed to admit Missouri without restriction and to preserve the sectional balance by adding the free state of Maine. For the future, slavery in the Louisiana Purchase could exist only in the region south of the southern boundary of Missouri. Old Republicans protested that states' rights barred Congress from interfering with slavery in any future state, but the House agreed to the compromise in a portentously sectional vote. Southerners and a few Northern allies agreed to the admission of Missouri, while a Northern coalition divided the Louisiana Territory in two, permitting slavery in one portion but banning it from the other. The question of slavery was so deeply divisive that very few congressmen would vote for both sides of this so-called Missouri Compromise.

As the Missouri crisis demonstrated, the apparent unanimity of the Era of Good Feelings masked some serious divisions about the nature and direction of American society. Following the congressional controversy from his library at Monticello, Thomas Jefferson saw its dangers with stark clarity. "I considered it at once as the knell of the Union," he wrote to a Northern sympathizer.

"A geographical line, coinciding with a marked principle, moral and political, once conceived and held up to angry passions of men, will never be obliterated; and every new irritation will mark it deeper and deeper." Jefferson acknowledged that slavery was the root of the looming threat to the Union and, as always, he regretted the existence of slavery. Like the Southerners in Congress, however, he feared a bloodbath if emancipation were not combined with deportation of the freedmen from America; the practical objections to this course seemed insurmountable. "As it is," Jefferson concluded painfully, "we have the wolf by the ears, and we can neither hold him, nor safely let him go. Justice is in one scale, and self-preservation in the other."

White Southerners who were less idealistic than Thomas Jefferson thought they saw the same dilemma. In the years ahead, they would opt for self-preservation without any of the misgivings that troubled the Sage of Monticello. They insisted on the sectional political balance that the Compromise protected and they would increasingly make the safety of slavery an important factor in guiding their course in national politics. At the same time, Northerners who desired to protect the Union sought to reassure the South without alienating their own section. These leaders would be very receptive to new alignments in politics that did not depend on Mr. Jefferson's "geographical line, coinciding with a marked principle." In part, the political parties of the Jacksonian era would be designed to meet such specifications.

Without entirely realizing it, Martin Van Buren's Bucktails had stumbled on a device that could bring coherence to social, economic, and political conflict in all the states and equilibrium to the national government. When rival political parties linked local and national issues, the sectional controversy that frightened Jefferson and many others could be evaded for a while, and the more manageable controversies aroused by the Market Revolution could be addressed in an orderly way. The revised party system would likewise leave ample room for personal rivalries and individual ambition, without allowing these potentially disruptive energies to gain destructive momentum. The second American party system would not be built in a day, however, and it could not even be attempted without a stronger national sense that amalgamation could not work. That sense began to build, however, in the waning years of James Monroe's Administration.

A Corrupt Bargain

IN JUNE OF 1826, Vice President John C. Calhoun of South Carolina addressed an unusual letter to General Andrew Jackson, complaining of the despotic menace of President John Quincy Adams. "In my opinion," Calhoun solemnly announced, "liberty was never in greater danger and such, I believe [*sic*], to be the impression of the coolest and most considerate of our citizens." Invoking revered formulas of republicanism, Calhoun put the matter bluntly. "An issue has been fairly made . . . , between *power* and *liberty*," he declared. Like a British monarch, President Adams was attempting to use "the power and patronage of the Executive" to make "the form of electing by the people a mere farce." Once the President could name his own successor, hereditary monarchy could not be far distant. But "I confide in the intelligence and virtue of the people," Calhoun concluded and pledged his support to Jackson in the next Presidential election. "That you may be the instrument, under providence, of confounding political machinations and of turning the attempts against the liberty of the country, into the means of perpetuating our freedom, is my sincere wish."

To be the instrument of divine providence was a role that Andrew Jackson relished. "I trust that my name will always be found on the side of the people," he replied gravely. "As their confidence in your talents and virtue has placed you in the second office of the government [I trust] that we shall march hand in hand in their cause." He thereby granted Calhoun what the South Carolinian had been seeking: tacit assurance that Calhoun could continue as Vice President in a Jackson Administration, with the hope of eventually succeeding Jackson as President.

Even in 1826, it was somewhat unusual for the Vice President to close ranks with the President's bitterest enemies, but the 1820s were unusual times. Calhoun's alarm about the future of republicanism grew most immediately from the nation's experience in the Presidential election of 1824. Republican Party unity had splintered irretrievably as five major candidates, Jackson and Calhoun among them, squabbled for the Presidency. The subsequent election of John Quincy Adams of Massachusetts had led to charges of corruption in high places, and Jackson and Calhoun were not the only Americans who feared that "the liberties of the country are in danger." Though Calhoun's warnings of despotism were highly exaggerated, the development of a new political order in the United States grew directly out of the situation that aroused the South Carolinian's anxieties.

Like his predecessors, James Monroe declined to serve a third term as President, but no one stood out as a superior candidate to succeed him. Except for the Administration of John Adams in the 1790s, the President had always been a Virginia planter and a Revolutionary hero, while the Vice President had often been a politician from New York. Since the election of Thomas Jefferson in 1800, the winning candidate had always been nominated by an unofficial caucus of congressional Republicans. This time, no Virginian seemed qualified, so other states rushed forward with their own favorite sons. Custom also required that these aspirants disclaim all ambition for the office; the example of Washington dictated that the office of President was too sacred to seek or to decline. Despite this injunction, no fewer than five major "candidates" (the word itself sounded inappropriate to the sternest old-fashioned republicans) jostled for position with thinly veiled ambition. Three of these men were members of James Monroe's Cabinet: William H. Crawford, John Quincy Adams, and John C. Calhoun. Henry Clay, Speaker of the House of Representatives, was a fourth, and General Andrew Jackson completed the list.

Logically speaking, there should have been some means to winnow this large field and facilitate reasonable comparisons between the candidates, but the congressional caucus was an awkward instrument for this purpose. It was not a true nominating convention—no one had selected the congressmen on the basis of their Presidential preferences, and nominating a President was not their constitutional responsibility. As an organ of the Republican Party, the caucus could only come up with one nominee and insist that all good Republicans support him. Since no other party existed to propose an alternative, the caucus procedure seemed to deprive voters of all meaningful choice in a transaction fraught with backroom deals and secret maneuvers. The caucus system was therefore unpopular, and many Americans denounced it. For a man like Martin Van Buren, however, the caucus was an essential tool of party unity, and party unity was essential to the safety of republicanism. He therefore labored assiduously to rebuild the New York–Virginia alliance that had dominated the government for so long, and to use the caucus to line up support for the favorite candidate of congressional insiders, William H. Crawford of Georgia.

Of all the candidates, Crawford came closest to the model of a traditional successor. Born in Virginia but reared in Georgia, he had many friends in Congress and served as Secretary of the Treasury. Enjoying close ties to the Old Republicans of Virginia, Crawford had also used Treasury positions to reward his friends and further his prospects. Though he had favored the Bank of the United States, his other views accorded with the "radical" states'-rights school, and his supporters were known as Radicals. As the candidate of "politics as usual," Crawford represented the greatest continuity with Monroe, though his talents seem meager in retrospect and he suffered a paralyzing stroke halfway through the campaign.

John Quincy Adams, the eventual winner, had originally stood with the Federalist Party of his father but deserted to Jefferson's side in 1807. He was thus the reluctant favorite of New England, whose leaders would have preferred a more faithful adherent to Federalism. Elsewhere, the Republican faithful remembered Adams's father with a shudder and doubted the sincerity of his Jeffersonian conversion. Southerners were especially suspicious of Adams's willingness to stand up for slavery. Experienced and erudite but personally stiff, he had begun his diplomatic career at the age of fourteen while secretary of legation to the U.S. minister to Russia. Later graduating from Harvard College, he served successfully in a variety of diplomatic posts, including chief of the U.S. delegation that negotiated an end to the War of 1812 and Secretary of State under President Monroe. Adams was admired for his accomplishments, but he had limited experience in elected office. Even more than his contemporaries realized in 1824, he was determined to use federal power the way Alexander Hamilton had hoped, to plan and fund a rapid but orderly transition to a commercial and industrial society.

Adams's South Carolina rival was John C. Calhoun, likewise brilliant and also serving in Monroe's Cabinet, as Secretary of War. Convinced that national economic development was a military and political necessity, he was still a vigorous supporter of internal improvements, the national bank, and even a mild protective tariff. Calhoun counted on support from Pennsylvania to demonstrate his broad national appeal; when that failed to materialize, he withdrew from the contest and ran successfully for Vice President.

Henry Clay of Kentucky vied for the Presidency as a spokesman for the West and as Speaker of the House of Representatives. A lawyer like the others, he had risen from modest circumstances in Virginia with the help of distinguished mentors. Moving to Kentucky as a young man, he attached himself to the hemp-planting interests of the Blue Grass region and opposed Kentucky's efforts to relieve debtors in the Panic of 1819. Also like Calhoun, Clay had strongly supported the War of 1812 and thereafter the nationalistic measures of innovative Republicans.

Even more than Calhoun and Adams, Clay put the needs of a market economy at the center of his social and political values. "The greatest want of civilized society is a market for the sale and exchange of the surplus of the produce . . . of its members," he informed the House of Representatives in 1824. "This market may exist at home, or abroad, or both, but it must exist somewhere if society prospers." Directly confronting the objections of Old Republicans, Clay scoffed at their fear that the "manufacturing system is adverse to the genius of our government, in its tendency to the accumulation of large capitals in a few hands; in the corruption of the public morals, . . . and in the consequent danger to the public liberty." Instead, he argued, "the greatest danger to public liberty is idleness and vice." To combat these evils, Clay suggested an intricate set of measures to encourage the Market Revolution that he called "the American System." In his proposals, high tariffs would protect America's infant industries, while steep prices for federal lands would provide the revenue for an expensive system of internal improvements. Clay hoped the American System would gain him the united support of the West and win him the election as the second choice of everyone else.

As an outsider in official Washington, General Andrew Jackson stood apart from the other candidates. Born in the Carolina backcountry in 1767, Jackson grew up on the frontier and fought as a young teenager in the guerrilla warfare that the Revolution brought to the Piedmont. When peace arrived, he was sixteen years old and bereft of both parents and siblings. After squandering a small inheritance in a few months of furious dissipation, he pulled himself together, read law, and headed for the Tennessee frontier. There he practiced law, married into a leading family, and quickly rose in politics.

Investing shrewdly in land and slaves, Jackson soon claimed the rank of a leading planter and a gentleman of substance. Like many of his peers, he engaged in several duels and killed one of his opponents. But after a brush with financial disaster in a mercantile and real estate speculation, Jackson pulled back from the unbridled pursuit of personal wealth and status that preoccupied most of his Nashville friends. Though briefly serving as congressman, senator, and judge, he turned instead to military service, winning election as major general of the Tennessee militia in 1802 and devoting himself to improving its preparedness while he struggled to repair his own private fortunes. Throughout Tennessee, he was winning a reputation as a commanding public figure, normally courteous and grave but quick to lose his temper and slow to forgive offenses, with an almost limitless capacity for firm personal loyalty and fierce personal hatred.

In the following decade, the War of 1812 gave Jackson the opportunity to prove himself on a larger stage, and he emerged a national hero. Still suffering from serious wounds incurred in a private brawl, he dragged himself from a sickbed in 1813 and led his Tennessee and Kentucky volunteers against Britain's Creek Indian allies. Along the way, Jackson's personal courage and determination won him the soldier's nickname "Old Hickory," after the tough, fibrous wood well known as the most durable natural substance on the frontier. Seizing huge chunks of Alabama and Mississippi wilderness from the Indians, Jackson in 1815 defeated the crack British regulars who had sought to capture New Orleans. In a war that had seen one American fiasco after another, culminating in the burning of Washington, D.C., Jackson's triumphs were received as a providential vindication of republicanism. With the editor of *The New Hampshire Patriot*, Americans rejoiced that "the brilliant and unparalleled victory at *New Orleans*, has closed the war in a blaze of Glory" and "placed America on the very pinnacle of fame." Henry Clay, Jackson's future rival, exulted, "*Now*, I can go to England without mortification." In the midst of the jubilation, no one minded that a peace treaty had been signed at Ghent two weeks before the battle took place but without the knowledge of the combatants.

The victorious general was immediately mentioned for the Presidency, but James Monroe had a prior claim, so Andrew Jackson waited. In the interim, he wrested more Indian territory in a series of ruthless treaty negotiations. While tracking an insurgent band of Seminoles in 1818, he invaded Spanish Florida, executed two British agents he blamed for the uprising, and provoked an international uproar. Monroe and his Cabinet contemplated a court-martial for the irascible commander, but the popularity of Jackson's actions dissuaded them. The United States acquired Florida lawfully the next year, and Monroe made Jackson governor of the territory in 1821 as a sign of his approval.

For many genteel Easterners, Jackson would always be a hot-tempered frontier outlaw. Van Buren remembered later that Richmond editor Thomas Ritchie "scarcely ever went to bed without apprehension that he would wake to hear of some *coup d'état* by the General." For others, Jackson was the model republican statesman who combined the common touch of the self-made man with the poise and determination of a natural aristocrat. His talents and virtues, wrote one typical admirer, demand "his elevation as the second Washington of America." He won the support of those who viewed the intriguing and manipulation of the other candidates as a disgrace to the Republic and a violation of public virtue. "If we would preserve the original simplicity of our institutions and perpetuate this grand republic," wrote another early supporter, "we wou'd choose our presidents not for the splendour of their manners, but their simplicity and plainness—not for the eloquence of their haranguing . . . , [nor] their pliancy and amiable accomodation [*sic*] of the ten thousand particular wills and wishes that assail them on every side, but a firm, dignified and commanding resistance of every thing not founded in *right*, and plain solid *republican utility*." By the early 1820s, Jackson himself was listening to these plaudits with increasingly serious attention, and he began to view himself as the restorer of virtue and justice to a much abused nation.

Despite his military honors, Jackson had virtually no standing as a prominent civilian statesman. For many months after his formal nomination by the Tennessee legislature, the other major candidates refused to take his prospects seriously. Then the worried letters began to trickle in. "The unfortunate nomination of Gen. Jackson has so possessed the public mind and the disorder has broken out in so many fresh places that your friends here have been unable to make much headway," reported a bewildered Clay supporter from Philadelphia. "The [Jackson] contagion is even spreading to this country," echoed another from Alabama. "Strange! Wild! Infatuated!" marveled another observer from Cincinnati. "Two thirds here are said to be for Jackson. But surely, in February last, his name was not mentioned in the Miami country." Surprising even Jackson's managers, his candidacy had caught the public imagination in diverse states, and the General began to gather endorsements from public meetings and state conventions throughout the Union.

The campaign methods of the other major candidates matched their assumptions about how the President would be chosen and who would make the key decisions. Six out of twenty-four states still chose Presidential electors in the state legislature, and lobbying in these states focused directly on the established legislative power brokers. Elsewhere, candidates and their close friends courted key state leaders who were thought to be capable of delivering their states. A favorite tactic was to accuse a rival candidate of corruption in his Cabinet post or of actions damaging to the state or section in question. Alone among the candidates, William H. Crawford put his faith in the power of the congressional caucus, while his rivals denounced the institution as an "aristocratic" instrument to control the popular will. When the caucus finally met, only 66 congressmen out of 291 dared to attend. Crawford won the nomination with 64 votes, but the prize brought him opprobrium rather than success.

Popular campaigning was limited to the eighteen states where electors would be chosen by voters themselves. Alert campaign managers were quick to line up newspaper support and local committees of correspondence, but the Jackson men seemed more ready than the others to employ mass meetings, "spontaneous" resolutions, and personal canvassing among the voters. Favorable letters to newspapers lauded Old Hickory as untainted by political intrigue, blessed by Revolutionary participation, and bound by the principles of George Washington. By contrast, Adams's campaign biography stressed the merits of his illustrious ancestors.

In all the closely contested states, direct appeals to the voters tended to expand the role of ordinary voters in a process dominated by locally prominent citizens in the past. In New York, a "People's Party" led by DeWitt Clinton capitalized on hostility to Van Buren's manipulation of the state and national caucuses to demand a popular choice of electors. In New Jersey and North Carolina, "People's tickets" carried their states for the Old Hero, riding popular resentment of established political cliques. Jackson himself insisted that he did not seek the office and that he would take it only as the free gift of the people, but in his correspondence he encouraged the popular or egalitarian dimension of his candidacy by soberly contrasting the political morality of "the people" with "the intrigues of designing Damagogues." He offered no programs to democratize society, but he defended the virtues of the old Republic in a manner that tended to magnify the importance of the electorate. "I am fast going out of life," he predicted prematurely, "but my fervent prayers are that our republican government may be perpetual, and the people alone by their Virtue, and independent exercise of their free suffrage can make it perpetual."

Every candidate couched his appeal in terms of republican principles, but alternatives in political program lent substance to the elusive differences of ideological nuance. "Radicals" promised that Crawford would oppose the wasteful and unconstitutional practice of protective tariffs and federal subsidy of internal improvements. Adams, Clay, and to a lesser extent Calhoun took the opposite tack and called for protection and transportation development. Jackson straddled the issue, promising to support "a judicious examination and revision" of the tariff in order to benefit American workingmen over European manufacturers, but resisting any program that would favor one state or section more than another.

This reply was designed to assist his cause in pro-tariff Pennsylvania without damaging it in the anti-tariff South, and to a large extent, it succeeded.

The final balloting was inconclusive. Jackson led with 99 electoral votes, followed by Adams with 84. The General had won most of his support from the South and West, as well as Pennsylvania and New Jersey, while Adams had carried his native New England. Van Buren's failure to deliver the vote of New York left Crawford with only 41 electoral votes; Clay trailed with 37, mostly from Kentucky, Ohio, and Missouri. In the popular vote, Jackson claimed 152,901 out of 361,120 votes cast, or 42.3 percent. Compared to other contemporary elections, not many voters participated in the balloting; nationwide, about one adult white male in four cast a ballot, and Maryland and Alabama were the only states where more than half the eligible voters appeared at the polls. Since no candidate won a majority of electoral votes, the House of Representatives faced a choice between the top three vote getters. In accordance with the Twelfth Amendment to the Constitution, each state delegation in the House would receive one vote in the election. As the eliminated candidate, Henry Clay thus found himself in the interesting role of kingmaker.

Clay began leaning to Adams before he left Kentucky for Washington in late November 1824. The two men disliked each other, but Adams supported the American System, Crawford rejected it, and Jackson equivocated. Moreover, it would be easier for Clay, as a Kentuckian, to follow Adams in the White House than to succeed a fellow Westerner. Despite the logic of his preference for Adams, however, Clay remained noncommittal. The situation in Washington was ripe for intrigue, and Clay apparently saw no reason why he should not protect his future interests while also following his best judgment for the good of the country. On the night of January 9, 1825, a month before the balloting in the House, Clay and Adams reached an understanding. The Kentuckian promised to support the New Englander and emerged from their private meeting with the conviction that he could have any position in the Cabinet that he chose, particularly the post of Secretary of State.

To preserve their consciences and the accepted proprieties of the day, the two men probably failed to state the bargain explicitly, but their gentlemen's agreement had violated the standards of strict republican morality. Throughout the campaign, all the candidates had been obliged to protest that they would make no secret deals to obtain the Presidency. Like Jackson, Adams had gone even further and insisted to his private correspondents that he did not seek the office, had never sought any office, and would serve only at the genuine behest of the people. Clay had acknowledged his feelings more honestly, but both men knew that personal ambition for the Presidency was thought to be corrupt, and that dickering for the office would arouse a public outcry. Since the Department of State was still regarded as a semiautomatic stepping-stone to the White House, for Adams to offer this Cabinet post in exchange for the Presidency would amount to an attempt to obtain his own election by appointing an inside successor. Trading favors later became routine in American politics, but the citizens of 1825 were quick to call this practice corruption. The political risks were therefore obvious as Clay began lobbying for Adams at the end of January 1825.

Talk began immediately that Adams and Clay had rigged the election with a "corrupt bargain." An anonymous congressman published charges that Clay would deliver his friends for Adams and collect the State Department as his reward. Clay denied it angrily and demanded an investigation, but his accuser turned out to be a crackpot congressman who refused to testify and whom no one in Washington took seriously except Andrew Jackson. Soon thereafter, the election took place, Clay's friends did vote for Adams, a number of old Federalists swung to him as well, and Adams became the President by a bare one-vote margin. Several days later, Adams asked Clay to be Secretary of State, and Clay accepted. It was the worst political mistake the Kentuckian ever made.

The reaction was instantaneous. "Expired at Washington, on the ninth of February," announced one newspaper, "of poison administered by the assassin hands of John Quincy Adams, the usurper, and Henry Clay, the virtue, liberty and independence of the United States." Vice President–elect Calhoun agreed. In his view, Adams's election and Clay's appointment was a flagrant attack on republican values, "the most dangerous stab, which the liberty of this country has ever received." Andrew Jackson was more grim. "The Judas of the West has closed the contract, and received the thirty pieces of silver. His end will be the same." For the rest of his life, Henry Clay would struggle with the charge of an infamous "bargain and sale."

Remaining calm in public, Jackson thought immediately of the election of 1828 and the chance it would give him to reestablish the supremacy of what he called "the will of the people." Though the House had been constitutionally free to select any of the top three candidates, Jackson felt that his share of the popular vote gave him the moral right to the office. In voting for Adams, moreover, the Kentucky delegation had violated instructions from the state legislature to cast their ballots for Jackson, and the General could point to similar evidence from other states to show that in fact he was the people's choice. In the aftermath of the "corrupt bargain," his conviction grew stronger that republican liberty could survive only if the power of the people was expanded. This would require him to run for President again. A powerful but unacknowledged craving for personal vindication fueled Jackson's drive for the White House, but he steadily justified his course in terms of democracy and republicanism rather than personal satisfaction. This proved to be a winning combination.

Taking office, President Adams was well aware of his political weakness, but he quickly made matters worse, if that were possible. Prudence required this minority President to play safe and not arouse unnecessary antagonism, but John Quincy Adams had great plans for the growth and development of the United States that he felt duty-bound to advocate, regardless of his precarious popularity. Most Republicans still believed that liberty and power were opposites, but Adams embraced heresy and advocated the contrary. "Liberty *is* power," he proclaimed in his first annual message to Congress and proceeded to outline a vast array of expensive projects for internal improvement, ranging from roads and canals to a national university and a national astronomical observatory. Adams knew his grandiose program would be unpopular with the voters, but he stubbornly plunged ahead. "The spirit of improvement is abroad upon the earth," he intoned. "While foreign nations less blessed with . . . freedom . . . than ourselves are advancing with gigantic strides in the career of public improvement, were we to slumber in indolence or fold up our arms and proclaim to the world that we are palsied by the will of our constituents, would it not be to cast away the bounties of providence and doom ourselves to perpetual inferiority?"

Congress was aghast. *Palsied* by the will of their constituents? Had the man no shame? His election itself was a monumental scandal. Did he need to go further to show his contempt for the sovereign people? "Before my God I declare," swore John Branch, an impassioned senator from North Carolina, ". . . I never will be *palsied* by any power save the Constitution and *'the will of my constituents,'* " and his colleagues scrambled to agree with him. Though many representatives still defended the Administration, few would go so far as to introduce bills for the President, and the nation's press heaped ridicule on Adams's plans for "lighthouses of the skies."

Adams's gaffe about "the will of our constituents" was symptomatic of his larger problem. Certain leading Republicans had come to accept the necessity of at least some government aid to economic development, but large numbers of ordinary Americans still suspected that the Market Revolution might corrupt the Republic. For these citizens, the effects of innovations such as fraudulent bank notes and the putting-out system had only stimulated greed, undermined virtue, and promoted social, economic, and political inequality. Adams's proposals would obviously further such developments, and his critics were quick to identify the "corrupt bargain" with the wider problem of social and political decadence. Like Hamilton before him, Adams would befriend a powerful "monied interest" that would tax and exploit the yeoman farmer until he was gradually reduced from republican independence to postrepublican dependence. High taxes and large public expenditures would create opportunities for embezzlement, graft, and conflicts of interest. Legions of useless officials would fatten at the public trough, using their money like King George's courtiers, to riot in luxury and rig elections to perpetuate themselves in power. Greed would triumph, virtue would fail, and republican society would perish.

Viewing it in the context of the President's larger political program, outraged Republicans concluded that the "corrupt bargain" with Clay was no isolated incident but an essential first step in a conspiracy to corrupt America as a whole. The very words "corrupt bargain" concisely conveyed the dual threat of an immoral and overly commercialized society that Adams's critics envisioned. Fighting back, they hurled the President's words about "palsy" back into his teeth, reasserting the power of the still-virtuous people to block all grandiose schemes and thereby paralyze the threat to the Republic.

In the absence of debatable Administration bills, dissent in Congress focused on Adams's request to send representatives to a Pan-American congress to be held in Panama. Congressmen denounced the proposal as an effort to compromise U.S. sovereignty, stretch the Constitution, repudiate the wisdom of George Washington, and condone the tolerant racial attitudes of Latin America. Arguments about strict construction and the dangers of executive power filled the Senate chamber and inspired Calhoun to write his message to Jackson that "liberty was never in greater danger." The climax came when John Randolph of Roanoke, the neurotic Old Republican from Virginia, denounced the corruption of the recent election. "Let Judas have his thirty pieces of silver," he shrieked. "They shall go to buy a Potter's field, in which to inter this miserable Constitution of ours, crucified between two gentlemen, suffering for 'conscience sake,' under the burden of the first two offices of this Government." Alluding to the personal habits of the straitlaced President and the loose-living Cabinet officer, Randolph called their coalition "the combination, unheard of till then, of the puritan with the blackleg." Unable to stand more abuse, Clay challenged Randolph to a duel, but both men survived it unscathed. For the rest of Adams's term, Congress and the President stood at a virtual deadlock.

Prudent use of patronage might have eased the stalemate, but Adams set his face against administrative methods that most political leaders were coming to take for granted. Then as now, the President could scarcely perform his duties without cooperative subordinates who shared his principles and confidence. State and federal executives were learning, moreover, that a judicious appointments policy could cement the loyalty of supporters, strengthen a political base, and create a reliable and coherent body of campaign workers. Republican morality warned against the corruption inherent in a spoils system of appointments, but resourceful politicians had always relied on it to some extent, and public acceptance of the system was growing. Unlike his peers, however, John Quincy Adams bent over backward to reward his enemies, punish his friends, and undermine his own Administration.

The opposition pointed endlessly to the Clay appointment as evidence of Adams's attempt to manipulate patronage and entrench himself in office as a monarch of corruption. With the exception of Clay's case, however, the charge was entirely false. Men who had worked tirelessly for the President's election, exposing themselves to taunts of "Federalist" and "aristocrat," could barely get so much as a limp handshake from John Quincy Adams, much less a federal appointment or a printing contract. "Such a system of [political rewards] would be repugnant to my very soul," Adams sniffed. Meanwhile, the large number of pliant workers whom Crawford had installed in the Treasury and elsewhere remained undisturbed, free to devote long hours to the cause of their new favorite, Andrew Jackson. Adams would never fire anyone—even a Cabinet secretary—except for official misconduct, and political opposition never counted as misconduct. Even when vacancies occurred naturally, Adams refused to give his well-qualified supporters any sign of his personal confidence and gratitude by asking them to join the government. At the height of his reelection campaign in 1828, for example, he appointed an active Jackson partisan to be postmaster of Philadelphia. This dogmatic indifference to practical politics drove pragmatists such as Henry Clay to despair. "The friends of the Administration have to contend not only against their enemies," he groaned, "but against the Administration itself, which leaves its power in the hands of its own enemies." Clay did what he could with the patronage of his own department, but this was very little.

Upon entering office, Adams had congratulated Americans that the "baneful weed of party strife was uprooted" in the palmy days of James Monroe. He urged his countrymen to go further and "discard every element of rancor . . . and yield to talents and virtue that confidence which in times of contention for principle was bestowed only upon those who bore the badge of party communion." He dismissed the ancient quarrel between Federalists and Republicans as obsolete, but took the latent conflict between North and South more seriously. He assured the South that its domestic institutions were not the business of federal government, and he urged the representatives of different sections to allow friendly relations in Washington to take the place of sectional prejudice. In other words, Adams tried awkwardly to extend the amalgamating policies of Monroe, yet offered nothing but wooden expressions of goodwill to replace the sectional antagonisms that always simmered beneath the courteous surface of life in Washington.

The President's favorite policies, however, were deeply offensive to plantation interests and sensibilities and did nothing to bridge the sectional gap. Though he expressed himself only to his diary, the President did hate slavery as much as Southerners had suspected. Many Northern leaders continued to side with the President because they admired his program or disliked Jackson, but they lacked any formal organization. To distinguish themselves from the Democratic-Republicans of the opposition, the President's supporters called themselves National Republicans during his reelection campaign, but they made few concrete efforts to weld themselves into a party.

The opposition was less bashful. An alliance gradually developed between the supporters of Jackson, Crawford, and Calhoun, with Jackson as standard-bearer and Calhoun as the candidate for Vice President. The task of unification was not simple, for Jackson and Crawford disliked each other and many outside the General's original camp had doubts about the emotional stability of the "military chieftain." After sizing up the situation, however, Martin Van Buren of New York determined that the union ought to be attempted. Van Buren's beliefs were staunchly Jeffersonian and he could not countenance the constitutional principles that Adams tried so ineptly to champion. He recognized Jackson as the only logical candidate for the opposition and thought that the other former Radicals would come around. Calhoun saw the same logic and joined the Jackson camp immediately. But Van Buren recognized that party organization would require concert, harmony, and discipline, qualities that the various state-level politicos would not find easy to tolerate. After mending his fences in New York, Van Buren put his formidable skills as an organizer to work and began to forge a national alliance that would come to be known as the Democratic Party.

Van Buren began at the top. He visited with Calhoun and restored congenial relations there. Calhoun prepared the way for an approach to Thomas Ritchie, editor of the Richmond *Enquirer*, head of the so-called Richmond Junto of leading Virginia Republicans, and the principal voice of Crawford's Southern supporters. On January 13, 1827, Van Buren addressed a carefully worded letter to Ritchie, spelling out the advantage of a party alliance "between the planters of the South and the plain Republicans of the North."

The New York senator began by urging the importance of a national convention of Republicans to bring about "the substantial reorganization of the Old Republican Party." Rejecting the anti-party sentiments of Adams and Monroe, Van Buren insisted that party divisions were inevitable and even beneficial. "We must always have party distinctions and the old ones are best," he explained, drawing on his experience with the Bucktails and the Clintonians. Specifically, Van Buren proposed to re-create the old New York–Virginia alliance of Republicans, designate Jackson as their nominee, and force Adams and company into the role of Federalists. He wanted to return to the pattern that prevailed when Ritchie's idol Jefferson battled with the forces of J. Q. Adams's father. The alternative, he predicted, was not an absence of parties but another outburst from Jefferson's "firebell in the night." "If the old [party distinctions] are suppressed," he argued, "prejudices between free and slave holding states will inevitably take their place." In effect, Van Buren proposed to stifle sectionalism by encouraging a party system that would cut across sectional lines. If Northerners and Southerners of one party felt more in common with one another than with Northerners and Southerners of the other party, neither section could rally all its forces against the other and the constructive tensions of party could mitigate the violent tensions of sectionalism. Paradoxically, party divisions would lead to national unity. The argument was persuasive. Ritchie joined the Jackson forces and brought most of the old Crawford men with him.

Having secured the South, Van Buren turned to New York, Pennsylvania, and the states of the Ohio Valley. This region was ethnically and economically diverse and politically rent with factions. Many voters there sympathized with Jackson's Old Republican values, but they also appreciated the advantages of commercial development. Unlike Southern planters, the commercial farmers of the middle states wanted tariff protection from imports, for they grew crops such as hemp and wool for American markets that faced competition from abroad. Manufacturers in these states wanted similar protection against imported finished goods. Since many of these farmers and mill owners were his own New York constituents, Senator Van Buren set out to do what he could for them.

Guided by Van Buren's Regency colleague Silas Wright, the

House produced a tariff bill in 1828 that gave generous protection to the Western producers of molasses, hemp, and wool, but imposed higher prices on the iron, rope, and sailcloth purchased by New England shipping interests. The costs of the bill would thus be paid by diehard Adams men, while the benefits would go to potential Jacksonians. Manufacturers of woolens protested that they had not received enough protection, so Van Buren satisfied them with an amendment in the Senate that increased the woolen duty just high enough to win votes from manufacturing areas, but not so high as to alienate congressmen whose constituents were more likely to buy blankets than sell them. It was an artful piece of legislative juggling, but it had little to do with the presumed republican principles of Andrew Jackson.

New England leaders acquiesced in the tariff of 1828, even though their section bore a heavy portion of its costs. Manufacturing and wool growing were spreading into their region also, and Yankee sentiment was shifting from free trade to protectionism. The South, however, was outraged and called the bill a "tariff of abominations." Except for the sugar interests of Louisiana and the hemp growers of Kentucky, Southern planters could get no benefit from protection of manufactures but had to pay the costs in higher prices for retail items and in lower foreign demand for their staples. The Virginia legislature called protection "unconstitutional, unwise, unjust, unequal, and oppressive." Alabama lawmakers described its supporters as "the allied powers of avarice, monopoly, and ambition" and its passage as "a palpable usurpation of a power not given by the Constitution; . . . a species of oppression little less than legalized pillage of the property of her citizens." Southerners did not desert the Hero's banner on account of the tariff issue, for they could not abandon him for Adams, but they would carry their outrage into national politics after the election was over.

With major sectional leaders satisfied, the Jacksonians' focus shifted to the battle for public opinion. Led by Duff Green, a Calhoun favorite who edited the *U.S. Telegraph* in Washington, a corps of newspapers spread the Jackson message across the country. In addition to Thomas Ritchie, prominent state editors included Regency spokesman Edwin Croswell of the Albany (New York) *Argus*, former Clay supporters Amos Kendall and Francis Preston Blair of the Frankfort (Kentucky) *Argus of Western America*, and Isaac Hill of the Portsmouth *New Hampshire Patriot*.

Scribbling busily in Nashville, the General's trusted friends Major John Henry Eaton and Major William B. Lewis headed a central committee of correspondence that answered campaign charges and attempted to keep all segments of the Jackson alliance informed of overall developments. By 1828, the opposition was united behind the General and a formal convention proved to be unnecessary.

National organizing efforts among Jacksonians were mostly undertaken by and for state-level leaders such as Van Buren, Ritchie, and Eaton. Insofar as possible, state leaders were counted on to encourage and coordinate local efforts to arouse the voters themselves. Acting on their own or after recruitment by statewide leaders, local activists tried to bring the campaign down to the level of the average citizen. Town and country organizers were men who had the time and resources to provide voluntary leadership; often they were lawyers with rhetorical skills and professional interests in politics. Whatever their occupation, they were likely to be wealthier and better educated than their fellow citizens, but they sought to persuade the voters rather than command them. Adams men organized like the Jacksonians, but do not seem to have reached quite so deeply into the ordinary citizenry. If the rival political committees of Cumberland County, North Carolina, were typical of the rest of the country, the Adams men were wealthier and tied more firmly to the commerce of the county seat, while the Jacksonians had closer ties to the rural hinterland.

Jackson's partisans used newspapers to reach the voters, but they also organized town, county, and district conventions, mass meetings, torchlight parades, barbecues, and hickory pole raisings to attract the voters' attention. Speeches, banners, songs, and party emblems spelled out the differences between the two candidates and pounded home the importance of the contest. A full year and a half before the election, a zealous Kentucky organizer reported to Jackson that he had "carried into full and successful operation last year, a plan, or System or Committees, from a Principle or Central Committee at Louisville, down to Sub-Committees into every ward of the Town, and [militia] Captains Company in the Country." As a result, this Jackson organizer boasted that he had listed every voter in his own and a neighboring county, with an indication of each man's preferences in state and national politics. When election day came, he would be sure that the Jackson men came to the polls. Most counties were not so well organized, but political operatives made great strides in bringing Presidential politics closer to popular attention.

Two themes stood out in the Jackson supporters' attempt to reach the public consciousness. Editors and speechmakers emphasized the moral unfitness of John Quincy Adams to be President and the undemocratic character of his elevation to the office. The charge of "corrupt bargain" blended these two themes perfectly, for Clay and Adams could easily be depicted as corrupt aristocrats who had undermined republicanism by an agreement that was immoral because it overturned the will of the people. A convention of Republican young men in Halfmoon, Saratoga County, New York, expressed their indignation in a typical resolution:

> *Resolved*, that the cause of Jackson, is emphatically *the cause of the people*—that the contest in which we are engaged, is between the *people* on the one side and the *aristocracy* on the other, between an *honest patriotism*, and a *devoted attachment to the spirit of our republican institutions*, on the one side, and an *unholy and selfish ambition*, and a *contempt of the free principles of our republic*, on the other; between the friends of the incorruptible JACKSON, and the *followers* of a corrupt and sinking administration.

In addition to his recent political crimes, Adams was denounced for his elitist education, his early association with European courts, his former Federalist allegiance, and to crown it all, his purchase of a billiard table and a chess set—gambling devices, supposedly—for the White House. Jacksonians even charged that Adams had procured an American virgin for the lust of the Czar while serving as a fourteen-year-old diplomat in St. Petersburg! Jackson's followers lost no opportunity to associate Adams with immorality and to promise the voters, as the Republican convention of Albany County, New York, put it, that divine providence was utilizing Andrew Jackson "to bring back the republic to the purity and simplicity of the democratic days" of yore.

The Adams forces resisted these critics by appealing to a similar fear that the Republic was endangered. In Washington, Joseph Gales and William W. Seaton used the *National Intelligencer* to purvey sober warnings against the antirepublican tendencies of a "military chieftain." They hinted strongly that a man such as Jackson could become a tyrant and lead the United States to the same tragic fate that had befallen Napoleonic France or the republics of antiquity. Even in private correspondence, National Republicans such as William Plumer of New Hampshire predicted that if Jackson were elected, "the freedom of the country will terminate, as that of all preceding republics have, in monarchy." To demonstrate Jackson's violence and unpredictable character, Philadelphia printer John Binns distributed the so-called Coffin Handbill, which provided readers with "Some Account of Some of the Bloody Deeds of General Jackson," underneath a vivid illustration of the coffins of six militiamen executed during the Creek War, and accompanied by a ferocious woodcut of Jackson running a sword cane through the body of a hapless Nashville pedestrian.

The most celebrated charge of the Adams press was that Andrew Jackson had "torn from a husband the wife of his bosom" and lived with her in a state "of open and notorious lewdness." In fact, Jackson's wife, Rachel, was an exceedingly pious woman who had once been married unhappily to one Lewis Robards. Believing (as they claimed subsequently) that Robards had obtained a divorce, Rachel and Andrew were married in 1794, but they remarried two years later when they discovered to their professed shock that the divorce had not yet been granted at the time of their earlier ceremony. Branding the General an adulterer and a bigamist, one prolific Adams pamphleteer sneered that "those indifferent to the character of the President's wife and those who conceive that a fallen female may be restored by subsequent good conduct, may conscientiously give General Jackson their support." Subsequent published reports identified Jackson as a mulatto and his mother as a prostitute.

Ordinarily, a man like Jackson would have dealt with such attacks by shooting or flogging the fool who dared to make them, but his position as a candidate for President with a violent reputation to overcome made him helpless. Neither Adams nor Clay was directly responsible for the worst gutter tactics, just as Jackson himself never charged Adams with pimping, but none of the candidates restrained their followers from the most extreme attacks. Jackson blamed Clay for the slurs on Mrs. Jackson's chastity, and described him as "the bases[t], meanest, scoundrel, that ever disgraced the image of his god," but he held himself back from public retort and left the job of replying to all charges to the Nashville committee of correspondence. Mrs. Jackson had already been in declining health, and she died soon after the election. The General, who had loved his wife intensely, promptly concluded that she had succumbed to mortification and grief. Her death significantly deepened his bitterness toward his opponents.

When each candidate's followers attacked the morality of his opponent, they were responding to the widespread public concern that the moral purity associated with the old Republic was deteriorating. The Republic was indeed changing rapidly, and Americans were primed by long-standing cultural precepts to interpret change as a warning sign of moral and political decay. While many Americans admired technological progress, they did not like all of its consequences, and the election campaign showed them expressing their doubts as a series of moral condemnations. For Adams supporters in the tidy villages of New England and the busy countinghouses of Philadelphia, Boston, and New York, republican virtue appeared in the orderly improvement of America's resources, and moral and material improvement were presumed to go together. If controlled development preserved a due inequality between those who were best and worst in both moral and material terms, that was only just. But if national expansion and social flux unleashed frontier brawlers and gave an opportunity for the rag, tag, and bobtail to put a barbarous military chieftain in the White House, the Republic was in serious moral trouble.

For Jackson supporters in the South and West, republican virtue consisted in the preservation of liberty for all white citizens. They already associated Massachusetts Yankees like Adams with the cheating peddlers of wooden nutmegs, and they more than likely considered themselves the victims of a "corrupt bargain" every time they ventured into a store. If the will of the people put a stop to the nefarious designs of intriguing aristocrats, that, too, was just. But if the highest office in the land was subject to "bargain and sale," their liberty was in danger and the Republic was in serious moral trouble from a different extreme. Trumped-up charges of unethical behavior came naturally to both sides in these circumstances, but the moralistic rhetoric reflected substantial differences in social vision and material ambitions.

Moral concerns gained force from the fact that liberty and power were indeed at issue in 1828. Farmers and artisans had taken the ideology of the American Revolution, matched it with the material opportunities of the New World, and devised an understanding of liberty that implied economic security and independence for the average family. Just as that libertarian vision was taking shape, however, it also began slipping away, for entrepreneurs, editors, and politicians could foresee a different kind of America, a mighty nation based on technological improvement, economic strength, and political power. These leaders could argue, often persuasively, that public liberty could not be secure without power available to defend it. They could therefore count on electoral support from many Americans who were not wealthy businessmen themselves but foresaw advantages for themselves and their country from the rise of an urban, industrial, and commercial civilization. These Americans were prepared to use political power to bring their vision of the future into being, even if popular liberty suffered as a consequence. As farmers in the crowded countryside lost the liberty to bequeath land to their large broods of children, and artisans in the booming towns lost the liberty to acquire their own shops, some Americans called these changes progress and others viewed them as corruption. On the symbolic level, at least, the election of 1828 pitted these two viewpoints against each other.

For the present, liberty found more friends than power. Andrew Jackson won 56 percent of the popular vote and 178 of the 261 electoral votes. He carried the South and the West with almost no opposition and captured Pennsylvania again, along with the other middle states. As before, Adams swept New England, while his only foothold in the South came from the tariff-conscious states of Kentucky and Louisiana.

Popular resentment at the outcome in 1824 had contributed to movements in the states to give the choice of electors directly to the people, so in 1828 South Carolina and Delaware were the only states where the Presidential election took place in the legislature. With the selection reduced to a head-on contest between two sharply differentiated rivals and with vigorous vote-getting efforts mounted by committed local activists, it is not surprising that popular turnout more than doubled, reaching 56.3 percent of the adult white male population. Turnout was even higher in states where both candidates stood a chance of winning, for each voter had a stronger sense that his ballot could make a difference. These states were still the exception, however; New Hampshire, New York,

New Jersey, Maryland, Kentucky, and Ohio were the only states to register turnouts in excess of 70 percent, and except for Kentucky, they were the only states where no more than ten percentage points separated the winning candidate from the loser. On the whole, these states were economically and socially diverse, with many competing internal interests and subcultures; electorates like theirs were much more ready to polarize over Presidential politics than more isolated and homogeneous areas like Georgia or Maine.

President Jackson took office as the friend of liberty and the foe of unwarranted power. His election campaign had appealed to republican nostalgia and contrasted the Tennessee general's supposed simplicity and virtue to the economic and political corruption symbolized by Adams. Beyond this, Jackson's plans were hidden. Clustering about the President, a host of would-be power brokers assured themselves that the simple frontier warrior would be easy to manipulate, but their assurances reflected more confidence than certainty. In keeping with his image, the General had wrapped his intentions in a toga of republican ambiguity, and he refused all calls to make specific pledges. Did his ambiguity conceal a program or only a set of reflexes? As Andrew Jackson entered Washington, no one really knew.

4

"Our Federal Union.
It Must Be Preserved"

THE INAUGURATION of Andrew Jackson drew vast crowds. Packing the taverns and filling the muddy streets, the General's well-wishers stared at the unfamiliar monuments of the nation's capital and buzzed with speculation about the country's new direction. "I never saw any thing like it before," snorted Daniel Webster, the conservative senator from Massachusetts. "Persons have come 500 miles to see Genl Jackson; & they really seem to think that the Country is rescued from some dreadful danger."

Mourning the recent death of his wife, the victorious candidate had consistently refused all offers of public parades and celebrations while he journeyed to Washington to start his term. Sympathetic to the General's grief, Jackson's supporters restrained their own joy for the victory of "the People's Will" until Inauguration Day itself. On the morning of March 4, 1829, they clogged Pennsylvania Avenue as the President-elect walked from his hotel to the Capitol, and stood in silence, twelve to twenty thousand strong, as he read a short, simple, and completely inaudible address. "It was grand,—it was sublime!" exulted Margaret Bayard Smith, a prominent hostess of Washington's high society. "A free people, collected in their might, silent and tranquil, restrained solely by a moral power, . . . was majesty, rising to sublimity, and far surpassing the majesty of Kings and Princes. . . ." When Jackson completed the oath of office, the crowd roared its approval and surged to follow as the new President rode slowly toward the White House.

The scene that ensued became a permanent feature of American political folklore. Presidential receptions had always been open to the public, but the genteel tone of previous Administrations had intimidated ordinary citizens and kept them at a distance. Those who planned the Jackson inaugural had assumed this reticence would continue, but they were wrong. "Country men, farmers, gentlemen, mounted and dismounted, boys, women and children, black and white," filled the streets and then the White House. China and crystal crashed to the floor as thirsty celebrants stretched for punch. Silk upholstery perished in shreds as frontiersmen with muddy boots scrambled for perches to view the people's hero. Jackson himself was so crushed that he had to be helped to escape the building, but the crowds did not begin to clear until vats of refreshment were carried onto the lawn. *"The Majesty of the People* had disappeared," Mrs. Smith lamented with a shudder. Careless planning was more responsible for the fiasco than ingrained popular barbarism, but Margaret Bayard Smith spoke for many well-to-do citizens when she concluded that unchecked democracy might yet bring a bloody revolution to America.

Fears of a bloodbath proved groundless, but Jackson's Administration did bring significant changes to Washington. Though left ambiguous in the campaign and in the inaugural address, Jackson's political creed became clearer as he confronted specific problems. The new President thought of himself as the restorer of traditional American values, but his principles marked a significant departure from those of his predecessors.

To begin with, Andrew Jackson believed strongly in majority rule. In his first annual message, Jackson referred emphatically to "the first principle of our system—*that the majority is to govern*—" and he remained convinced that his defeat in 1824 had resulted from a violation of this maxim. A good Jeffersonian, moreover, Jackson rejoiced that the majority of American citizens were well suited for the preservation of a republic. "The wealth and strength of a country are its population," he would later declare, "and the best parts of that population are the cultivators of the soil. Independent farmers are everywhere the basis of society and true friends of liberty." At the same time, Jackson often reminded his countrymen that majority rule must be softened by consideration for the interests of minorities. "The exercise of [majority] will in a spirit of moderation, justice, and brotherly kindness," he explained, "will constitute a cement which would forever preserve our Union."

Over the course of his Administration, Jackson recommended various measures to protect selected political minorities, but his favorite was to restrict the power of the federal government, on the assumption that legitimate but threatened interests could then seek the protection of individual states. In his fourth annual message, Jackson spoke of his "hope of reducing the General Government to that simple machine which the Constitution created," and to do so he consistently favored low taxes and low federal expenditures, limitation of federal authority in favor of states' rights, and a reluctance to use federal power to stimulate economic change. Nevertheless, Jackson still believed in what he called "the just authority of Government." Majority rule meant that certain federal powers must be exercised, regardless of local objections. As the only federal official elected by "the great body of the people," Jackson saw himself as the sole and rightful representative of majority power. He intended to exercise his strong if limited powers to their utmost. Some of the most controversial episodes of his Presidency erupted over the balance that Jackson chose to strike between the strengths and the limits of his powers, particularly in resolving problems of national expansion and economic development. Before tackling these questions, however, Jackson put his own Administration in order by selecting his Cabinet and establishing a policy on appointments to federal office.

As inaugural crowds dispersed homeward without further incident, official Washington still feared that Jackson might dismiss vast numbers of the civil servants appointed by previous Administrations. Jackson had promised "reform" in his campaign and in his inaugural address, and he firmly believed that official corruption was largely responsible for Adams's previous capture of the Presidency and the country's other problems. Cleansing "the Augean stables" would thus be his first priority as President. Leading Jacksonian newspapers expanded on this theme and gloated that a vast corps of Adams appointees would soon be swept from power and replaced by hungry and deserving Democrats. Uncertain of Jackson's intentions and lacking any legal protection, honest bureaucrats naturally feared for their jobs and struggled to conceal their worries during the inaugural festivities.

Cabinet positions were the most important appointments to be made, and speculation about them was rampant. Many observers assumed that Jackson was a figurehead who would serve a single term and be dominated by his advisers. They identified Martin Van Buren and John C. Calhoun as the likeliest men to manipulate Jackson while he was President and to succeed him thereafter. Acting on these assumptions, the followers of Van Buren and Calhoun naturally started jockeying for position well before the inauguration. Presumably, the composition of the Cabinet would tell the world which intriguer had successfully overawed the President and won the position of heir apparent.

John C. Calhoun was already Vice President and could not join the Cabinet. Jackson balanced Calhoun's prominence by asking Van Buren to be Secretary of State, the most prestigious post and a traditional stepping-stone to the Presidency. For the other Cabinet officers, Jackson surprised everybody by choosing mediocrities—"plain, business men," he called them—who could not possibly dominate him or distract the government by vying for higher office. Treasury went to Samuel Ingham, a Pennsylvanian whose views on the vital tariff issue fell somewhere between the strong protectionist demands of his own state and the even stronger free trade views of his personal friend Calhoun. John Branch and John MacPherson Berrien, two wealthy Southern planters, became Secretary of the Navy and Attorney General respectively. The Post Office went briefly to John McLean of Ohio, who resigned in favor of Kentucky lawyer William T. Barry, an undistinguished Jackson loyalist who kept clear of all intrigues between the General's possible successors. Instead of designating a voice behind the throne, the Cabinet choices indicated that Jackson would dominate the government himself.

The most controversial appointment was Tennessee Senator John Henry Eaton as Secretary of War. As one Administration insider put it, Jackson had long determined "to have near him a personal and confidential friend to whom he could embosom himself on all subjects." Eaton was a longtime friend and neighbor who had served with Jackson in the Creek War, written the General's campaign biography, and launched his drive for the White

House. Perhaps most important, the Secretary of War would be responsible for Indian affairs, concerning which Jackson and Eaton held identical opinions. To Jackson, Eaton was a perfect officer, but official Washington felt differently.

Just before the inauguration, Eaton had married one Margaret O'Neale Timberlake, a beautiful and lively widow who was also the daughter of Eaton's landlord, a Washington tavern keeper. Peggy, as she was known, had regularly defied conventional standards of female decorum, which demanded modest and retiring behavior from all ladies. Genteel society condemned her unanimously as "frivolous, wayward [and] passionate." What was worse, the leaders of Washington society condemned the innkeeper's daughter as a notoriously promiscuous woman who had long been intimate with Eaton (and a series of other politicians before him) not only prior to their marriage, but even before the rumored suicide of her late estranged husband, a naval officer who often spent many months at sea.

By the flagrant double standard of the nineteenth century, the mere suspicion of extramarital sex condemned Peggy Eaton as an irretrievably fallen woman, while Eaton himself was only blamed for presumption, in attempting to foist off his mistress as a virtuous female. Washington's most prominent ladies, including the wives of the other Cabinet officers, promptly refused to associate with Mrs. Eaton, to invite her to their parties, or to return her social calls. What might have been a minor scandal in any other city became a major crisis, since Washington protocol demanded a regular round of balls, receptions, and dinner parties at which all Cabinet officials and their wives were expected to receive equal treatment. The ostracism of the Secretary of War and his wife thus obstructed Cabinet harmony and hamstrung Jackson's government from the outset.

Remembering the cruel sneers that he blamed for his own wife's death, Jackson doggedly defended Peggy Eaton's reputation. He was soon convinced that his enemies had invented the stories about her to drive Eaton from the Cabinet and to paralyze the Administration. Striking back, Jackson shocked his own supporters by launching an obsessive and fruitless campaign to force the Cabinet wives to call upon Mrs. Eaton.

Observing the new Cabinet and its antics from the sidelines, disappointed politicians scoffed that Jackson's appointments had brought in "the millennium of the minnows" and fumed that the old frontiersman had refused to take directions from the nation's established elite. Calhoun's friends were particularly miffed. "All the talents of the Union were at his command," complained John Floyd, governor of Virginia and Calhoun admirer. "[I] did believe in common with all others of his friends, that he would call around him the talented and distinguished men throughout the confederacy. . . . Instead . . . , he has surrounded himself with men of narrow minds, some of them hardly gentlemen and none of them have much character and no principles, moral or political, except Ingham and Branch."

Calhoun could take a little comfort from the Administration's party newspaper, the *U.S. Telegraph*, edited by his firm supporter, Duff Green of Missouri. Since the days of George Washington, embattled politicians had found a national party newspaper to be indispensable to their struggles, and Jackson was no exception. Speaking unofficially but authoritatively, the *Telegraph* conveyed the Administration's views to its supporters in Congress and around the country, rallying the faithful and rebutting the opposition. Except for the Vice President himself, Green was the most influential Calhounite in Washington, doing what he could to promote the Vice President's interests. As for the rest of the Administration, Calhoun shared his friends' misgivings, but there seemed to be little he could do.

When undistracted by "Eaton malaria," Jackson continued his reforms of the government bureaucracy. Republican doctrine taught him that corruption was the deadly inner rot of all attempts at self-government. For Jackson, "corruption" meant a variety of problems ranging from a general decay of society's moral standards, to interference with the electoral process, to downright embezzlement of public funds. Convinced that all forms of corruption were rampant in Washington, Jackson attacked them as soon as he got down to work. Poring over department accounts, the President and his aides collared a significant number of officials whose financial records looked suspicious. Defective statutes against corruption frustrated most efforts to prosecute these men, and Jackson soon asked Congress to correct the situation. In the meantime, some embezzlers went to prison and others absconded, but most accused officials just lost their jobs. Also quick to get the ax were those accused of incompetence, alcoholism, or active involvement in the more scurrilous aspects of the Adams campaign.

Jackson filled these and other vacancies with his own supporters. One especially important appointee was Amos Kendall, a gaunt Kentucky editor who became Fourth Auditor of the Treasury and a vigilant foe of corruption in his department. In Kentucky, Kendall had fought stalwartly for the old Republic, battling banking interests and the friends of Henry Clay. Jackson came to rely very heavily on Kendall's abilities as political confidant and phrasemaker. Another Treasury post went to Major William B. Lewis, an old Tennessee comrade who actually lived in the White House and advised the President continually on party matters. The President's nephew and private secretary Andrew Jackson Donelson also lived in the White House, while his wife, Emily, served as Jackson's official hostess. Together with other insiders who joined them later, Kendall, Lewis, Eaton, and Van Buren composed a circle of informal advisers around the President whom opponents derided as the "Kitchen Cabinet." Established Washington leaders felt that nationally known politicians in the official, or "Parlor," Cabinet ought to be closest to the President, but tension on the subject of Mrs. Eaton had led Jackson to suspend its regular meetings. Instead, Jackson shrugged off the objections of outsiders and sought advice from whomever he chose.

Most of Jackson's appointees were honest and qualified men, but some were worse than their predecessors. The President insisted, for example, on giving the collectorship of the port of New York to his professed admirer Samuel Swartwout, despite the misgivings of other New York Jacksonians. Swartwout later fled to England, taking with him more than $1.2 million in stolen public funds. This scandal left the President deeply chagrined, but it illustrated the dangers of Jackson's frequent tendency to make important decisions on the basis of personal loyalty.

Opponents quickly charged that Jackson's program of "reform" was itself an example of corruption. Remembering the British ministries that controlled elections by filling royal payrolls with slavish placemen, Clay and Adams supporters assumed that Jackson's removals were largely motivated by a desire to reward Jacksonians with powerful jobs. Once in office, these partisans would become Jackson's personal tools, loyal to no one but their chief and eager to further his dictatorial ambitions. From the National Republican perspective, nothing could be more corrupt. According to the *National Intelligencer*, Washington's leading anti-Jackson newspaper, partisan appointments reduced "all the patronage, and all the Interests of the Government, to the schemes of the mere demagogues for their personal aggrandisement." One irate Senate committee later charged that to fill public offices as Jackson had would "convert the entire body of those in office into corrupt and supple instruments of power, and . . . raise up a host of hungry, greedy, and subservient partisans, ready for every service, however base and corrupt." Similar charges have long been repeated by historians, and the impression is now widespread that Andrew Jackson demolished a sound civil service by wholesale introduction of the "spoils system."

Jackson saw the matter differently. After ten months in office, he explained to Congress that serious abuses had developed under previous Administrations. "Office is considered as a species of property," the President declared, "and government rather as a means of promoting individual interests than as an instrument created solely for the service of the people." No one in a republic had an inherent right to public office, he reasoned, so no one could complain if he lost a public job in favor of someone more honest, more competent, or more in agreement with elected officials who carried a popular mandate. Jackson went on to attack the notion—widely promoted by the enemies of his removal policy—that no one except a tiny elite had the training or experience to qualify for public office. "The duties of all public officers are, or at least admit of being made, so plain and simple that *men of intelligence* [italics added] may readily qualify themselves for their performance." This was obviously no plea for the appointment of incompetents but a demand that public duties be shared among the large body of qualified citizens to avoid the creation of an entrenched and corrupt bureaucracy.

Jackson thus made "rotation in office" a cardinal principle of his Administration, though he followed the principle more flexibly than his enemies tended to think. During Jackson's first term in office, the President removed no more than one federal officeholder in eleven. By carefully comparing the backgrounds of Jackson's appointees with those of his predecessors, historical sociologist Sidney H. Aronson has found that Jackson's choices possessed the same levels of education and experience as those of earlier Administrations, though the Jacksonians included more men from provincial families whose qualifications would probably have been overlooked by previous Presidents. If the real extent of corruption was no wider than the relatively modest number of men who were removed, moreover, then the rhetoric of Jacksonian reform was more significant than the practice itself. Nevertheless, Jackson's appointments policy did correct some real abuses in several government departments. Rotation in office was also a solidly democratic principle that brought greater openness to the government.

In fairness to Jackson's critics, it must also be said that those discharged for suspected corruption or incompetence had no guaranteed chance to refute these charges and may have been fired unfairly. If Jackson himself did not use the appointment power to discharge qualified public servants and pack the government with incompetent partisans, there was nothing to prevent him or some less capable successor from doing so. The potential for abuse was obvious. It remained for later generations to create a civil service system that was less susceptible to political manipulation than Andrew Jackson's.

The President's war on corruption and Washington society's war on Peggy Eaton both seemed to draw strength from a widespread fear that America was losing its republican virtue. That fear had affected both sides in the recent Presidential election and would continue to influence politics in the years ahead. It originated in a set of very real conditions, for social and economic changes had brought unprecedented and self-interested political demands from some citizens and bitter opposition from others. As in every Presidency, symbolic issues and private feuds such as the Eaton affair continued to have a significant impact on public policies. On the whole, however, squabbles over patronage and etiquette had less to do with the Administration's effort to restore the old Republic than substantial problems of pressing national concern.

Of all these problems, Jackson viewed the Indian question as particularly urgent. By the end of the 1820s, most Indians were gone from the Atlantic Seaboard, while the tribes of the Old Northwest had been seriously weakened and demoralized. In the states of the Old Southwest, however, some sixty thousand Cherokees, Creeks, Choctaws, Chickasaws, and Seminoles still constituted a serious obstacle to the expansion of white America. During and after the War of 1812, General Jackson had wrested huge territories from these tribes, but they had kept control of large and valuable portions of Alabama, Mississippi, Georgia, North Carolina, and Tennessee. As President, Jackson was determined to secure these lands for white people.

Prior to Jackson's Presidency, Indian policy suffered from the inconsistencies generated by a mixture of ignorance, benevolence, and greed. Since the days of earliest settlement, many whites had believed that the American continent was reserved for them by Providence and that Indians should accordingly surrender it and disappear. Legally, however, white Americans had treated the tribes as sovereign nations with fundamental rights to their own soil that could be transferred only by a voluntary agreement embodied in a formal treaty. On this basis, the federal government had contracted numerous treaties with the Eastern tribes, agreeing to purchase set amounts of territory and solemnly guaranteeing the Indians' right to remain on whatever was left unsold. As this process continued, Presidents and other officials began to express the expectation that the Indians would soon quit the East altogether, trading their ancestral lands there for new territories beyond the Mississippi. At the same time, these officials often professed great regard for the Indians, hoping that they would give up hunting and other aspects of traditional culture in exchange for the way of life practiced by whites. To this end, Congress appropriated substantial sums for Indian schools and for gifts of seeds, plows, and livestock to prospective Indian yeomen.

Some proponents of the Indian education policy hoped that sedentary farming would promote white acquisition of more Indian land, as the tribes sold off the territory they could not till. Others assumed that "civilizing" measures should be combined with removal to the West, so that Indians could be protected from lawless white frontiersmen while they changed their culture. Few considered the possibility that Indians would use the skills learned from whites to strengthen their abilities to hold on to their remaining traditional territory, but that was what actually happened.

The Cherokees, Creeks, Choctaws, Chickasaws, and Seminoles had gone furthest in adopting useful portions of white technology and culture, thus gaining a reputation among whites as the "Five Civilized Tribes." These Indians had never followed a nomadic lifestyle but had lived in permanent farming villages since pre-Columbian times. By the 1820s, many of their communities were led by chiefs of mixed white and Indian descent who encouraged the process of cultural adaptation. Often living in log cabins or frame houses and dressing like white Americans, these Indians raised corn and livestock much like their white neighbors. The wealthier chiefs lived like planters and used the labor of black slaves to cultivate cotton and other staple crops. Many Indians sent their children to schools operated by white missionaries, and some had embraced the Christian religion. Cherokees had devised their own written language and published a tribal newspaper in English and Cherokee. At the same time, the Indians continued to hold their tribal lands in common and showed increasing unwillingness to sell any more of it to white people. As a tribal council of the Creeks put it to one insistent federal negotiator, "we would not receive money for land in which our fathers and friends are buried . . . We love our land; it is our mother; and we do not think anyone would take it from us if we did not wish to part with it."

White leaders' determination was quite as firm as the Creeks'. The Indians were sitting on some excellent cotton soils. Their territory was an attractive haven for runaway slaves, much to the planters' irritation. Since Indian land was held in common and not by individual owners, it could not be bought and sold like a commodity in the commercial economy of the whites. Most of all, perhaps, Indian sovereignty represented an affront to the racist principle that none but white men were fully entitled to republican rights and privileges. In his memoirs, Georgia's future governor Wilson Lumpkin wrapped racial, civic, and economic arguments together to express a common conviction. Cherokee Georgia, he explained, "embrac[ed] five or six millions [of acres] of the best lands within the limits of the State. . . . The resources of Georgia could never be extensively developed by a well-devised system of internal improvements, and commercial and social intercourse with other portions of the Union, especially the great West, until this portion of the state was settled by our industrious, enlightened, free-hold population—entitled to, and meriting, all the privileges of citizenship." Sharing such views, many frontiersmen would be clamorous for Indian land no matter how much vacant territory was already available to them.

Pressures for action were especially strong in Georgia. Whenever Indian land became available in that state, the government used a state lottery to determine which lucky citizens would win the privilege of buying farm-sized parcels at below-market prices. This gesture to republican equality gave every white family in Georgia a personal stake in Indian removal, as struggling farmers from the older sections of the state won a new chance for bonanza with every cession of Indian territory. By the same token, the stubborn persistence of the Indians could appear to every hopeful yeoman as an outrageous obstacle to his own aspirations.

Seeing their opportunities, politicians in the Deep South vied eagerly to see who could be most aggressive in promoting white equality by demanding Indian lands. In particular, Georgia Governor George M. Troup commanded a political faction among the rice and cotton gentry of the state and needed an issue to bolster his appeal to the common man. Indian baiting was the answer, and during the Adams Administration, Troup pressed ahead with plans to survey and distribute Creek lands before the legal niceties of federal sale had been completed. When Adams objected, Troup threatened armed confrontation on the grounds of Georgia's sovereign right to its own territory. "From the first decisive act of hostility," Troup taunted Adams and his supporters, "you will be treated as a public enemy . . . , and, what is more, the unblushing allies of the savages whose cause you have adopted." Georgia's frontiersmen loved this rhetoric and they cheered when Troup's posturing brought a hasty compromise at Creek expense. They also voted for Andrew Jackson in 1828, satisfied that the doughty old Indian fighter would give them every assistance as white Georgians turned their attention from the defeated Creeks to the still-defiant Cherokees.

Like his Georgia allies, Andrew Jackson held Indian land claims in contempt. Treaties with Indians he had long regarded as "an absurdity," for he believed that the tribes were not sovereign nations but "subjects of the United States." Though Jackson himself had negotiated many Indian treaties, he had done so in bad faith, privately believing that Congress and the states had the right to seize all Indian lands at pleasure, treaties or no treaties. Legally, Jackson pointed to guarantees of state sovereignty in the U.S. Constitution and assurances there that no state could be dismembered without its own consent, and insisted that these clauses made the existence of an independent Indian state in Georgia unconstitutional. This argument ignored the long series of treaties guaranteeing Cherokee sovereignty which preceded the U.S. Constitution and which the Constitution presumably could not abrogate, but Jackson remained inflexible. As a practical matter, he continued to go through the motions of treaty-making, realizing that Congressional consciences and Indian pride both demanded the face-saving fiction of a voluntary agreement in place of any naked act of expropriation. Faced with Cherokee refusals to submit voluntarily to such a formula, Jackson needed some means of coercing the Indians without appearing to do so.

Events in Georgia ultimately gave him this chance. In 1827, the Cherokees had taken a dramatic step to protect their sovereignty further. Discarding their traditional form of tribal government, the Indians declared themselves an independent republic with a written constitution. Shortly afterward, gold was discovered in northern Georgia and prospectors swarmed in, heedless of Indian protests. Responding to prospectors' demands and retaliating for the Indians' republican pretensions, the Georgia legislature extended its law over Cherokee territory, declaring all tribal laws to be null and void, and effectively reducing all Cherokees to the approximate legal status of free Negroes.

The effects were dramatic and immediate. Intruders surged over Cherokee country, seizing Indian farms, homes, and gold mines. When the tribe sought protection from resident federal troops, Georgia asked the President to withdraw them, and Jackson cheerfully complied, declaring that the federal government had no authority to interfere within a state. Indians who resisted white intruders were beaten or threatened, with impunity, for Georgia courts could not admit Indian testimony against whites. Unlicensed traders flooded the district with whiskey, encouraging credit purchases, and using the white-controlled courts to seize Indian property in payment. Anticipating the Cherokees' rapid departure, state officials coolly began to survey the land in preparation for the lottery that would soon distribute it to white people. Following Georgia's example, Alabama and Mississippi also extended their laws over the Indian territory in their midst, placing all tribal cultures under nearly intolerable pressures.

Under the circumstances, it was unnecessary for Andrew Jackson to produce a plan to force the Indians to move. If he simply declared his legal inability to protect the Indians from the onslaughts of their white neighbors, the frontiersmen would provide the force for him. As the pioneers did just that, Jackson struck a pose as the Indians' rescuer. He could not save the Cherokees from Georgia, he announced, for the states were indeed sovereign within their borders. But the Indians could save themselves by voluntarily relinquishing their Eastern lands, and moving beyond the Mississippi River, outside the jurisdiction of any state. There they would be subject to Congress, and Congress could set aside land for them in perpetuity, where they could retain their own tribal structures and adopt the customs of white civilization at their own pace. Alternatively, individual Indians could remain where they were and receive legal title to their own farms and homes. But those who stayed behind would be subject to state laws (which branded them as free persons of color) and could not continue their existence as a tribe. Few expected that individual Indian landholders, surrounded by hostile neighbors and by the unfamiliar demands of the market economy, could hold out against continued white harassment. Before long, they too would sell their claims and move. After Jackson outlined these principles in his first annual message, loyal supporters introduced bills embodying them in both houses of Congress in the early months of 1830.

The proposals provoked immediate controversy. Northern Protestants had invested great sums and high expectations in missions to the Southern Indians, hoping to show that moral suasion and Christian benevolence could lead these "savages" to salvation. Encouraged by Indian cultural change, pious men and women were convinced that Jackson's professed regard for the Indians was false and his removal policy a smokescreen for downright theft. Echoing their constituents, Northern congressmen denounced the sham of "voluntary" Indian removal. "Do the obligations of justice change with the color of the skin?" taunted New Jersey Senator Theodore Frelinghuysen. "Is it one of the prerogatives of the white man, that he may disregard the dictates of moral principles, when an Indian shall be concerned?" Congressional debaters also attacked Jackson's constitutional arguments. Whatever the proper balance between states' rights and federal power, they claimed, the Constitution could not obliterate the prior legal rights of third parties, particularly Indian tribes whose claims on American soil long predated white settlement and whose rights had supposedly been guaranteed by numerous treaties both before and after its ratification. Other opponents pointed out that Indians who remained in the

East would have no effective legal protection in the states and that the government had made no preparations for a safe journey or for finding good lands in the West.

Southern and Western proponents of removal were quick to reply to these arguments. Yes, they answered their critics, whites did have greater rights than nonwhites. Indians "were a race not admitted to be equal to the rest of the community," declared Georgia's Senator John Forsyth. The free and equal citizens of his state would never "submit to the intrusive sovereignty of a petty tribe of Indians" and demanded the right to legislate for all persons within its borders. "The jurisdiction claimed over one portion of our population may very soon be asserted over *another*," Governor Troup added, with a dire hint to his region's slaveholders. Mangling logic but speaking bluntly, a Jacksonian editor reasoned that "if the general government has a right to make treaties with the Indians living within the states because they are red, it has an equal right to make treaties with the negroes because they are black." With some justice, moreover, Jacksonians charged opponents with hypocrisy, citing National Republican support for Indian removal when John Quincy Adams had endorsed it. Steamrolling the opposition, the Jacksonians beat back all amendments and passed the Indian Removal Act of 1830 by a thin margin, less than three months after its introduction.

The Cherokees fought back undaunted. Employing William Wirt, a former Attorney General and a distinguished constitutional lawyer, they obtained two landmark decisions from Chief Justice John Marshall's Supreme Court. In the case of *Cherokee Nation* v. *Georgia* (1830), Marshall ruled that the Indian tribes were not foreign countries but "domestic dependent nations" which possessed some attributes of sovereignty but not the crucial right to sue the state of Georgia. Two years later, in a decision more favorable to the Indians, Marshall declared in the case of *Worcester* v. *Georgia* that the state's extension of Georgia law over the Cherokees was unconstitutional and void. Unfortunately for the Indians, the Court had no power to compel Georgia to obey its ruling, and in Jackson's words, the opinion "fell still born."

Despite their increasingly gloomy situation, the Cherokees still refused to sign a removal treaty. Led by the "mixed-blooded" chief John Ross, most of the tribe continued to cling to their homes. Finally, in 1835, the Administration signed a treaty with a small faction who falsely claimed to speak for the whole tribe. Using this Treaty of New Echota as a pretext, the U.S. Army rounded up the remaining Cherokees in 1838 and sent them on a "Trail of Tears" to what is now the state of Oklahoma. Their journey was a tragic one: clothing was inadequate, rations were stolen, wagons and other vehicles were insufficient, the winter was bitterly cold, and disease was rampant. Out of eighteen thousand captive Cherokees, almost four thousand died along the way.

The Jackson Administration eventually signed some seventy Indian treaties, receiving some 100 million acres of land in the East in exchange for $68 million and 32 million acres in the West. Both north and south of the Ohio, almost all the tribes between the Appalachians and the Mississippi were forced to sign, though most were quite reluctant to do so. When some of the Creeks, Seminoles, Sauks, and Foxes finally took up arms to resist removal, the U.S. Army crushed their rebellions and deported them by force. Thousands of Indians died along the way, but Jackson remained convinced that the operation had been for the tribes' own good. "While the safety and comfort of our own citizens has been greatly promoted by their removal," he concluded solemnly, "the philanthropist will rejoice that the remnant of that ill-fated race has been at length placed beyond the reach of injury and oppression, and that the paternal care of the General Government will hereafter watch over them and protect them."

Some careful students of federal-Indian relations have concluded that Andrew Jackson should not be blamed for his removal policy. Jackson was no Indian-hater, they declare, for he often expressed affection for individual Indians and even adopted an Indian orphan as a playmate for the other children in his household. The Indian problem was too complex for a simple solution, they point out. The Indians were unwilling to subject themselves to state law and the states could not tolerate the existence of separate political entities within their borders. Since the government was never willing to exterminate the Indians altogether, removal was the sole alternative.

It can only be argued in reply that the one real reason why the tribes could not remain as "domestic dependent nations" within state boundaries—which is where the Indian reservations are located today—was the intransigent greed and racism of the whites who surrounded them. While no participant in the Indian removal tragedy could have stepped outside the values of his own time and place, no irresistible force compelled Congress to embrace the values of Governor Troup over those of Senator Frelinghuysen. Jackson's role was one of condescending paternalism—not benevolence—that refused to take the Indians seriously as competent adults. To Jackson, they were his "red children," he was the "Great Father," and Jackson never doubted that father knew best. Jackson's professed benevolence to the Indians must thus be viewed with skepticism as possibly sincere but undoubtedly self-serving.

The removal of the Indians was not an isolated incident, for it had close connections to better-known aspects of Jacksonian history. By attacking the Indians, Jackson impressed Americans with his powerful blows for white equality, states' rights, and frontier values. He thus spelled out the basis for his popular appeal as President, cemented his coalition of Southern and Western supporters, and laid the basis for his party's future strength. By the same token, the congressmen and missionary supporters who resisted Indian removal assembled many rhetorical themes that would continue to characterize the President's opposition. According to them, Jackson was a tyrant, a bully, a man of violence, a traducer of the law, a friend of slaveholders, and an enemy of evangelical causes. Later in Jackson's Administration, these accusations would again be pressed into political service.

Within the states, moreover, the attacks on Indians by Governor Troup and his counterparts foreshadowed a crucial development in popular political culture. Voters increasingly responded to politicians who could point to a conspicuous enemy of public liberty and equality and pledge to destroy the "monster." The pugnacious stance that had worked against the Cherokees would soon be directed against other targets. Particularly in the South, even planter politicians who opposed the President's basic program and received meager support from nonslaveholders could gain a measure of public approval by directing attacks against alien enemies: Indians first, then the federal government and its tariff policies, and finally the abolitionists. In their turn, Northern voters were also learning to follow these attacks, first against certain secret societies, then against banks, immigrants, Roman Catholics, and finally the "slave power." Popular electioneering played a central role in the development of political parties and ultimately, of sectional conflict.

Most immediately, Indian removal showed the benefits of an aggressive attack on federal policy by states that felt aggrieved by it. When Georgia defied federal prerogatives on the Indian question, Adams and Jackson had both retreated, though Adams was reluctant and Jackson was eager. Perhaps the same approach could be used against other objectionable federal policies. In particular, Georgia's neighbor South Carolina hated the federal tariff and was moved to action when the Georgians' strategy paid off.

The protective tariff was an issue that cut straight to the heart of America's political and economic future. The proponents of a manufacturing economy argued insistently that America's "infant industries" needed protection from British competition. Without the protective tariff, they maintained, America would always remain in a colonial relationship to Europe, supplying unprocessed staples such as cotton in return for every variety of manufactured product. Not only would this condition be humiliating for a great nation, but it would leave America unable to provide its own means of defense in wartime. Using such nationalistic arguments, protectionists had secured the nation's first protective tariff in 1816 and had steadily raised its rates thereafter. By 1830, most imports competing with American-made goods were taxed between one third and one half of their value.

The protective tariff was especially associated with the political ambitions of Senator Henry Clay. As Clay described his famous "American System," a high tariff wall would protect American manufactures and encourage urban and commercial growth to complement the nation's strong rural and agricultural society. As towns and cities grew, Clay predicted, farms would improve also, as farmers left the stage of primitive self-sufficiency and learned the benefits of exchanging their crops for the products of their new urban customers. Improved transportation would be a crucial part of the process, knitting a vast nation together more tightly. To pay for it, Clay proposed to keep the price of federal lands high and to distribute the proceeds of federal land sales to the states, earmarking them for internal improvements. Some supporters even hoped that federal revenues could promote the emancipation of slaves, by financing a colony of freed Negroes in Africa. To oversee this extensive process of tax collection, public expenditure, social reform, internal trade, and manufacturing enterprise, a strong Bank of the United States would exercise powerful controls on the availability of credit and the strength of the currency. It was a grandiose vision, with something promised for everybody, and Clay perpetually hoped that the nation would embrace its principles and in the bargain make him President.

Though many Americans shared Clay's hopes, others were far less enthusiastic. High prices for federal lands would discourage westward migration, critics charged, hampering the growth of the Western states and depriving poor Easterners of their only chance for a fresh start. Factories might make the nation strong and powerful, others insisted, but they could not make it a virtuous republic without a stable and prosperous farming economy. Tariffs, banks, and internal improvements spelled privilege for a few at the expense of the many. Missouri Senator Thomas Hart Benton became the spokesman for an alternative vision of the future, one that promised cheap lands, low taxes, westward expansion, noninterference with slavery, and a continued reliance on agriculture as the mainstay of American life. Not surprisingly, Benton became an ardent Jacksonian (despite a history of personal conflict with the General), while Clay remained a steadfast opponent of Jackson's policies throughout his life.

Opposition to the American System, and especially to the high tariffs that lay at its core, prevailed in most of the plantation regions of the southeastern states. The planters of cotton, rice, and tobacco all depended on the export of their crops to Europe, not on sales to growing American cities. If the price of manufactured goods were protected by a tariff, they would pay inflated prices for the goods they bought for themselves and their slaves, while selling their crops in an unprotected foreign market. Even worse, by reducing the volume of European sales to the United States, the tariff would inevitably reduce the volume of European purchases of American plantation staples. In the planters' eyes, the tariff and the American System were sinister devices to rob the plantation in favor of the city, and to enrich the Northern manufacturer at the expense of the Southern slaveholder. As such, opponents reasoned, these discriminatory measures violated the U.S. Constitution, though biased federal courts might rule otherwise.

These feelings ran especially strong in South Carolina. In contrast to the other Southern states, almost all parts of the Palmetto State were suitable for the plantation system. A powerful elite of intermarried cotton planters spread across its landscape, undis-

tracted by the internal sectional rivalries that forced their counterparts elsewhere to compromise with nonslaveholding neighbors.
Political power in South Carolina often derived from kinship connections and other forms of local dominance that had little to do
with service to particular interests, leaving planter-statesmen free
to indulge a lofty feeling of liberation from the sordid calculations
of mere politicians. A touchy sense of honor and independence
flourished in this special political environment, fed by the heady
sense of mastery that the ownership of dozens or hundreds of
bondsmen gave to most of its leading participants.

The planters' love of command was tinged by fear. By 1830,
South Carolina was the only state in the Union in which a majority
of the population was enslaved. Along the coastal marshes where
rice and the exotic long-staple cotton were the principal crops, the
ratio of blacks to whites reached as high as ten or twelve slaves
for every white person. In these conditions, the slightest distur-
bance to slavery seemed to threaten local whites with the specter
of destruction and race war. The tariff seemed to present such a
challenge, for a plantation system could hardly maintain itself when
crushed by taxation. Planters were also acutely aware that a major
slave rebellion had been barely averted in Charleston in 1822 and
again in nearby Georgetown in 1829. Surveying the international
scene, the planters knew that a small band of English abolitionists
had persuaded Parliament to ban the African slave trade in 1807
and were on the verge of winning emancipation for the slaves of
the British West Indies. Though yet small, an antislavery movement was growing in the North. Could not American abolitionists
wreak the same havoc in South Carolina as their English counterparts had done in Jamaica, either by promoting legislative interference with slavery or by emboldening slaves to take matters
into their own hands? Whether or not they came from large slaveholding districts, almost all South Carolina representatives had
strong personal interests in slavery and were determined to protect
it from every possible threat, including the tariff.

It is therefore not surprising that South Carolina politicians led
the assault on the federal tariff or that they attacked it with a fury
that almost led to bloodshed. The state's politicians had little use
for legislative give-and-take. They were thoroughly convinced that
liberty for whites depended on a healthy plantation economy and
on the total subordination of blacks that made it possible. They

were hypersensitive about slavery, and recent events at home and abroad had made them even more so. And they were bound together in a dense web of personal and family connections that united leaders from all sections of the state in their firm determination to preserve their way of life.

Of these leaders, first among equals was the nation's Vice President, John C. Calhoun. Born to an up-country gentry family in 1782, Calhoun had a brilliant mind, a Yale education, a low-country bride, and the ample fortune she brought with her. Elected to the House of Representatives in 1810, Calhoun distinguished himself as an advocate for war with Great Britain and as a zealous proponent of victory. His nationalism continued after the war, leading Calhoun to favor internal improvements, the encouragement of manufactures, and a national bank. In 1817, President Monroe had recognized Calhoun's efforts on behalf of the military by asking him to take the post of Secretary of War. As Calhoun's talents continued to attract attention, friends began to mention him as a Presidential candidate. Though disappointed in 1824, Calhoun kept his spirits up and hoped to follow Jackson in the White House.

Not all Carolinians shared Calhoun's optimistic nationalism. From the beginning, rivals such as Senator William Smith had argued that Calhoun's favorite programs depended on loose construction of the federal Constitution and that loose construction could destroy the rights of the states. In particular, a powerful federal government in the hands of a Northern majority could attack the institution of slavery, the foundation of South Carolina society. Though Smith and his followers never won control of South Carolina, their warnings found a broader audience in the aftermath of the Panic of 1819, as prosperity faded, tariffs mounted, and slavery's critics grew bolder. By 1827, the president of South Carolina College was defiantly predicting that the South could never save itself in a nation ruled by Yankees. "We shall ere long be compelled to calculate the value of our union," Thomas Cooper warned, "and enquire of what use to us is this most unequal alliance?" When Congress ignored such sentiments and imposed the so-called tariff of abominations in 1828, the mood in South Carolina grew increasingly bellicose.

Faced with mounting planter outrage, Calhoun and his associates in state politics looked for a militant anti-tariff position that still stopped short of Cooper's frank secessionism. Where Jackson had insisted on majority rule, Calhoun and his friends sought protection for what they saw as minority rights. The doctrine known as nullification became their answer. During the summer of 1828, Calhoun became the secret author of an "Exposition and Protest" that spelled out the features of this policy. The South Carolina legislature soon adopted the essay as its official position in the tariff controversy, though Calhoun still hoped that his position in the Jackson Administration could moderate the tariff and forestall all radical action.

According to Calhoun's "Exposition," the federal Constitution was a compact between sovereign states. In case of a disagreement about the meaning of the compact, the states themselves still retained the power to interpret its provisions. In other words, the states and not the federal courts had the final authority to pass on the constitutionality of federal laws. If a state such as South Carolina felt that the tariff was unconstitutional, but despaired of finding relief in Congress or the courts, it could call a special state convention to proclaim the law in question null, void, and unenforceable within its borders. Such an act of nullification would force the other states to confront the problem. If two thirds of Congress and three quarters of the states could agree that the act in question was in fact legitimate, they could amend the Constitution to correct its ambiguity. The aggrieved state could either live with this decision or secede. Alternatively, it might persuade the other states of the justice of its complaint and win national endorsement of its position. Far from threatening the Union, supporters argued, nullification would strengthen it by offering a safe and orderly means for an oppressed minority to obtain relief without secession. Even so, the doctrine's emphasis on minority rights offered a radical challenge to the Jacksonian position that majority rule was the essence of a republic. "Constitutional government and the government of a majority are utterly incompatible," the "Exposition" declared, "it being the sole purpose of a constitution to impose limitations and checks upon the majority. An unchecked majority is a despotism—and government is free, and will be permanent in proportion to the number, complexity, and efficiency of the checks, by which its powers are controlled." The nullifiers' defense of minority rights was far from absolute, for they did not hesitate to abuse the minority rights of white South Carolinians

who disagreed with them. Nevertheless, the nullification controversy would bring these two competing versions of republicanism
to the brink of war.

Clinging to the possibility of a peaceful solution, Calhoun hoped
that he could guide President Jackson and his party toward a low-
tariff policy in time to avert a clash between state and federal
governments. These hopes were gradually eroded, however, as the
Administration's first year in office wore on. Calhoun supporters
watched helplessly as the friends of Martin Van Buren scooped
up the choicest appointments and won the President's confidence.
Before long, Jackson's suspicious eye had even fixed on John C.
Calhoun as the author of Peggy Eaton's troubles. John Henry
Eaton, after all, was a Van Buren ally and a supporter of the tariff
of 1828, while Floride Bonneau Calhoun had turned a very cold
shoulder to Peggy. By the fall of 1829, Jackson had become convinced that the South Carolinian had whipped up the Eaton scandal, as he later explained, "to coerce me to abandon Eaton, and
thereby bring on me disgrace for having appointed him, and
thereby weaken me in the affections of the nation, and open the
way to his preferment or my ruin." Fearing his premature death
at the end of 1829, Jackson denounced Calhoun's Presidential
aspirations in a private letter to an old friend, and endorsed Van
Buren as his successor. The hopes of South Carolina's moderates
were thus slowly demolished in the bitter quarrel, partly personal
and partly political, between Andrew Jackson and his proud but
powerless Vice President.

The gathering conflict between South Carolina and the Union
won a flood of national publicity in the winter of 1830 when a
minor proposal by a New England senator touched off a major
congressional debate about the meaning of the Constitution.
Shortly after the session opened, Senator Samuel Foot of Connecticut introduced a resolution to limit the sale of Western lands,
a proposal that would slow the growth of frontier states and cut
into public revenues, forcing the government to continue its reliance on a high tariff. Foot's resolution brought angry replies from
Thomas Hart Benton of Missouri and Robert Y. Hayne of South
Carolina. Both accused New Englanders like Foot of conspiring
to injure the South and West. Massachusetts Senator Daniel Webster then rose to defend his section. In doing so, he scoffed at
South Carolina's constitutional theories and referred to the blight-

ing effects of the slave economy, suggesting that the free-labor system would always make allies of the North and West.

Webster's suggestion that Southern problems could be blamed on slavery touched a raw nerve. As Vice President Calhoun nodded approvingly from the chair, Hayne lashed back at Webster with a fiery defense of the peculiar institution. Hayne insisted that slavery was a blessing, not a curse, that blacks were wholly unqualified for liberty and far better off in slavery than in the "savagery" of Africa or the penury of freedom. As for Southern backwardness, that was the fault of the tariff. South Carolina would defend itself against Yankee thievery despite the sophistry of Massachusetts.

Hayne then summarized the case against the tariff and spelled out the argument for nullification as the last resort of a beleaguered minority. Quoting from the Virginia Resolutions of 1798, which had been passed in opposition to the Alien and Sedition Acts, Hayne reminded his colleagues "that in case of a deliberate, palpable, and dangerous exercise of other powers not granted by the said compact, the States who are party thereto, have the right, and are duty bound, to interpose, for arresting the progress of the evil." According to Hayne, liberty itself depended on the compact theory of government, for an all-powerful or "consolidated" Union would destroy the rights of states and individuals alike.

The debate had wandered far from the subject of the public lands and even from the tariff, but Hayne's reply gave Daniel Webster the perfect opportunity to present an alternative vision of the American Republic, based on a larger view of the nation and its destiny. Rising to his fullest rhetorical powers, the Massachusetts orator swore passionately that he held no enmity toward the South or any desire to disturb its institutions. Though he disapproved of slavery, Webster would leave its disposition to the states. Regardless of slavery's merits, however, Webster rejected the compact theory of the Constitution. Harking back to a theme in the *Federalist Papers*, Webster the constitutional lawyer insisted that the Constitution was created by the whole American people, not the states. Using words that foreshadowed Lincoln's Gettysburg Address, Webster proclaimed that the national charter was "the people's constitution, the people's Government; made for the people; made by the people; and answerable to the people." When the Constitution had been ratified, "We, the people of the United States of America" had granted certain powers to the federal government, granted certain other powers to the states, and retained still others as individuals. In their wisdom, the people had provided that disagreements about the respective powers of the state and federal governments should be settled by the United States Supreme Court, not by twenty-four separate state conventions. To believe otherwise would plunge the Union back to the dark and turbulent days of the Articles of Confederation. America did not need to choose between personal freedom and national greatness, Webster promised, for the country could have both. "Liberty and Union," he proclaimed, "now and forever, one and inseparable!"

The Hayne-Webster debates were a brilliant display of grandiloquence. For generations thereafter, Northern schoolchildren would memorize the peroration of Webster's "Second Reply to Hayne" as the perfect embodiment of American nationalism. The debate itself settled nothing, however, for as speaker followed speaker in the months ahead, Foot's original resolution was forgotten and discussion gradually collapsed from exhaustion. Many of the issues raised by the debate would be settled only by the Civil War, but Hayne and Webster had spelled out two compelling and mutually exclusive visions of the Republic's meaning and destiny. So far as the tariff and nullification were concerned, the practical question was: Where did Andrew Jackson stand?

The answer was quickly forthcoming. On April 13, 1830, all the leading Republicans in Washington gathered at a special banquet to honor Thomas Jefferson's birthday. States'-rights sympathizers controlled the program and put Robert Y. Hayne on the podium as principal speaker. When Hayne concluded his stemwinder in support of strict construction and the defiant actions of the state of Georgia, a parade of lesser states'-rights militants followed with supporting toasts. When these had died away, all eyes turned expectantly to Andrew Jackson. Protocol compelled the President to offer the first "volunteer" toast, and the provocative rhetoric of the nullifiers had now obliged him to bless or condemn what they had said. Knowing Jackson's strong adherence to states'-rights principles, the nullifiers expected an endorsement. Instead, they were stunned when Jackson lifted his glass defiantly and offered the uncompromising nationalist sentiment "Our Federal Union. *It must be preserved.*"

By stressing the supremacy of the Union without hedges or qualifications, Jackson had effectively repudiated the whole nullification movement. A hush fell over the room while the President's meaning sank in. As Vice President, Calhoun came next. "The Union," the Carolinian countered, his hand trembling with emotion, "next to our liberties, the most dear." He thus returned Jackson's challenge, praising the Union but insisting—in contrast to Webster and Jackson—that liberty and Union did not always hang together. If necessary, South Carolina would choose liberty first. The President and Vice President were now locked in public combat, with the basic principles of republicanism standing between them.

Why had Jackson taken this path? He was a cotton planter himself and just as injured by the tariff as any man in South Carolina. He was also a large slaveholder and presumably as wary of slave revolts as any other prudent master. Perhaps more important, he was a well-known friend of states' rights and strict construction. As Senator Hayne had just reminded the audience, Jackson had also acquiesced in the wholesale nullification of federal laws and court decisions by the state of Georgia. What made tariff policy different from the Indians?

The fact that Jackson and Calhoun were enmeshed in a bitter private quarrel involving the Eatons certainly aggravated the enmity between them, but the President's stand on nullification did not reduce to personal pique. As a planter and a slaveholder, he was sympathetic to the legitimate complaints of his section, but the finespun theories of the nullifiers left him wholly unconvinced.

Like most other white Southerners of the 1830s, Jackson was removed from the special conditions that surrounded South Carolina planters, and as yet felt impatient with their overwrought fears and obsessive insecurity. He had known financial hardship as a planter and had survived it. He did not worry that a temporary federal tax could push the plantation system into a downward spiral of bankruptcy. While he had no sympathy for the infant abolition movement, Jackson knew full well that the federal government would never interfere with slavery as long as he was President, and unlike Calhoun, he did not brood about the future. While a significant number of planters in other states were coming to share the South Carolinians' concerns, most Southern politicians still shared Jackson's optimism and rejected the extreme response of South Carolina.

Recognizing the strong feelings which the tariff provoked among others, Andrew Jackson had always approached the subject of protection with great care. In his view, the great importance of the tariff was to stimulate the production of military necessities and to raise the needed revenue for repaying the national debt. Beyond these two purposes, Jackson felt that the alleged effects of the tariff in promoting manufactures and in penalizing agriculture were highly exaggerated on both sides. He therefore always felt that the subject should be compromised. When he first ran for the Presidency, Jackson committed himself to a "judicious" tariff but left his supporters to guess what levels he actually meant by that. By the end of his first term, Jackson could foresee that the national debt would soon be repaid and thus looked forward to reducing import duties, but he still insisted that sectional interests must be compromised. "In the exercise of that spirit of concession and conciliation which has distinguished the friends of our Union in all great emergencies," Jackson told Congress, "it is believed that this object may be effected without injury to any national interests."

Despite his interest in low tariffs and his willingness to compromise, Jackson could not agree that a protective tariff was unconstitutional or that individual states could overturn a legitimate act of Congress. While he supported the rights of Georgia to legislate for Indians and to exercise all sovereignty within its own state borders, the tariff was a policy that regulated the commerce between the United States and foreign countries. Though states should enjoy great latitude in their internal concerns, each could not go its own way in matters that concerned the whole Union. Here Jackson's military background may have been decisive. As President, Old Hickory was not prepared to lead a government that could be stymied by a single state, any more than he would command an army that could be halted by a single soldier. In the Creek Wars, when deserters had threatened the strength and unity of Jackson's forces, Old Hickory had approved their execution by firing squad. He would soon be threatening nullifiers with a similar fate if they dared to defy him or obstruct the laws of the United States.

Soon after the dramatic confrontation at the banquet, the personal rupture between President and Vice President became complete when friends of Van Buren leaked an ancient secret. In 1818 Jackson had provoked international outrage when he invaded

Spanish Florida without permission and executed two British subjects whom he suspected of arming and inciting the Seminole Indians. Within the privacy of President Monroe's Cabinet, Calhoun,
as Secretary of War, had joined others in protesting Jackson's
insubordination, calling for an official censure or even a court-
martial. In the end, Monroe had suppressed such talk and Jackson
failed to discover exactly who had attacked him. In the ensuing
years, however, Jackson continued to feel acutely defensive about
the whole incident, so Calhoun kept quiet about his opposition
and allowed the General to believe that he had endorsed his conduct in the affair. Though rumors of Calhoun's true actions sometimes reached him, Jackson continued to give the Carolinian the
benefit of the doubt and dismissed contrary rumors out of hand.

As the controversy over nullification and the Eatons intensified,
the recollection of Calhoun's old loyalty was the one remaining
prop of the Vice President's standing with the President, so Calhoun's enemies in Jackson's inner circle soon seized the opportunity to knock it loose. Soon after the Jefferson's-birthday
banquet, they arranged for Jackson to see a letter from William
H. Crawford, Monroe's old Secretary of the Treasury and an old
enemy of both Jackson and Calhoun, detailing the truth about the
Carolinian's former secret attack.

Already angered by the Vice President's political course, Jackson was infuriated by the proof of his personal disloyalty and
hypocrisy and demanded an explanation. When Calhoun replied
with an evasive self-justification, an acrimonious exchange of letters followed, dragging on for most of a year and leading to a total
breakdown in the relationship between President and Vice President. Making matters worse, Calhoun later spurned the chance
for a reconciliation and published this correspondence in the spring
of 1831. He apparently hoped to create a ground swell on his own
behalf, by convincing the public that Jackson was a rash and vain
old man, helpless against Van Buren's wily manipulation. Unfortunately, Calhoun only convicted himself of bad judgment, for the
quarrel with Jackson was of his own making, not Van Buren's.
Far from being manipulated by Van Buren, Jackson probably manipulated Calhoun, taking grim delight at the spectacle of the Vice
President's progressive self-destruction. Eventually, Calhoun also
publicized his full endorsement of nullification. The two publications sealed his political fate, leaving Jackson, the Democratic

Party, and the Union on one side of a deep gulf and Calhoun, South Carolina, and nullification on the other.

As the rupture deepened between Jackson and Calhoun, the President decided that he needed a different newspaper to communicate his views to his party and the public. Duff Green, his first press spokesman, had consistently used the *U.S. Telegraph* to promote the cause of the Vice President and could not be trusted any longer. After consulting with Amos Kendall, Jackson asked Francis P. Blair of Kentucky to come to Washington and establish the *Globe* as the voice of the Administration. Back in Kentucky, Blair and Kendall had edited a paper together, and Blair's opinions were as close to the President's as Kendall's. By the end of 1830 the *Globe* was turning out hard-hitting copy for the inspiration of Jacksonians everywhere. Blair was soon a central figure in the Kitchen Cabinet and his paper defined the standards of Jacksonian party orthodoxy. Striking back, Duff Green published Calhoun's pamphlet on the Seminole controversy, while his *Telegraph* defended Calhoun and sniped at Van Buren until the two leading Jacksonian newspapers were in a state of open warfare.

Internal dissension grew so intense in the early spring of 1831 that Secretary of State Martin Van Buren resolved on a dramatic step to break the impasse. As matters stood, the President was scarcely on speaking terms with the Vice President and most of his Cabinet, while official Washington was divided between armed camps of feuding Jacksonians. Worse yet, from Van Buren's perspective, his own reputation for intrigue lent support to Calhoun's published innuendos that the Administration's breakdown was the fault of the Little Magician and his sinister influence over the Old Hero. To get on with his own agenda, the President needed to shake off all backbiters, surround himself with loyal subordinates, and prepare for a second term. Not coincidentally, an internal housekeeping would protect Van Buren from charges that he alone was responsible for the Administration's difficulties, thus clearing the way for his succession to the Presidency after Jackson's retirement. In the spring of 1831, Van Buren decided to relieve the President's embarrassment and protect his own future by offering to resign as Secretary of State. He broached the idea to Jackson on one of their daily rides and the General agreed to think it over.

It took all of Van Buren's persuasive skills to convince Jackson that his resignation would be an act of service and not desertion.

But when John Henry Eaton offered to follow Van Buren's example, the way was cleared for a general Cabinet purge. Jackson's personal loyalty to Eaton had prevented him from asking the Secretary of War (and his controversial wife) to step aside for the sake of peace. When Eaton impulsively volunteered to follow Van Buren, however, the other participants in the "petticoat war" could be asked to depart without personal disgrace, freeing the President to reconstruct his Cabinet completely. Jackson was quick to see the advantages and promptly sought the resignations of Ingham, Branch, and Berrien. Only William T. Barry, the loyal but plodding Kentuckian at the Post Office, was suffered to remain.

When the *Globe* announced the resignations of Van Buren and Eaton on April 20, politicians and editors were shocked by the sudden shake-up of the government and the dangerous instability it portended. Matters were not improved when the *Telegraph* proclaimed to the world that Jackson had turned out his Cabinet because the secretaries would not command their wives to receive a notoriously immoral woman. The dismissed secretaries had refused to go quietly, moreover, and were soon spreading their own lurid versions of events, portraying an Administration in the grip of petty jealousy and self-serving manipulation. Ex–Secretary of the Navy John Branch published an account that accused Van Buren of exercising a "malign influence" over the helpless President, while using the pretext of the Eaton scandal to stir up a quarrel with virtuous statesmen like Calhoun and expel all low-tariff supporters from the Administration. Even the President's closest friends worried that the avalanche of dirty linen could topple Jackson's Presidency, but the President himself rejoiced that the purge had rid him of discordant voices in his official family. He concluded that Van Buren's act of self-sacrifice proved him to be a "pure republican who has laboured with an eye single to promote the best interests of his country," while Calhoun stood exposed as the antithesis of a virtuous statesman, a malicious intriguer who followed ambition rather than principle.

In the round of appointments that followed the Cabinet purge, Jackson rewarded Van Buren with the mission to Great Britain while bringing the incumbent, Louis McLane, back to Washington as Secretary of the Treasury. Edward Livingston, a New York lawyer turned Louisiana planter, became Secretary of State. Hugh Lawson White, the President's old friend from Tennessee, vexed

Jackson by refusing the post of Secretary of War. The position went instead to Lewis Cass, territorial governor of Michigan and an enthusiastic supporter of Indian removal. Levi Woodbury of New Hampshire took charge of the Navy, while Roger Brooke Taney of Maryland completed the Cabinet as Attorney General. With the exception of Van Buren, the preceding Cabinet had lacked distinction, but the President found his new officials highly satisfactory.

The consequences of the Cabinet shake-up did not end with the appointment of new secretaries. Though Jackson remained popular with the voters, senior political leaders were increasingly alarmed by the apparent success of Van Buren and the Kitchen Cabinet in winning the President's ear and displacing established leaders like Calhoun and the dismissed members of the Parlor Cabinet. Still convinced that voters would defer to the prestigious judgment of the Senate, they determined to end Van Buren's career by denying him confirmation as minister to Britain. By prearrangement, the Senate vote was tied and Vice President John C. Calhoun took pleasure in casting the negative vote that ended Van Buren's diplomatic tour.

Angered by his enemies' continued efforts to humiliate him, Jackson retaliated sharply. The *Globe* began a spirited campaign to give Van Buren the second spot on the ticket when Jackson ran for reelection in 1832. Gathering in Baltimore in May 1832, the first national convention of the Democratic Party endorsed this proposal. As expected, Jackson won reelection over rivals Henry Clay of the National Republicans and third-party candidate William Wirt. Van Buren then replaced his archrival from South Carolina as the second-ranking official in the country and first in line to succeed the President on his retirement. In national politics, Calhoun's destruction seemed complete.

Shorn of all pretensions to influence over the Administration, Calhoun could no longer restrain the radicals in his own state who longed for a tariff showdown. When Jackson signed the Tariff Act of 1832, lowering duties somewhat but preserving the principle of protection, they pushed the tariff struggle to a climax. Nullifiers captured the South Carolina assembly and called for the election of a sovereign state convention. Gathering in November 1832, the convention solemnly declared the tariffs of 1828 and 1832 to be null, void, and of no effect in South Carolina. After February 1,

1833, it would be illegal to enforce the tariff laws there. State loyalty oaths would bar all dissenters from this policy from holding public office or even sitting on a jury. If the federal government used force to execute its laws, the nullifiers warned, South Carolina would secede from the Union and fight back. Though Calhoun's term as Vice President would not end until Inauguration Day in 1833, he resigned his position at the end of 1832 and returned to Washington as senator from South Carolina, girding himself to defend his native state from the floor of Congress itself.

For Andrew Jackson, South Carolina's latest actions far exceeded the legitimate bounds of states' rights. In his view, the Constitution clearly gave Congress the right to impose tariffs, while the principles of majority rule required South Carolina to submit to positive congressional decisions. In his annual message of December 1832, Jackson criticized nullification and indicated his intention to enforce the laws. A week later, he issued a special proclamation to refute the claims of South Carolina.

Written with the help of Secretary of State Edward Livingston, Jackson's proclamation of December 10, 1832, was a vehement assertion of federal power that echoed many of Daniel Webster's arguments in the debate with Robert Y. Hayne. "The Constitution of the United States . . . forms a *government*, not a league," it declared. "The power to annul a law of the United States, assumed by one State, [is] *incompatible with the existence of the Union, contradicted expressly by the letter of the Constitution, unauthorized by its spirit, inconsistent with every principle on which it was founded, and destructive of the great object for which it was formed.*" Furthermore, said Jackson, secession was as illegal as nullification. "Disunion by armed force is *treason,*" he insisted and treason he would not tolerate. Lest anyone mistake his meaning, Jackson soon asked Congress to pass a "Force Bill" containing new legislation giving him the power to use force to collect the revenue. Privately, he raged to everyone within earshot of his determination to march into South Carolina at the head of an army and wage war, if necessary, to hang Calhoun and his cohorts.

Jackson's proclamation whipsawed the prevailing coalitions in Congress and the states. Habitual enemies of Jackson's such as Henry Clay and Daniel Webster were as pleased as they were astonished by the President's nationalist stand. Protectionist legislators in Pennsylvania passed prompt resolutions of support, followed by their counterparts from New England, the middle states, and the Old Northwest. The nullifiers themselves were delighted by Jackson's militant stance, for they hoped the President's violent threats would frighten his traditional supporters in the states'-rights camp. "It is not *now*, whatever it may heretofore have been, a doubtful question of political economy," a Calhounite newspaper reflected. "It is now a question of right on one side and power on the other."

Still unconvinced by the tortuous constitutional logic behind nullification, most Southern politicians rejected South Carolina's radical course but worried seriously about the implications of the proclamation and the Force Bill. The Virginia legislature condemned both nullification and protectionism and defended its long-standing concern for states' rights. Grimly underscoring his state's opposition to consolidated federal power, one prominent Virginian told a reporter that "the Executive can never march troops against South Carolina, through eastern Virginia, *but over our dead bodies*." The North Carolina and Alabama legislatures likewise condemned nullification but refused to back the Force Bill and called for compromise to resolve the crisis. The President's near-unanimous Southern coalition began to split, as the plantation districts warmed to South Carolina's theories and bridled at all talk of coercion. Mississippi planter spokesman John A. Quitman put it clearly: "Carolina tho' she may be wrong has taken the field in our cause."

As South Carolina and the President staked out rival and extreme positions in the crisis, initiative passed to Congress to resolve the issue. In addition to the Force Bill, the Administration called for rapid tariff reduction to meet the just complaints of South Carolina, and the nullifiers reciprocated by extending the date when their ordinance would take effect. In late December 1832, Representative Gulian C. Verplanck of New York introduced a measure, with Jackson's approval, drastically lowering the tariff of 1832 over the course of two years, but stopping short of ending protection altogether. Speaking for the manufacturers, Daniel Webster strongly opposed this bill and was joined by the other protectionist congressmen. Even the Calhounites rejected the Verplanck bill, partly because it continued the policy of protectionism and partly because they hated to give a pro–Van Buren congressman any credit for resolving the controversy.

Seeing his opportunity, Senator Henry Clay waited until the Verplanck bill seemed hopelessly deadlocked and then introduced an alternative. His compromise would begin by lowering the tariff very gradually, to give manufacturers time to adjust, but would end by renouncing protection entirely by 1842. Webster and Jackson both resented Clay's plan because it seemed to capitulate to Calhoun while it added to the laurels of the Kentuckian, but they could offer no feasible alternative. The compromise tariff bill won the support of a coalition of low-tariff supporters and moderately protectionist congressmen, while the Force Bill passed with the votes of National Republicans and Northern Jacksonians. Few congressmen voted for both measures, but Jackson signed the two of them into law on March 2, 1833. Soon afterward, South Carolina claimed victory and rescinded its nullification of the tariff, though the convention stuck by its principles and defiantly nullified the Force Act. National authorities ignored this provocation and rejoiced that the crisis had passed without bloodshed.

In the course of the nullification controversy, South Carolina had spelled out an extreme version of the states'-rights dogma, including a claim for the right of secession. Jackson, Webster, and other unionists had proclaimed an alternative doctrine, the idea that the Union was perpetual, that the national government was supreme in its field, and that an effort to end the Union was an attack on republicanism itself. Neither of these views prevailed in the short run. Adroit congressional negotiators had evaded the constitutional issue with a compromise that gave substantive relief to the South, at a pace that manufacturers could bear, and gave unionists a symbolic assertion of federal supremacy in the Force Act. The underlying constitutional questions could not be settled finally until the aftermath of the Civil War.

In practical terms, however, it was clear that the great states'-rights battles of the early Jackson Administration had been settled in favor of those who opposed the use of federal power to promote industrialization, urbanization, and economic innovation. When the national government failed to protect the Indians against Georgia but expelled the Eastern tribes instead, it made available vast new acreage for the continuation of an agrarian republic of slaveholders and yeomen. When the same government discarded the protective tariff while offering no more than symbolic condemnation of South Carolina's challenges, it again favored agrarian interests over economic development. It had also chosen slavery over free labor, since most of the affected Indian lands were in the South, while tariff reduction might threaten the jobs of Northern wage earners. Over the long run, Jackson proved to be right: the effects of the tariff were exaggerated, and the loss of tariff protection did little to slow the pace of economic change. But for voters and politicians in the Jacksonian coalition, the reaffirmation of traditional values was more reassuring than the trend of economic indicators. For the present, these republicans would be glad that the nation seemed to stand for physical expansion over qualitative change, slavery and agrarian stability over dangerous innovation. It was a stance that would continue to dominate American public life for most of the antebellum era.

Not all citizens were so satisfied. The nullification controversy also gave the opponents of Andrew Jackson a chance to identify one another and test their strength. The election of 1828 had been won by a sectional coalition that seemed to leave northeastern proponents of economic development in a hopeless minority. Nullification opened up fissures in this coalition that later party activists could exploit. While many Southern planters rejected Calhoun's tactics, they could only sympathize with his goals. The Virginia tidewater, the Georgia cotton belt, and the Alabama and Mississippi river bottoms all held voters who worried about the tariff, the future of slavery, and the heavy hand of federal power. These voters were also wary of Jackson's appeal to unqualified majority rule, and the threat that political egalitarianism might pose to their property rights and to their leadership of state and local governments. Many of these planters had been old supporters of William H. Crawford who had come around quite reluctantly to Andrew Jackson when they lacked any other alternative. The nullification crisis once more roused their worries about this unpredictable General.

Ironically, the South's agricultural businessmen shared with their Northern protectionist enemies a lively concern for the mechanics of national and international markets, world trade, long-distance credit relations, and a stable national currency. By contrast, neither nullifiers nor manufacturers had much in common with the backwoods adherents of self-sufficiency or the urban artisans and wage earners who clamored for "Equal Rights." In the coalition between Clay and Calhoun that led to the compromise tariff of 1833, many saw an awkward marriage of convenience that could not last. More prescient observers saw the seeds of an important coalition of anti-Jackson forces that could bring the President to heel. All they needed was another controversy to organize around. Even while the nullification crisis had been building, Jackson's economic policies were giving them the issue they desired. The permanent organization of Jackson's opposition would arise from the President's war on the Bank of the United States.

Killing the Monster

IN THE AFTERMATH of the nullification crisis, President Jackson decided to celebrate with a "Grand Triumphal Tour" of New England. The "land of steady habits" had never warmed to the headstrong Tennessee General, but the descendants of the Puritans and Federalists had a powerful attachment to the Union and cheered the retreat of South Carolina. In the spring of 1833 they cheered even louder for Old Hickory as the newly reelected President made his way by railroad, steamboat, and horse-drawn carriage through all the major cities of the East and the towns and villages of eastern Massachusetts. To the chagrin of John Quincy Adams, Harvard College presented the frontiersman with an honorary doctorate, and one lively wag started a colorful tradition by imagining the self-educated President's Latin reply: "*E pluribus unum*, my friends, *sine qua non*." Everywhere large crowds applauded him as the man who had saved the Union from collapse, and even the Brahmin leadership of Boston was impressed with his dignity and poise. Jackson stood at the height of his popularity.

The confrontation with South Carolina demonstrated that Andrew Jackson was determined to preserve the Union and to make the federal government—in its proper sphere—superior to the power of the states. But what should be done with federal power once its supremacy had been achieved? Should the government devote itself to the goals of John Quincy Adams and Henry Clay, continuing to stimulate the nation's rapid transformation to a commercial economy? Or should it follow Jefferson's precepts and seek to maintain a society of family farms and independent producers? Defining the relationship between state and national power formed one major theme of Jackson's Presidency, while establishing the federal stance toward economic development constituted a second. When they fully understood his approach to that question, the leadership of New England would not be half so pleased as they had been earlier.

When he first took office, Jackson's inclination was to halt federal efforts to promote further economic change in the United States. Though his official messages never failed to congratulate Americans on the growth of their prosperity, he regarded the direct productions of the earth and human hands as the only reliable basis for material improvement and remained hostile to the social and political implications of paper wealth, machine technology, and large-scale production. Socially, Jackson felt that the advance of commerce, banking, and industry tended to undermine the independence, virtue, and equality that made a republic possible. Politically, he believed that the practice of giving special subsidies to some economic activities and not others opened the door to immediate abuses, as special interests scrambled to win favors by bribery and other improper activities. In other words, Jackson associated government assistance to the Market Revolution with long- and short-term forms of "corruption," the traditional bane of republican government, and he regarded its advocates with deep suspicion.

As his first term proceeded, Jackson's initial views had hardened and took the form of specific policies. In addition to his stand on the protective tariff, he came to oppose the national bank, the circulation of paper money, and most federal aid to internal improvements. Jackson hoped these policies would cripple the economic developments that tended to restrict the "liberty" and "virtue" of America's small farmers and independent producers. As he declared in his fourth annual message, directly paraphrasing Jefferson, "independent farmers are everywhere the basis of society and the true friends of liberty," and Jackson did what he thought was necessary to protect their strength and freedom of action.

Jackson's economic program was highly controversial. The President's rousing stand in favor of the liberty and independence of small producers encouraged Americans who felt trapped or threatened by economic change and helped to bring them into the Democratic Party. Other voters felt just as strongly that progress required the expansion of markets, the development of transportation systems, the establishment of reliable networks of credit, and the concentration of capital for larger and larger tasks. Their goals implied a relative transfer of power and wealth from independent producers to the capitalists who controlled banks, corporations, and extensive enterprises. In exchange for the loss of independence, the friends of progress promised that average citizens could win a higher standard of living as they traded the burdens of self-sufficiency for the comforts of a cash income paid in bank notes, and many Americans were willing, even anxious, to make the switch. Others found that they had no choice but to change and decided to accept the new reality by supporting the institutions that had created it.

In Jacksonian eyes, the bank notes of the new cash economy were not likely to be worth much. Even when they were, the citizens who gave up republican independence for material wealth had surrendered to a corrupt bargain in their own lives. Nevertheless, thousands resented Jackson's efforts to stand in the way of their conceptions of personal and social improvement. Jackson's economic policies pertained directly to a pervasive debate on the nation's future and touched on the daily realities of countless American families.

Andrew Jackson's war on banks and internal improvements did not secure an agrarian future for America, but they did shape the political landscape of his generation. A debate over economic development was already agitating the politics of states and communities. Jackson's words and actions drew a connection between local and national controversies and forced voters and political leaders to take sides. In order to support a popular but beleaguered President, Jackson's advisers organized themselves into a revitalized Democratic Party and emerged with a stronger sense of who they were, what they wanted, and how they wished to pursue their goals. Jackson's opponents went through a similar, if contrary experience as they formed themselves into the Whig Party to wage a counterattack. The resulting pattern of two-party competition was one of the most significant and enduring consequences of Jacksonian politics. Even more important, Americans elaborated their ideas of equality and democracy in this controversy and created the fundamental ideological legacy of the Jacksonian years. The debate over federal aid to economic development, and especially the dispute over rechartering the second Bank of the United States, was thus the central event of Andrew Jackson's Presidency.

Jackson's view of economic development was ambiguous. He frequently cited material improvement as evidence of the benefits of free institutions or of white society's superiority over the Indians. As he asked in his second annual message, "what good man would prefer a country covered with forests and ranged by a few thousand savages to our extensive Republic, studded with cities, towns, and prosperous farms, embellished with all the improvements which art can devise or industry execute, occupied by more than 12,000,000 happy people, and filled with all the blessings of liberty, civilization, and religion?" When his tour of New England brought him to the factory village of Lowell, Massachusetts, Jackson was fascinated by the wonders of its machinery. Perhaps because the operatives were mostly women, and thus excluded from his notions of republican rights, Jackson did not ask his guides how workers' liberties had fared under industrialism. On the other hand, where the liberty of white male citizens was concerned, Jackson was very sensitive about the social and political consequences of economic development. As his words and actions in office would make clear, he would not condone economic progress which in his view was founded on unequal privileges or which resulted in the permanent domination of some citizens by others. Instead, Jackson was in favor of economic well-being that was founded on hard work and personal achievement, and productive of more personal liberty rather than less. In practice, this vision would put serious limits on the degree of commercial and industrial progress that the President could endorse.

Early in his Administration, Jackson showed how the suspicion of economic development could become a partisan shibboleth and the basis for a popular government policy. In the spring of 1830, Congress passed legislation authorizing a purchase of $50,000 of stock in the Maysville, Washington, Paris, and Lexington Turnpike Company. The planned road would begin at the terminus of the National Road on the Ohio River and cut across the state of Kentucky. Eventually, the directors hoped to extend the road to the

Tennessee River in northern Alabama, thus linking two major river systems and allowing their enterprise to qualify as a national rather than local project. Despite its attractive features, the Maysville Road became a controversial test of the internal improvements policy.

Led by James K. Polk of Tennessee, congressional Jacksonians condemned the bill as expensive, unconstitutional, and excessively local in its impact, not least because it brought special benefits to the home state of Henry Clay. The bill also caught the attention of Secretary of State Martin Van Buren. The New Yorker was no friend of federal expenditures for internal improvements. His own Bucktail faction had once ridiculed plans for "Clinton's Big Ditch" and resisted efforts to get federal support for the project. Once the Erie Canal had proved successful, however, the Regency had no interest in using federal funds to subsidize rival projects in other states. Moreover, as the head of the old pro-Crawford wing of the party, Van Buren knew how much his Southern friends worried about expansion of federal power. He therefore urged the President to veto the appropriation for the Maysville Road.

Jackson needed no urging. He shared the fears of Presidents Madison and Monroe that federal subsidies to internal improvements projects were unconstitutional. Despite these doubts, if Congress did have the power to build national improvements, the Maysville Road could not qualify because it lay entirely within a single state. Moreover, Jackson's highest fiscal priority was the repayment of the national debt. Congress had already appropriated all the remaining funds in the Treasury; the Maysville Road—any system of federal improvements—would increase the debt, not lower it. In May of 1830, Jackson had Van Buren and Polk weave these themes into a Presidential veto message that would put a stop to all such projects in the future. Several weeks later, he reinforced the message with a veto of a second turnpike and pocket vetoes of some similar legislation.

Still thinking that political success would depend on the views of established community leaders—the sort of men who usually longed for better transportation facilities—Western Jacksonians had warned against a veto on grounds of political expediency. Jackson himself thought differently. "The voice of the people from main [sic] to Louisiana during the last canvass for the Presidency has answered this in the negative," he reflected privately. "They have cried aloud for reform, for retrenchment in the public expenditures, and economy in the expenditures of the Government." The Maysville veto would be popular, Jackson predicted, despite the disappointment of ambitious promoters. A system of federal expenditures in the states, moreover, would undermine republican virtue and violate the Constitution. "The Govt. of the United States owning half the capital in each state corporation will wield the state elections by corrupting and destroying the morales of your people . . . This is not a power granted to Congress, and of course is an infringement upon the reserved powers of states, and at once destroys that harmony that by the framers of the constitution was intended to exist between the two govts."

The President's estimate was correct. The Maysville veto became the first of several measures that spelled out Jackson's initially ambiguous principles, reaching over the heads of established leaders to the opinions of ordinary voters, cementing the loyalty of the like-minded and forcing lukewarm supporters into opposition. To the friends of Old Republican John Randolph of Virginia, the message "fell upon the ears like the music of other days." One Pennsylvania congressman protested against the veto until reports from his district forced him to admit that "the General . . . had known his constituents better than he himself had known them." "The line . . . has been fairly drew," Jackson exulted afterward. "Where [the veto] has lost me one, it has gained me five friends, and in Kentucky has done me no harm." Tennessee supporter Felix Grundy confirmed this view, though he had opposed the veto himself. "Altho your friends may not be numerically increased, their attachment is now of a stronger texture," the congressman wrote. "Formerly, it consisted in a degree of affection for the man and an admiration of his character & public services and confidence in his virtues. Now is added, an adherence to political republican principles."

The new policy on internal improvements did not rule out all federal expenditures for transportation, only those that were too expensive or merely "local" in scope. Jackson also demanded that publicly financed projects be free to everyone and not the property of private corporations. When Jackson was convinced that these conditions were met, as in the case of lighthouses to protect federal ports of entry, he signed the appropriations. Ultrastrict constructionist Thomas Ritchie thus regretted that the veto did "not exactly come up to our Virginia Doctrines." Spotting the same inconsistency, contemporary and subsequent critics have charged that the Maysville veto was nothing more than a hypocritical "*electioneering document* sent to Congress for political effect." Such criticisms ignore Jackson's strong beliefs that the federal government did possess definite if limited powers, particularly in the areas of commercial protection and national defense. Though tempered by the same pragmatism that allowed him leeway on the tariff question, the Maysville veto made it clear that Jackson would tolerate no national network of federally financed roads and canals, as called for by Clay's American System. The integration of the national market economy would thus proceed more haltingly than it might have otherwise, a result that few Jacksonians seemed to mind. John Quincy Adams agreed. Reviewing the consequences of his defeat at Jackson's hands, the ex-President reflected, "I fell and with me fell . . . the system of internal improvement by national energies."

As Jackson's internal improvement policy became settled in the aftermath of the Maysville veto, attention shifted to the related question of banking and currency. Even more than improved transportation facilities, money and credit were the driving forces behind the transformation of the American economy. Though supporters of internal improvements could carry on their projects without federal assistance, financial leaders insisted that the national system of banking and currency required some central direction by the Bank of the United States. They therefore hoped to see the Bank rechartered when its original charter expired at the end of Jackson's second term. Andrew Jackson thought otherwise and decided to destroy the Bank. His struggle with the "Monster Bank" and its supporters became the centerpiece of his Presidency.

The power of the B.U.S. grew out of its size and its privileges as the government's own bank. In the course of ordinary business, federal officials and other customers were constantly making deposits of state bank notes at the many branches of the Bank of the United States. At the insistence of Bank president Nicholas Biddle, the B.U.S. then presented these notes to the banks that issued them and demanded specie in return. The Bank's demands were so regular and so large that state bankers were always obliged to keep a generous supply of specie on hand, and to limit the volume of notes they issued, in order to be sure of having enough cash to satisfy the B.U.S. This policy acted as a brake on the lending practices of the state banks, curbing any tendency they might have had to make excessive loans, print too many notes, and thus generate an inflationary boom. In times of financial stringency, moreover, Biddle could relax his customary demands for specie, giving sound state banks more breathing space and counteracting the tendency to deflation. Biddle's monetary policies thus gave the B.U.S. some power to regulate the nation's money supply to balance the business cycle and meet the needs of the commercial and industrial economy.

Just as many had opposed a federal role in transportation development, not everyone supported the federal bank. Soberminded state bankers recognized its value in stabilizing the business climate for everyone, but other observers noted that the B.U.S. was fundamentally a private institution with primary obligations to its stockholders and not to the general public. Because the notes of the B.U.S. were known and respected everywhere, and also legal tender for the payment of federal taxes, customers preferred them to the notes of other banks and accepted them at nearly par value throughout the Union. The B.U.S. seemed capable of driving the state bank notes from circulation and establishing a monopoly of national currency, which it could then manipulate at pleasure. For citizens who still thought of power and liberty as polar opposites, this was not an attractive prospect. Americans who feared the inegalitarian and antirepublican tendencies of economic development were not reassured to learn that the goal of the Bank of the United States was to make the process as smooth and efficient as possible.

Resentment of the Bank of the United States could easily lead to resentment of banking in general. A popular and articulate expression of this feeling came from banking critic William M. Gouge, a journalist and self-trained economist who published *A Short History of Paper Money and Banking in the United States* in 1833. Written in a simple but hard-hitting style, Gouge's book became the favorite reference of Jacksonian bank critics. Gouge emphasized the unreliable aspects of paper money currency and went on to denounce the pernicious consequences of economic development that was based on corporate charters and other unequal privileges bestowed by the state. Gouge predicted that paper money finance could eventually make America as rich as Europe but at a terrible cost. "With every year," he warned, "the state of society in the United States will more nearly approximate to the state of society in Great Britain. Crime and pauperism will increase. A few men will be inordinately rich, some comfortable, and a multitude in poverty." If banking charters were only repealed, Gouge hoped that progress would continue more naturally and more justly, "wealth becoming the reward of industry, frugality, skill, prudence, and enterprize, and poverty the punishment of few except the indolent and prodigal." Depending upon the observer, the expansion of banks could thus appear as the crowning ornament of republican society or the cause of its downfall.

Andrew Jackson agreed with Gouge. In the 1790s he had lost a great deal of money at the hands of a commercial speculator in Philadelphia, and he associated banks with the fraudulent manipulations that made such losses possible. Because the U.S. Constitution blocked states from issuing paper money, he inferred that it likewise banned state banks from doing the same thing. Nor did Jackson see any constitutional authority for a federal bank, regardless of what John Marshall's Supreme Court may have said about the subject. As he frankly declared in his first official interview with Nicholas Biddle, "I do not dislike your Bank any more than all banks. But ever since I read the history of the South Sea Bubble [an eighteenth-century British financial scandal] I have been afraid of banks." At the beginning of his Administration, Jackson seemed to be interested in a radical overhaul of the existing Bank, but as he grew more convinced that every aspect of the American System ought to be dismantled, he determined to destroy the B.U.S. and replace its paper money with a "constitutional currency" of gold and silver coins. In his eyes, the Bank had become a "Monster" and a "hydra of corruption," impossible to reform and inimical to republican society and politics.

Despite the President's strong convictions against the Bank, its friends were numerous and well placed. Most of them would have supported the Bank out of conviction in any case, but their friendship was also reinforced by tangible benefits. In Kentucky, Henry Clay had served as the Bank's attorney for many years. In Washington, Daniel Webster argued its cases before the Supreme Court and earned handsome fees for his services, but sometimes not as promptly as he would have liked. In 1833, he complained to Biddle that "my retainer has not been renewed, or *refreshed*, as usual. If it be wished that my relation to the Bank be continued, it may be well to send me the usual retainer." Other congressmen won generous loans from the Bank, without having to provide the usual securities and sometimes without having to pay them back. Prominent editors could also gain favorable terms at the Bank's offices; Duff Green of the *U.S. Telegraph*, Mordecai Noah and James Watson Webb of the New York *Courier and Enquirer*, Joseph Gales and William W. Seaton of the *National Intelligencer*, and Thomas Ritchie of the Richmond *Enquirer* all borrowed from the Bank. Not all of them supported the B.U.S. editorially, though the New York *Courier and Enquirer* made a dramatic shift in the Bank's favor when a critical loan came through in 1831. All in all, downright bribery had little to do with the Bank's support, though anti-Bank propagandists had a field day with such examples of "corruption" when they eventually leaked out.

Pro-Bank sentiment was so widespread among political leaders that even Jackson's own supporters were divided. Many leading Cabinet members endorsed the institution, including Louis McLane, who succeeded Samuel Ingham as Secretary of the Treasury, and Edward Livingston, who followed Van Buren as Secretary of State. Indeed, in the official Cabinet, only the new Attorney General, Roger Brooke Taney of Maryland, fully shared the President's anti-Bank outlook. Among Jackson's informal advisers, many old friends and supporters in Tennessee had close ties to the Nashville branch of the B.U.S. In the Kitchen Cabinet, Jackson had to rely on the support of Amos Kendall and Francis P. Blair of the *Globe*. Both men had won their political spurs in the political wars that had racked Kentucky after the Panic of 1819 and both accordingly brought with them a powerful hatred of banks and paper money when they came to Washington. Even before his appointment as party editor, Blair had written Jackson that the B.U.S. was buying votes and subverting elections in favor of the friends of Henry Clay. Later on, hard-hitting anti-Bank propaganda became staple fare in the columns of the Washington *Globe*.

During the early years of Jackson's Administration, friends of the B.U.S. struggled tactfully but unsuccessfully to win the President's acquiescence in a recharter of the existing Bank. In his first annual message, Jackson criticized the Bank on constitutional grounds and denied that it had created a uniform national currency.

A year later, at the end of his second annual message, Jackson declared that the Bank "can not continue to exist in its present form without . . . perpetual apprehensions and discontent on the part of the States and the people." He proposed a "modification" that would have abolished Biddle's Bank altogether and replaced it with an agency of the Treasury. The third annual message merely stated that the President's views had not changed. At the same time, Jackson continued to appoint Bank supporters to key posts and to give a patient ear to their arguments. Conflicting signals from the Administration kept Bank supporters off balance for most of the President's first term.

In the meantime, Jackson's old enemies in the National Republican Party longed to unseat the frontier upstart in the election of 1832. Their choice for President was Senator Henry Clay of Kentucky, witty and urbane author of the American System and long-time friend of the Bank of the United States. Alongside Clay, Massachusetts Senator Daniel Webster stood opposed to the Administration as the voice of New England's manufacturing and shipping interests. Though they remained poles apart from the National Republicans on the issue of the tariff, South Carolina's nullifiers generally agreed with them about the need for a national bank and resented Van Buren's ascendency at the expense of Calhoun. As the election of 1832 drew near, therefore, Clay and Webster urged Biddle to join them and to use the election to force Jackson's hand. Nullifiers such as Calhoun and South Carolina's George McDuffie, chairman of the House Ways and Means Committee, likewise signaled their willingness to join in using the Bank issue against the President.

In November of 1831, Clay asked Biddle to submit a petition for a new charter and predicted that Congress would consent. If Jackson then signed the bill, well and good. National Republicans would charge him with inconsistency. If he vetoed it, indignant voters would make Clay President instead, and so much the better. To this simple argument, the Kentuckian added a subtle threat. If Biddle's cooperation and Jackson's veto sent him to the White House, Clay left no doubt that he would support recharter of the existing Bank. On the other hand, if Biddle remained neutral in an effort to placate Jackson, Clay implied that the victorious National Republicans could find another way to provide for the needs of the currency. Though his better judgment told him that an application for recharter in an election year would reduce the Bank to a political football, Biddle finally despaired of winning Jackson's support and accepted Clay's proposal. His request for recharter reached Congress in January 1832.

In Congress, Jacksonians responded with a demand for an investigation into the Bank's conduct, charging it with a variety of legal, moral, and political offenses. A packed committee quickly ratified the accusations, though sophisticated Bank critics agreed with the pro-Bank minority that the report was biased and uninformed. Biddle and his allies then agreed to certain modifications of the charter that might make it more acceptable to some opponents, and the bill to recharter the second Bank of the United States passed Congress July 3, 1832.

Jackson left no doubt among his intimates about what he would do. The day after the recharter bill passed the House, Martin Van Buren called at the White House and found Jackson lying sick but determined to do battle. Clutching his lieutenant by the hand, Jackson explained his illness. "The bank, Mr. Van Buren, is trying to kill me, *but I will kill it!*" A week later, Jackson released his inevitable veto.

Prepared by Kendall and Taney, the veto message crackled with democratic outrage. In harsh but colorful phrases, it condemned the Bank as "unauthorized by the constitution, subversive of the rights of the States, and dangerous to the liberties of the people." Starting off in measured tones, the message reviewed a long catalogue of reasons why Jackson found the recharter neither *"necessary* nor *proper,"* and ended with a stirring conclusion that became a mobilizing testament of faith for Jacksonian Democrats everywhere. Bristling with debater's points, the veto had an argument for everyone and served to rally the greatest possible constituency for the President's position.

Jackson began by denouncing the charter as an unjust grant of unequal privileges to the stockholders. The Bank, said Jackson, "enjoys an exclusive privilege of banking under the authority of the General Government, a monopoly of its favor and support, and, as a necessary consequence, almost a monopoly of the foreign and domestic exchange." Dismissing any possible public benefits that might result from this arrangement, the President focused directly on the fact that the monopoly was worth a great deal of money to the individuals who received it, far more money than they would have to pay for it. Stripping aside what he regarded as the pretense that banking and the provision of a paper currency were forms of community service, Jackson insisted that "banking, like farming, manufacturing, or any other occupation or profession, is *a business*," just a way of making money. Why should not anyone have the right to enter this business? Why should Nicholas Biddle and his aristocratic friends get special advantages?

Many of these stockholders were foreigners, Jackson added repeatedly, and to his audience, that meant "British." The others were "a few hundred of our own citizens, chiefly of the richest class," and "by this act the American Republic proposes virtually to make them a present of some millions of dollars," all of which "must come directly or indirectly out of the earnings of the American people." Obviously, Jackson objected vigorously to these features. The Republic should never grant exclusive privileges, but if it did, the recipients should pay a fair price. At all events, such an awesomely powerful institution should be "*purely American*," lest national security be threatened. If wealthy British aristocrats should dominate the American economy, Jackson was asking, how could the Republic be safe? "Will there not be cause to tremble for the purity of our elections in peace and for the independence of our country in war?"

The veto also pointed to the sectional features of the Bank of the United States. Most of its loans were made in the South and West, while most of the stock was owned in the East. In effect, Jackson claimed, the Monster exploited frontiersmen, because "it is obvious that the debt of the people in that section to the bank is principally a debt to the Eastern and foreign stockholders . . . and that it is a burden on their industry and a drain on their currency, which no country can bear without inconvenience and occasional distress." What was more, the charter gave tax advantages to foreign stockholders, who would quickly absorb the majority of shares and "place the whole United States in the same relation to foreign countries which the Western States now bear to the Eastern." Every patriot could see what Jackson was driving at: the Bank would recolonize America, reverse the results of the American Revolution, and deliver the Republic into the hands of British financiers.

Jackson addressed the question of the Bank's constitutionality at great length. Though the Supreme Court had affirmed that the

Constitution permitted Congress to charter a national bank, Jackson did not feel bound by the Court's decision. "Each public officer who takes an oath to support the Constitution swears that he will support it as he understands it," he maintained, "and not as it is understood by others." The Court had declared that a Bank was constitutional if the President and Congress found it "necessary and proper"; Jackson explained why it was neither, in his view, and therefore unconstitutional.

His list of reasons was long and detailed. The charter promised the Bank a monopoly for fifteen more years, but Congress had no right to bind its successors in this way. The taxable status of Bank stock would encourage its sale to foreign investors, to the detriment of the national interest. It was unconstitutional for the Bank to own land within the states or to choose for itself the location of its branches. Other provisions of the charter stripped states of their right to tax the B.U.S. like other banks, while the advantages that state banks enjoyed over individuals in doing business with the Bank would weld local and national banks together in a formidable financial colossus, "erecting them into an interest separate from that of the people." As Jackson hastened to point out, "it is easy to conceive that great evils to our country and its institutions might flow from such a concentration of power in the hands of a few men irresponsible to the people."

The veto's detailed bill of particulars touched one raw nerve after another among Americans who were already anxious that the Market Revolution was spinning out of control. The appeal to states' rights attracted Southerners and many others who felt that state governments, being close to popular control, were crucial barriers against powerful outside incursions. Citing repeated violations of the Constitution's sacred text founded the veto's reasoning firmly on the eighteenth-century republican tradition, not on mere expediency. The resentment of Great Britain, of special privilege, of judicial dictation, all addressed the real concern of citizens who felt that the simple, natural economy of a true republic was already in the grip of alien powers. In his veto, Jackson reassured these citizens that firm, steady resistance could save the Republic from corruption.

Jackson brought the veto's tumultuous themes to a roaring crescendo in the message's final paragraphs. "It is to be regretted that the rich and powerful too often bend the acts of government to

their selfish purposes," he began. Firmly refusing to level all social
and economic distinctions, the President acknowledged that perfect equality was impossible in a republic, for "equality of talents,
of education, or of wealth cannot be produced by human institutions." Jackson viewed these inequalities as natural and pledged
to protect them, but a bank charter was an unnatural advantage
that deserved different treatment.

> In the full enjoyment of the fruits of superior industry, economy,
> and virtue, every man is equally entitled to protection by law; but
> when the laws undertake to add to these natural and just advantages
> artificial distinctions, to grant titles, gratuities, and exclusive privi-
> leges, to make the rich richer and the potent more powerful, the
> humble members of society—the farmers, mechanics, and laborers—
> who have neither the time nor the means of securing like favors to
> themselves, have a right to complain of the injustice of their
> Government.

The injustice of the Bank would have disastrous practical consequences, according to Jackson, for it would feed dissatisfaction
that could undermine the Union and ultimately republicanism itself. "Many of our rich men have not been content with equal
protection and equal benefits, but have besought us to make them
richer by act of Congress," Jackson explained, alluding to the
pending tariff showdown as well as the Bank controversy. "By
attempting to gratify their desires we have in the results of our
legislation arrayed section against section, interest against interest,
and man against man, in a fearful commotion which threatens to
shake the foundations of our Union."

What was the solution? Exclusive privileges such as the Bank
charter must be withdrawn and equality should become the basis
of government policy. Only by treating all citizens exactly alike
could the Union expect to endure. Even more important, the Republic must return to first principles, to reevaluate the entire course
of its history since the founding and halt its moral and political
decay. "It is time to pause in our career, to review our principles,"
the President warned solemnly, "and if possible revive that devoted
patriotism and spirit of compromise which distinguished the sages
of the Revolution and the fathers of our Union." He disavowed
any intention to overthrow legally vested interests, but he warned

against creating any new abuses and called for renewed dedication to Divine Providence and the wisdom of ordinary citizens to turn back the tide of pernicious change. "Through *His* abundant goodness and *their* patriotic devotion our liberty and Union will be preserved."

The veto message struck the nation like a manifesto for social revolution. Its vivid rhetoric pitted rich against poor and middling Americans more stridently than any other Presidential pronouncement before or since, and has repeatedly led historians to consider the Jacksonian movement in terms of class struggle. Without question, in the words of historian Marvin Meyers, its language "address[es] a society divided into classes invidiously distinguished and profoundly antagonistic." Though the message appealed in separate parts to farmers, workers, Westerners, and slaveholders, however, no single group by itself was its primary audience. Instead, as Meyers observed, Jackson saw society as "a whole body, the sovereign people, beset with aristocratic sores."

In the logic of the veto message, the problems of America did not derive from conflicts which were built into the structure of society itself and which could be addressed only by more or less continual social struggle. The problem instead was a foreign and corrupting influence in a basically healthy system. The Bank and its minions had fastened corruption on the Republic; their operations were destroying the equality that an old economy had supposedly guaranteed. By eliminating the Bank, Jackson could restore the stable, peaceful world that the Founding Fathers had governed. Such a commonwealth would contain no clashing interests, no more class conflict, no exploitation, no degrading servitude of white men to creditors, employers, or to the marketplace itself. Power would return to honest republican citizens who gained their bread without guile or special privileges, who cherished their own liberty as they respected the liberty of others. Virtue would be restored. For a period, at least, the Republic would be safe from corruption, monopoly, and aristocracy, and the great body of the people could breathe easily once more.

The veto message thus addressed a great popular majority instead of a single social class. In it, Jackson took for granted that an economy of small owners and producers would always predominate in America, so long as privileged forces did not destroy it. If such an economy did exist in Jackson's own day, however, it would not long remain so. The thrust of the Market Revolution, and the Bank that assisted it, was to undercut such a world in favor of mass production, big business, and mass markets. In the America that was taking shape, the rhetoric of the Bank veto would become the language of protest, the slogans of embattled groups such as farmers or workers who still thought of themselves as "the people," even when the rest of the country was ready to dismiss them as mere "interest groups." Even in his own day, the republican language of Jackson's veto message was readily embraced and embellished by nascent radical movements among urban workingmen, and its populist uses would expand in the future. Though it was not originally formulated as the banner of continuing class conflict, the themes of Jackson's veto message would take on that role as American society continued to change.

In retrospect, it is easy to dismiss Jackson's vision as naïve or even fanciful. Realistically speaking, the egalitarian commonwealth he envisioned had never existed in America and could not be "restored." In any event, the forces of economic change were greater than any one institution, no matter how powerful, and could not be stopped by a single veto. It is even true that many of the Americans who rejected the larger political implications of the Market Revolution were also experimenting with its material benefits and could thus be charged with hypocrisy, or at least confusion about who they were and what they wanted for the country.

Such a hasty dismissal should be resisted. The arcadia envisioned by Jackson may not have existed in strict reality, but it was close enough to the truth to serve as a valid social ideal for generations of Americans who lived between the Revolution and the Civil War. Most Americans in this era were still rural dwellers with relatively easy access to farms of their own. In town, shops were small, and artisans were only beginning to realize that the status of master would slip further out of reach for most workers. Jackson won his greatest support, moreover, in those areas where this small-producers economy remained strongest. It is thus not true that most Jacksonians were living a double reality, thinking in one way and behaving in another. No matter how archaic their thinking may appear today, it was not in conflict with the reality of their daily lives. Instead, it grew out of that reality and drew credibility from it.

Jackson's veto was virtually unprecedented. Previous Presidents had held that Congress possessed the exclusive power to legislate. They had used the veto power a total of only nine times, always on the grounds that the proposed law was unconstitutional. In the Bank veto, however, Jackson claimed the right to participate in lawmaking directly, to be consulted in advance about proposed legislation, and to use the veto power against laws that he merely disapproved. These demands horrified the opposition. "The idea of going to the president for the project of a law, is totally new in the practice, and utterly contrary to the theory of the government," Henry Clay protested, and went on to denounce the idea "that each public officer may interpret the Constitution as he pleases." "If these opinions of the President's be maintained, there is an end of all law and all judicial authority," cried Webster, likening Jackson's stand to the tyranny of celebrated despots such as James II of England and Louis XIV of France. If Jackson saw the Bank as a threat to the Republic, conservatives saw the same threat coming from Jackson himself.

The legal and financial arguments of the Bank veto message were likewise vulnerable to logical rebuttal. Daniel Webster attacked the central argument of the veto that the charter was primarily a gift to its owners. "Congress passed the bill, not as a bounty or a favor to the present stockholders . . . , but to promote great public interests," he pointed out. If the stockholders benefited from a new charter, who could object? Every bank had to have some stockholders, and the public would benefit even more than they. He likewise scoffed at the notion that capital gains from a hypothetical increase in the market price of Bank stock could constitute a "present of some millions of dollars" torn from "the earnings of the American people." Nor did the Bank oppress the West and South, Webster maintained; it provided desperately needed credit for the development of those regions, and Americans should be grateful that foreign capital was available for this purpose. If Jackson's claims were true, Clay and Webster both asked, and it was difficult for the West to pay interest on its debt to the Bank, how much more difficult would it be to repay the entire principal in the four short years before the existing charter expired?

None of these arguments touched the central appeal of the veto message. In the public mind, the broadest promise of the American Revolution was to make every white man his own master. Throughout the country, ordinary citizens had struggled to free themselves from habits of deference to the village squire, only to face new and unsettling forms of social domination in the aftermath. For journeymen and pieceworkers in the infant industrial economy, the prospect of a lifetime working for scanty wages made a mockery of the promise of independence. For yeoman farmers drawn to commercial agriculture, the uncertainties of price fluctuations and credit gyrations made dependence on the growing market economy both a worrisome burden and a source of needed income. If the promise of independence was thus undermined, or in other words, if personal and political liberty was truly in danger, these citizens wanted to know whom to blame and how to find redress. Jackson persuasively told them to blame the Bank. The threats to liberty had not come from any natural source or from any defect in republicanism. Instead, sinister forces had conspired to extract special privileges from the state and had used these advantages to accumulate power over others. If the privileges were withdrawn, the power would crumble and liberty would be safe. Personal fortunes might rise and fall according to an individual's just deserts, but without government assistance "aristocracy," or the permanent concentration of power over others, could never triumph in America.

The veto also promised state political leaders that the central authority would not attempt to dictate the direction of local development. "In thus attempting to make our General Government strong we make it weak," Jackson assured them. "Its true strength consists in leaving individuals and States as much as possible to themselves." The message thus appealed successfully to a wide range of voters and elected officials and withstood all the refutations that were hurled at it.

Supporters of the Bank thought that the veto's doctrines would so alienate voters that Jackson would stand no chance of reelection. "It has all the fury of a chained panther biting the bars of his cage," sneered Biddle to Clay. "It is really a manifesto of anarchy . . . and my hope is that it will contribute to relieve the country from the dominion of these miserable people." He accordingly spent substantial sums of the Bank's funds to reprint the message and distribute it widely, along with sober essays by pro-Bank authors, in the confident expectation that the comparison would send community leaders and their constituencies hastening to the side of Henry Clay in the upcoming Presidential election.

The election of 1832 was actually a three-sided contest. In the Northeast, a popular outcry had arisen against the supposedly nefarious power of the Masonic fraternity, and an Anti-Masonic party took shape to combat its political influence. To nominate former Attorney General William Wirt for President, the Anti-Masons borrowed a familiar device from state politics and gathered in Baltimore for the first national Presidential nominating convention. The National Republicans followed suit and nominated Henry Clay, as expected, with B.U.S. attorney John Sergeant of Philadelphia as his running mate. In the South, many Jacksonians were frightened by Van Buren's success in displacing Calhoun and advocated the choice of slaveholding Philip P. Barbour for Vice President in place of the New Yorker. Despite their objections, the Democrats completed the round of national conventions by assembling in Baltimore to "concur" in Jackson's previous nominations by state and local bodies and to nominate Van Buren for Vice President.

In the campaign that followed, the principal issue was concerned less with the Bank than questions about power and republicanism that the effort to recharter it had raised. According to a typical Democratic newspaper from Pittsburgh, the worst aspect of the Bank was its threat to popular government—operating by loans and favors to corrupt political leaders, "it maintains its political party—cherishes its political favorites, bribes and corrupts the public press, and unfeelingly crushes all within its reach who may be so honest and fearless as to express disapprobation at its course and character." Like many Democrats, the editor moved easily from the narrow question of the Bank's political power to the larger problem of inequality posed by the concentration of wealth. The Bank War, he argued, showed "how necessary it is for freemen to watch the insidious movements of a monied aristocracy—who with peculiar subtlety, are ever ready to rise, grapple with, overpower, and bind the liberties of any people." The *Globe* agreed. "The Jackson cause is the cause of democracy and the people, against a corrupt and abandoned aristocracy," Blair thundered, and insisted that the future of liberty in both state and society demanded the suppression of the Bank. In the process, he did not fail to remind voters of the President's personal role in confronting the Monster. "It is difficult to describe in adequate language," he rhapsodized, "the sublimity of the moral spectacle now presented to the American people in the person of Andrew Jackson."

Supporters of the Bank took the opposite tack. To be sure, they praised the Bank for its practical economic benefits, but their strongest language was aimed at Jackson's alleged abuse of power and dictatorial ambitions. A Philadelphia assembly protested the veto by defining liberty as the freedom to defend private property against political interference. According to its resolutions:

> The principles of that message . . . would leave no man safe in the enjoyment of his property; would place the honest earnings of the industrious citizen at the disposal of the idle, the profligate and the vicious, would subvert every pillar of the constitution, and re-move every landmark of the law, and would substitute for a gov-ernment of perfect freedom and perfect equality, a system of anarchy, corruption, and misrule, naturally terminating in absolute despotism.

Washington's *National Intelligencer*, the leading newspaper of the National Republicans, repeated the theme. "The Constitution is gone!" shrieked an editorial. "It is a dead letter and the will of a DICTATOR is the Supreme Law!" Embellishing their warnings from the elections of 1824 and 1828 that a "military chieftain" could not be trusted with civilian power, Jackson's enemies agreed with Democrats that liberty was in danger, but maintained that "ex-ecutive usurpation" was principally to blame.

Even the Anti-Masons, who feared the power of a Masonic conspiracy more than the Monster Bank, echoed the common theme of republican subversion. According to their platform, "re-publicanism offers a more majestic and reverend image of sub-stantial glory, than can otherwise result, from the labors, and sufferings, and virtues of our race," but the principles of repub-licanism "were in never danger so imminent."

> Their foe is rich, disciplined and wily. He obeys no rules of civilized warfare, no restraint of truth, no injustice, no pleadings of humanity. He already occupies the principal posts heretofore relied on, as the chief defence of our liberty . . . and assails, by a thousand ambus-cades, and by all sorts of weapons the most envenomed and con-

demned, the watchful, thoughtful, steadfast, and unconquerable
friends of free principles. Such a foe is freemasonry.

Though Whigs, Democrats, and Anti-Masons all pointed to different sources of menace, all were clearly troubled for the future
of free government and all drew on traditional republican rhetoric
to express themselves. In the case of the Whigs and Democrats,
these fears had just as clearly originated in the complicated debate
over economic development that the Bank War epitomized. The
rhetoric of the Anti-Masons demonstrated, however, that the fear
of republican subversion could spread far wider than the controversy over a bank charter, and could lead some Americans to point
to enemies of republicanism that no one had previously suspected.

The Presidential contestants in 1832 relied on more than rhetoric
to take their message to the voters. Parades, dinners, barbecues,
speeches, songs, and torchlight processions all enlivened the campaign and brought the issues home to voters who tended to nod
over long columns of fine print. Democrats were especially skilled
at these techniques; one typical procession featured a hickory pole
entering a country town accompanied by fife and drum and Democrats bedecked with foliage. "Astride on the tree itself," Michel
Chevalier remembered, "were a dozen Jackson men of the first
water, waving flags with an air of anticipated triumph, and shouting
Hurrah for Jackson!" In Washington, Amos Kendall led the "Central Hickory Club" in a letter-writing campaign to notable Jacksonians in every state, urging the importance of local organization.
"Every neighborhood must be reached to meet the slanders and
falsehoods of our adversaries," he exhorted. "We are to have 'war
to the knife and knife to the hilt.' " With the name of a "good,
honest 'whole hog' Jackson man" in each locality, Blair and Kendall flooded the country with copies of the *Extra Globe* and sought
to persuade each voter that the war to preserve virtue and repel
corruption demanded popular endorsement of the President's veto
message.

The National Republicans' efforts were more restrained and
more likely to include a formal public dinner for local leaders of
the opposition than an uproarious mass meeting. Nevertheless,
their campaign literature circulated widely, criticizing Jackson for
his stance on the Bank, the tariff, the spoils system, the removal
of the Indians, and the authority of the Supreme Court. In Wash-

ington, a National Republican young men's convention assembled to meet Henry Clay and carry home his enthusiasm. In the larger cities, National Republican rallies attracted thousands and an active party press kept attention on the issue of "executive usurpation." "One more opportunity—*perhaps the last*—is yet afforded us," warned one typical Ohio sheet, "of strangling the monster of despotism before it shall have become too strong to be resisted. The power still remains in our hands. Let us so use it as men who are to render an account to our God, to our country, to the world—and all will be well."

In the end, Jackson triumphed handily, with 219 electoral votes to Clay's 49. The Kentuckian had carried his own state, most of New England, plus Maryland and Delaware. Vermont had fallen to the Anti-Masons, while South Carolina's legislature had given its votes to John Floyd, the pronullification governor of Virginia. All else belonged to the Hero. The popular vote totals were closer, and Jackson's 1828 majority may have been diminished, though irregularities in state record keeping make it difficult to be sure. The Democrats rejoiced and pressed forward, convinced that Jacksonism enjoyed a broad popular mandate.

The winter following the election was taken up by the nullification struggle, but the Bank issue was never far from Jackson's mind. The Bank was still in business under its old charter, and the President warned his congressional ally James K. Polk that "the hydra of corruption is only *scotched, not dead*." His fear was that Bank lobbyists might persuade the new Congress to reconsider the issue and grant a new charter by a two-thirds majority, making it possible to override a second veto.

To forestall such a step, Jackson decided to attack the Monster preemptively. Assuming that the Bank's lobbying process would include additional "loans" to undecided editors and congressmen, he determined to weaken the Bank's ability to lend by withdrawing all federal deposits and placing them in selected state banks. Stripped of the funds of its biggest customer, the Bank would be seriously limited in its ability to fight for a new charter or a more favorable Congress. When the old charter finally expired in 1836, the Monster would perish at last.

The intended step was far more drastic than the earlier veto. By law, the B.U.S. was entitled to the government's deposits unless the Secretary of the Treasury—not the President—directed otherwise. If the secretary did take this step, he was required to explain his reasons to Congress. A cautious House of Representatives had just declared that government money was safe at the B.U.S., so any effort by Jackson to force the Secretary of the Treasury to remove the deposits would appear to violate the wishes of Congress, long-established custom, and the spirit of the law. The appearance of illegal and arbitrary action would provoke a storm of outrage, even among moderate critics of the Bank, and would lend credence to National Republican charges that Jackson had become a dictator.

Even the Cabinet resisted removal of the deposits. The veto itself had shocked the secretaries, and most of them still hoped to cooperate with Congress and establish some sort of modified federal bank. Van Buren also asked that the President wait until after Congress had reconvened so that lawmakers might be consulted, but Jackson remained adamant. Explaining his motives to the Cabinet in a statement later published in the *Globe*, he insisted that the "experiment" with state banks was "necessary to preserve the morals of the people, the freedom of the press, and the purity of the elective franchise." Jackson also claimed the authority to act without congressional consultation on the grounds that the recent Presidential election had been fought on the question of the Bank's existence and the people had given him the mandate to crush it. No previous President had ever described his election as a popular plebiscite on a matter of policy, or asserted such an unlimited power to act in the name of the whole people, independently of their elected representatives in Congress.

Jackson listened patiently to the dissenters in his Cabinet but steadfastly ignored their protests. As Secretary of the Treasury Louis McLane was especially insistent on delay, Jackson moved him to the vacant position of Secretary of State. When William J. Duane, the new Secretary of the Treasury, also refused to follow orders, Jackson eventually fired him and appointed the Attorney General, inveterate bank foe Roger Taney, in his place. Beginning on October 1, 1833, Taney ordered that all federal revenues would be deposited in seven carefully selected state banks, while federal withdrawals would be taken from the B.U.S. Opponents called the government's new depositories "pet banks," while Jacksonians simply referred to them as "deposit banks." The government's balance in the B.U.S. would thus be drawn down gradually until the account was closed and all government business with the Monster was finished.

Congress took the news rather badly. Like the Cabinet secretaries, congressional Democrats wished to support the President, but few of them fully shared his uncompromising animus against the Bank. Practical men who usually enjoyed the support of the leading economic interests in their districts, they, too, had come to feel the benefits of commerce, credit, and development even as they hymned virtue and damned corruption on the stump. Their own sense of prudence and a due regard for the prerogatives of the legislative branch of government made them reluctant at best to see the nation's financial system dismantled by the unilateral action of the executive. Even in the House of Representatives, where Jacksonians held a nominal majority, opponents of deposit removal seized control and launched a blistering oratorical attack on the President's alleged abuse of power. In the Senate, the stronghold of Jackson's enemies, Clay, Webster, and Calhoun went even further in denouncing his high-handed actions.

Henry Clay led off with a set of resolutions that rejected Taney's reasons for deposit removal as "unsatisfactory and insufficient" and censured Jackson for his conduct in the matter. "We are in the midst of a revolution," Clay proclaimed ("hitherto bloodless," he added ominously), "but rapidly descending towards a total change of the pure republican character of the Government, and the concentration of all power in the hands of one man." As Clay put it, picking up a theme of his unsuccessful Presidential campaign, a republic was a government of limited powers and restrictions on the popular will, with no one branch of government able to dominate the others. For Clay, Jackson's claim to overturn established laws and institutions on the basis of a Presidential election meant that America was a republic no longer.

Other senators echoed Clay's charges. Webster repeated his arguments in favor of the Bank and branded deposit removal as illegal. According to Calhoun, Julius Caesar had also invaded the public treasury on his way to destroying the Roman Republic. The aspiring emperor had committed his robberies boldly, "but the actors in our case are of a different character—artful, cunning, and corrupt politicians, and not fearless warriors." Particularly in the South, deposit removal frightened political leaders who had acquiesced in the earlier veto, and former Jacksonians declared against the President. Senator Willie P. Mangum of North Carolina spoke for this group when he declared in debate that it was no longer a question of "bank or no bank" but of "law or no law, constitution or no constitution."

Boosted by such support, Clay's resolution of censure passed the Senate on March 28, 1834, by a vote of 26–20. In the House, patient maneuvering by Polk recaptured the situation for the Administration and the Democrats passed resolutions condemning recharter and rejecting restoration of the deposits. Jackson replied to his censure with a protest message that asserted even more explicitly than before that the President was "the direct representative of the people." Short of formal impeachment, he claimed, congressional objections to his official conduct were equivalent to attacks on popular government itself. Pro-Bank leaders were distressed by these assertions, but there was little they could do. The deposits were gone and resolutions could not bring them back.

Nicholas Biddle was not yet ready to surrender. If the time for reasoned argument was past, he concluded, bare-knuckle tactics might be more successful. "This worthy President thinks that because he has scalped Indians and imprisoned Judges he is to have his way with the Bank," the banker noted grimly. "He is mistaken." As the government slowly emptied its account at the B.U.S., Biddle was forced to call in loans to compensate for the loss, and businessmen who normally depended on Bank credit to finance their affairs faced a money shortage. From a period of relative prosperity, the nation's commercial centers quickly felt the sting of panic.

Though some contraction was unavoidable, Biddle lost his head in the crisis and cast aside all distinctions between the public welfare and the future of his own Bank. Hoping that popular distress might create sufficient political pressure for recharter, Biddle consciously pushed the contraction further than necessary. A short and sharp recession became his deliberate tool for political influence. When the Bank of the United States unexpectedly refused to renew the notes of its customers and demanded repayment instead, the money market suddenly dried up. Many mercantile businesses failed for lack of credit and unemployment mushroomed in commercial centers. The poor suffered most when jobs disappeared in urban warehouses and construction projects, but every-

one in credit-sensitive industries suddenly felt the pinch. Protests
from businessmen flooded Congress during the "panic session" of
the winter of 1833–34, most of them complaining of sudden financial stringency and demanding a restoration of the deposits as the
key to renewed prosperity.

Jackson and his loyalists brushed the protests aside. "Go to
Nicholas Biddle!" he roared to delegations of petitioning businessmen. "We have no money here, gentlemen." Privately he
added to Van Buren, "the golden calf may be worshipped by others
but as for myself I will serve the Lord." Rather than accept dictation from a private institution, one furious congressman likewise
declared, "I for one, say perish credit; perish commerce; . . . give
us a broken, a deranged, and a worthless currency rather than the
ignoble and corrupting tyranny of an irresponsible corporation."
Chairman of the House Ways and Means Committee James K.
Polk spoke firmly but more temperately. Regardless of the abstract
merits of a national bank, he declared, Biddle's attempt to create
a recession in order to coerce the government proved that the
Bank had forfeited its claims to legitimacy. "The Bank of the
United States has set itself up as a great irresponsible rival power
of the government. . . . The question is in fact whether we shall
have the Republic without the Bank, or the Bank without the
Republic."

Despite the determined posture of the Democratic loyalists, it
was evident that deposit removal had galvanized Jackson's opposition like no other issue. In the East, the business community
was livid and used the economic crisis to appeal to workers and
artisans to join in defending an orderly currency and a stable business climate. In the South, planter-politicians who had not dared
to embrace nullification found deposit removal a far safer ground
for denouncing "executive usurpation." In the West, the Bank
War likewise drove a wedge between "whole-hog Jackson men"
and those who cheered the President's personal qualities without
supporting his policies.

The outcry over "executive usurpation" so transcended the limits of the old National Republican Party that Clay and other leading
critics began calling themselves "Whigs" at the height of the debate
over the censure resolution in the spring of 1834. The new name
was taken from the party in English politics that had traditionally
resisted the prerogative power of the Crown and that had led the

American colonies to revolt against the arbitrary power of King George III. Unlike "National Republican," "Whig" was a name with popular drawing power in the struggle against "King Andrew I," and a "Whig" ticket soon entered the field in New York City's spring elections. Other Whig coalitions formed locally for the summer and fall elections, and by 1835 a new political party was coming into existence.

As Jacksonians noted derisively, the Whig Party in its infancy was an unstable compound of diverse elements. Clay and Webster stood at its head, but Calhoun also acted with them at first. Many Anti-Masons were inclined to join them, as were former Democrats who favored internal improvements, high tariffs, and of course the Bank of the United States. Other early Whigs were strict constructionists who deserted the President because they feared that he had stretched the Constitution even more than the outright supporters of broad construction. Initially, all they had in common was a resentment of the methods or the substance of Jackson's Bank policy, but the coming years would see the Whigs develop a coherent national program and an impressive level of unity. As the Whigs grew in strength they became a permanent opposition party to the Democrats, and U.S. politics settled into a stable pattern of two-party competition.

When Congress adjourned in the summer of 1834 without overturning Jackson's Bank policy, Nicholas Biddle was forced to acknowledge that his credit-tightening measures had accomplished nothing. On the contrary, the artificially created recession had alienated leading businessmen who favored the B.U.S. in principle but resented the crude pressure tactics that damaged them far more than rural or anticommercial Jacksonians. Biddle accordingly reversed himself, expanded the Bank's loans, and allowed prosperity to return to the nation's wharves and countinghouses. When his federal charter finally expired in the spring of 1836, Biddle obtained a state charter and continued his business as a purely private institution called the Bank of the United States of Pennsylvania, but he never again held center stage in the drama of national monetary policy.

Following the relaxation of credit in the fall of 1834, business conditions did more than improve; they boomed. While Democrats in Washington had been making war on the Bank of the United States, state legislators had chartered some 347 new state banks between 1830 and 1837. Fueled by an influx of foreign capital, these banks made new loans, and the money supply by 1836 rose more than two and one-half times over its level in 1829. Industry and commerce flourished in the rapidly developing Northeast; shoe and textile production quickened, railroad construction moved ahead to match the mileage of the nation's canal network, and cast-iron production nearly doubled to meet the new demand.

The price of cotton—always a bellwether of prosperity for the South and for the export trade—rose by more than half its level at the beginning of the decade. Aspiring planters responded by rushing to the southwestern land offices and snatching up the offerings of public lands. Throughout the West, land prices soared as entrepreneurs mapped out towns in the wilderness and projected fertile fields in virgin forests, prairies, and even swamps. Feeding the enthusiasm, states planned major new projects for internal improvement, opening up previously isolated areas for development and promising overnight riches to anyone shrewd enough to snap up lands along the rights-of-way. Though political conflict persisted between Democrats and fledgling Whigs, the get-rich-quick psychology of the "Flush Times" began to compete with political rhetoric for public attention. The "Alabama Feaver" of the post-1815 boom had struck Americans once more.

Unfortunately for working people, inflation lifted rents and prices powerfully, while wages moved much more sluggishly. Throughout the mid-1830s, protests quickened in the working-class neighborhoods of Eastern cities. An early union movement tested its wings and "workingmen's" candidates challenged the established leadership of Whigs and Democrats alike. In the winter of 1836–37, the price of flour rose so rapidly that many New York families went hungry, and resentment boiled over into riot against merchants who profited from popular distress. The prosperity of the Flush Times did not spread with anything like equality.

The onset of the most feverish land speculation roughly coincided with the transfer of government deposits from the B.U.S. to the "pet" banks. Contemporaries and later historians have consequently assumed that one event caused the other—that the pet banks lacked the responsibility of Biddle's B.U.S. and loaned the government's money to all comers, kicking off a credit boom that lifted prices and expectations out of sight, especially in the Western land market. More careful research by economic historian Peter

Temin has shown that the Bank War had little to do with the contemporary level of prices and investment. Instead, a combination of international circumstances conspired to bring more Mexican silver to the United States (which fueled more bank loans), to elevate the British demand for cotton (which increased its price), and finally, to persuade British investors to subscribe more heavily to American state bonds (which encouraged internal improvements). It was these forces which generated the speculative boom of the mid-1830s, not the gunplay between Andrew Jackson and Nicholas Biddle. Even so, the causes of the boom were less important than its effects, so far as the participants were concerned, and the last years of Andrew Jackson's Presidency witnessed a frenzy of speculation that seemed to mock the rhetoric of republican asceticism coming from the rostrums of anti-Bank assemblies.

The boom psychology of the Flush Times distressed President Jackson, who had hoped that the Bank War would initiate an entirely different spirit of slow and steady prosperity based on hard work and personal achievement. Instead, the passing of the "hydra of corruption" appeared to clear the way for a plague of secondary monsters that seemed less controllable but every bit as vicious as their parent. "I did not join in putting down the Bank of the United States to put up a wilderness of local banks . . . ," fumed Thomas Hart Benton. "I did not strike Caesar to make Anthony master of Rome." Belatedly, Jackson began to express his critique of the economy in terms of the "money power" or the "credit system" instead of a single Monster Bank. Late in his second term, he consulted with Kendall about another major step to protect "the safety of our currency, . . . check the paper system & gambling menace that pervades our land & must if not checked ruin our country & our liberty," but nothing came of it, for Jackson's time in the Presidency was running short and his health and energy had suffered. In the final months of his Administration, loss of blood from pulmonary hemorrhages and physicians' bleeding nearly killed the sixty-nine-year-old veteran. Instead of grand new initiatives, Jackson continued to try to turn the nation to a currency of gold and silver, in the hope of further limiting the influence of note-issuing banks.

Ironically, his efforts were frustrated by several circumstances stemming from earlier successes. Removal of the federal deposits from the Bank of the United States meant that a few pet banks enjoyed the enormously profitable business of holding the government's money. On the whole, state bankers were a cautious lot who saw the advantages of the Bank of the United States and favored its recharter, but once the Bank was definitely eliminated as a government repository, they were all eager to share the spoils of its defeat. Through their representatives in Congress, they began to press for a dramatic expansion in the number of banks that were entitled to hold the government deposits. Jackson was opposed to these demands, for a wider dispersal of the government's money would increase the problems of making sure that it was kept in safe hands, but his war against the B.U.S. had been waged against the principle of monopoly, and how could he defend a monopoly for seven banks any more than for one?

A second problem arose early in Jackson's second term, when the President's stubborn insistence enabled the United States government to pay off the federal debt completely for the first and only time in its history. Because the Compromise of 1833 left the tariff temporarily at high levels, however, federal revenues did not decline when expenditures for debt service came to an end, and an embarrassing surplus began to accumulate in the federal treasury. At one time, Jackson had suggested that constitutional barriers to federal support of internal improvements might be overcome by distributing any possible federal surplus to the states, who might then construct the projects on their own. By the time the surplus actually materialized, however, the struggles over the tariff and the Bank had convinced him that government should have nothing to do with such projects, and he dropped his support for distribution in any form. Whigs found the idea of distribution very attractive, however, and began to press it very strongly. In addition to a one-time distribution of the existing federal surplus, moreover, Henry Clay championed a permanent policy of distributing the proceeds from the sale of public lands, to be used by the states to finance internal improvements. Clay's measure had the merit of earmarking the proceeds from the sale of a permanent national asset for capital improvements rather than for current expenditures, but it would also create pressure for high land prices and a permanent protective tariff to replace the lost federal revenues. Simon-pure Jacksonians opposed Clay's land policy because they feared it would reopen the tariff controversy, reduce opportunities for yeoman farmers to acquire land, and stimulate the corruption they associated with government support for economic development, but the measure found support among Democratic moderates. Despite opposition, moreover, the federal surplus continued to grow and pressure to do something about it increased.

Congressional pragmatists hammered out a compromise in the Deposit Act of 1836. This measure sharply increased the number of deposit banks and provided that the surplus of $37 million be distributed to the states, in proportion to their federal populations. The distribution was nominally termed a "deposit," and not an outright grant, but everyone understood that the government would never ask for its money back, and it never has. The states were thus free to spend the windfall as they pleased, and most chose to finance public schools or internal improvements. In many cases, states did both, by investing in potentially profitable banks or transportation companies and reserving the dividends for education. Unwittingly, the new influx of cash, credit, and construction contracts fueled the boom psychology even further, adding even greater expectation of quick riches to the feverish promoters of the Flush Times.

Jackson resisted the Deposit Act because he feared that distributing the surplus and scattering the federal deposits would further encourage the inflationary boom. He almost vetoed the measure, but he had to accept the fact that it was popular even in his own party and that a veto might well have been overturned. Instead of vetoing the bill, he demanded the inclusion of a feature to promote an all-metallic currency. The act barred deposit banks from issuing or accepting paper notes of less than five dollars' value and gradually lifted the limit to twenty dollars by the end of his term. Jackson hoped that this provision would induce Americans to use coin instead of paper in their ordinary transactions. He had become especially sensitive to the problem of businessmen who cheated their employees and customers by deliberately paying them in the worthless or devalued currency of distant banks. By forcing small bills out of circulation, Jackson at least hoped to protect workers and farmers from the fluctuations of the "rag money" preferred by speculators. Pinning his future hopes on a metallic currency, he reluctantly signed the Deposit Act of 1836, but instructed Francis Blair to condemn it in the *Globe* and to agitate persistently for the repeal of all but its anti–paper money features.

Acting to curb speculation in the public lands, Jackson took another step against bank notes with the Specie Circular of 1836. This directive ordered purchasers of large tracts of public lands to pay with coin after August 15, 1836, though actual settlers could continue to pay for their plots with notes. The order produced immediate outrage among bankers, Whigs, and speculators, all of whom complained about the trouble and expense of hauling bullion across the continent from Eastern banks to Western land offices, when the banks needed the metal to support their own note issues. Political opponents likewise labeled it a new act of executive usurpation, possessing, in the words of the *National Intelligencer*, "the same arbitrary character as the removal of the public deposits in 1833, emanating from the imperious will of an irresponsible Magistrate, the execution of which will not effectually cripple the deposit banks but produce a derangement of all business of the country."

The Specie Circular was so unpopular among business and political leaders that Congress attempted to repeal it, an impertinence that Jackson stifled with a pocket veto on the last day of his second term. His Administration thus ended in financial stalemate: the Bank of the United States was finished as a public institution, but the public funds were perilously lodged in unstable private banks and the nation was still very far from a specie currency. Despite his best endeavors, Jackson left office with the Republic still vulnerable to corruption by the forces of economic transformation, but he could make no further efforts at reform after issuing the Specie Circular. The remaining problems must be left for his successor.

The closing years of Jackson's second term were hardly uneventful. In 1835 he escaped harm in the first Presidential assassination attempt. Indian affairs continued to demand attention, as the Cherokees persisted in staving off removal and Seminoles went to war to defend their lands and homes in central Florida. In 1835 Chief Justice John Marshall died—the last real Federalist in Washington, it seemed—and Jackson fought successfully to replace him with Roger Taney, the committed Jacksonian theorist who had contributed to the Bank veto message as Attorney General and withdrawn the deposits as Secretary of the Treasury. For the next quarter century, Chief Justice Taney would be writing Jacksonian doctrine into the nation's basic constitutional law. The following year, a quarrel flared with France until the offer of British mediation led to a satisfactory settlement. Soon afterward, Americans living in Texas won their independence from Mexico, prompting Jackson to recognize their republic in the last hours of his Presidency. Finally, just before Jackson left office, a Democratic majority in the Senate acceded to a campaign launched by Senator Thomas Hart Benton and "expunged" the resolutions of censure that had been introduced by Henry Clay and passed in the aftermath of the deposit removal episode. The Senate's official journal was mutilated as a result, but the Old Hero was deeply gratified by this act of vindication.

Despite the significance of these events, Jackson's main preoccupation had become the preservation of his earlier accomplishments and the codification of his legacy. He wanted to make sure that Vice President Martin Van Buren won the right to succeed him in the White House and continue his policies, and he wanted to leave a strong Democratic Party to perpetuate his principles. For the most part, Jackson watched from the sidelines while Van Buren and other subordinates undertook the tasks of party-building and electoral campaigning. Their efforts were rewarded, and Van Buren triumphed narrowly over a divided Whig opposition in the election of 1836.

Pleased by the outcome of the voting, Jackson turned his mind to a Farewell Address that would spell out the lessons of his Presidency and put its experiences in perspective. Drafted by Taney after careful consultation with the President, the address was the last major statement of the Jacksonian creed and expressed the President's strongest counsels to his posterity.

As in previous pronouncements, Jackson's major themes were liberty, equality, and the Union. He began by praising the experience of fifty years under the federal constitution. Despite many doubtful moments, Jackson declared that faithful adherence to the wisdom of the framers had brought the United States freedom, stability, and prosperity, respect from foreign nations, and deliverance from the menace of the Indians. Union and the Constitution had brought these blessings, but departure from them would bring calamity. "At every hazard and by every sacrifice," he concluded, "this Union must be preserved."

How could the Union be saved? Like Jefferson, Van Buren, and other prescient leaders, Jackson pointed to sectional conflict as the foremost enemy of national unity. Recalling George Washington's

Farewell Address, Jackson interpreted the first President's warnings against the "spirit of party" as a stricture against geographical
alignments that could divide the North and South. As everyone
realized, slavery was the basis of sectional tension, and Jackson
urged his fellow whites to tolerate different views of that subject.
He warned Southerners against secessionism and the tendency to
reject nonslaveholders such as Van Buren as candidates for President. Even more strongly, he condemned the infant abolition
movement and denounced "all efforts on the part of people of
other States to cast odium upon [Southern] institutions." Implicitly
denying that slavery had any moral significance, Jackson argued
that the Union was diverse and that its diversity must be respected.
In effect, Southerners must accept the free states' decision against
slavery among themselves, while the North must absolutely respect
the need for continued slavery in the South. As for the views of
Afro-Americans, Jackson ignored them.

During Jackson's Administration, the divisive potential of the
slavery question had appeared most clearly during the controversy
over tariffs and nullification. Here slavery merged with questions
of economic development that shaped the other central episodes
of Jackson's Presidency. As always, Jackson claimed to favor economic progress, but he insisted that promoting it by a policy of
unequal subsidies was unnecessary and unconstitutional. Americans must be especially wary against the temptation offered by
Henry Clay to justify a protective tariff by using the proceeds to
pay for internal improvements. The Maysville veto had been directed against the folly of using one constitutional violation to
justify another, and its lesson must not be forgotten.

Jackson saved his sharpest warning for the related problems of
money and banking. The experience of the Bank War had taught
him that this was a deeply serious problem that went to the heart
of the question of liberty's future. No longer a question of a single
Monster Bank, the problem in his mind had become "the money
power" and "the paper system." The ability of the B.U.S. to
mobilize state bankers, merchants, even artisans and shopkeepers
in the petition campaigns of 1833–34 had deeply impressed Jackson
even as he had breathed defiance against it. Now these former
protesters were committed members of the Whig Party and Van
Buren had barely succeeded in defeating them. The nation must
be fully warned of their menace.

With an air of saddened patience, Jackson reviewed once more the evils of paper money. Its value, unlike gold's, was based on public confidence and would therefore fluctuate. Unwitting farmers and laborers would usually be the victims of any downward movements. Even worse, the ebb and flow of credit undermined republican virtue by "engender[ing] a spirit of speculation injurious to the habits and character of the people." The easy availability of borrowed paper currency in good times would "foster this eager desire to amass wealth without labor; . . . and inevitably lead to corruption." Worst of all, said Jackson, "the paper-money system of this country may be used as an engine to undermine your free institutions." The Bank War and Biddle's contraction proved how liberty would be threatened by a concentrated money power, for had the Bank been successful, "the Government would have passed from the hands of the many to the hands of the few, and this organized money power from its secret conclave would have dictated the choice of your highest officers and compelled you to make peace or war, as best suited their wishes." All but the vestiges of republicanism would have vanished.

The Farewell Address went far beyond the Bank veto in its analysis of economic conditions and political consequences. Where the veto had been aimed at one outstanding case of corruption, the address envisaged a perpetual struggle of "the agricultural, the mechanical, and the laboring classes" against "the great moneyed corporations," and their network of supporters in distant places, their influence over the press, their large circle of clients and retainers. These Jackson referred to as a "crowd of dependents about them who hope to grow rich without labor by their countenance and favor, and who are therefore always ready to execute their wishes." In other words, corporations were creating a complex social formation to support them, which aspired to forms of political power unknown to traditional republicanism. Though Jackson was still no leveler, he had grasped a significant truth about his changing society, and his Farewell Address spoke the language of class conflict even more clearly than his Bank veto.

Jackson expressed confidence that the experience with the Bank of the United States would preclude the charter of another national bank. But now he worried about "the multitude of corporations with exclusive privileges which they have succeeded in obtaining in the different States." These interlocking institutions could obtain from the states what the federal government had denied to the Monster Bank, and the Republic would be just as badly off as before. What could save it?

An all-metallic currency would help, since it would strip the banks of their power to control the economy as a whole by manipulating the value of paper money. Even more important, equality and majority rule would also operate in favor of liberty. "Never for a moment believe that the great body of the citizens . . . can deliberately intend to do wrong," Jackson declared. But in the end, nothing could stave off corruption but watchfulness and virtue. "You must remember, my fellow citizens, that eternal vigilance by the people is the price of liberty." Unhappily, even this resource was vulnerable. Experience in the Presidency had shown Jackson that many Americans actually wanted the new society with its material benefits, even at the cost of deviations from what he regarded as the true republican faith. Ultimately, even the people were corruptible. "It is from within, among yourselves—from cupidity, from corruption, from disappointed ambition and inordinate thirst for power—that factions will be formed and liberty endangered."

At the pinnacle of republican success, it seemed, liberty was still in danger. Eight years under Andrew Jackson had not been enough to make it forever safe, for the spirit of corruption was unsleeping and the people themselves were the ultimate source of the threat. In his closing warning, Jackson suggested that even the people were fallible, that they must constantly be reminded of their duties and their destiny lest they forget their sacred trust. Jackson did not say who would offer the necessary reminders in his absence, but he clearly hoped that the memory of his parting words would help. Beyond that, his other writings clearly indicated his hope that the Democratic Party might succeed where the people themselves could fail, in keeping alive the spirit of the old Republic.

Andrew Jackson thus ended his Presidency as he had begun it, on a note of ambiguity. But while he had entered the White House with an unspecified plan of "reform," he left it with a clear designation of the paths to salvation and destruction. To save itself, America must preserve the Constitution and a flexible but unbreakable Union based on equal tolerance for freedom and slavery. Rather than respond to Jefferson's firebell in the night, the Republic must grapple with other enemies. As of old, liberty was in danger from power, and virtue was prey to corruption. But the locus of concentrated power was not King George, it was "the great moneyed corporations," and the other agents of commerce, industry, and the international market economy. These were the sources of corruption that could overcome the Republic. Jackson had not succeeded in destroying these "monsters," but he promised a victory if every American citizen were treated with absolute equality. Elsewhere, he had called equality of legal rights "the great radical principle of freedom," and he insisted on its importance in all his major state papers. Equality would mean that the enemies of republican society could not obtain the help they needed from government and would therefore be doomed to perish.

As expressed in the Farewell Address and other major documents, Jackson's economic vision is open to a number of cogent objections. Jackson himself was a rich man, and some Jacksonians in state politics were closely connected to banks, transportation companies, and the other "monsters" that party orators denounced. From this perspective, Democratic slogans pitting the poor against the rich have a hollow ring. Jackson's favored panaceas also seem completely inadequate to his professed goals; in hindsight, the destruction of the B.U.S. and the promotion of hard currency look like very feeble weapons against the gathered forces of revolution in transportation, commerce, and industry. Even the withdrawal of all "privileges," or government encouragement to economic development, seems insufficient to have staved off change for long. Even if we concede their sincerity, the Jacksonians' obsession with monsters, conspiracies, and cure-all solutions seems so unrealistic that we are tempted to dismiss them as hopelessly neurotic or simple-minded. Finally, we who live in a world the Jacksonians fought to prevent may find it hard to believe that the battle was really worthwhile. "You can't fight progress," we are inclined to say, and from our perspective, banks and internal improvements were indisputably progressive and much more compatible with true democracy than the slave plantation that Andrew Jackson owned and lived on.

These considerations have led some historians to dismiss Jacksonian rhetoric as "claptrap" and to look beyond Old Hickory's words for the true motives of his actions. One popular explanation has been that the Jacksonians were not opposed to economic development itself, but only to the special privileges that aided some businessmen more than others. The true Jacksonian, it has been argued, was a "man on the make" who was anxious to enrich himself by clearing away institutions such as the B.U.S. that sought to restrict the benefits of growth to those who were already well established and well connected. From this perspective, Jacksonian talk about preserving the society of the old Republic was no more than confused nostalgia at best and hypocritical cant at worst.

There is something to be said for this interpretation. Some professed Jacksonians were unquestionably hypocritical, and Jackson himself was a pragmatic politician as well as an ideologue. Like his support for a "judicious tariff," even his most strident pronouncements left room for a shade of ambiguity, holding open the possibility that he would tolerate economic developments that did not violate his political objectives. In practice, this might mean that he could do business with Democratic bankers, if not with Whigs. At the least, it is clear that Jackson's language was always carefully honed for political effect and was designed to affect immediate electoral results as well as long-term social trends.

A close examination of Jackson's program in its context ought to show, however, that the President and his key spokesmen meant what they said, even if they were misguided or eventually ineffectual. Their ideas and actions were logically derived from their eighteenth-century heritage, especially from the still-vivid ideology of the American Revolution and its aftermath, as well as from the experience of their own lives. Though Jacksonian slogans such as "That government is best which governs least" were later used to resist government restrictions on business, it is clear that they were not formulated for that purpose. Jackson wanted to keep government out of business in order to starve the "monster" in its cradle, not to liberate it from democratic controls.

Jackson was not opposed to "prosperity," but his plans for the Republic were based on a nostalgic vision of society in which no white man could permanently coerce or dominate another. In reality, this kind of society had never existed in America, but the Old Hero and his followers certainly believed that it had and did their best to defend it. When they pointed to corporations and the "paper system" as agents that undermined their notions of equality, they may have erred in details but they sensed an important truth. The growth of commerce and, later, of industrial capitalism did indeed produce an interdependent society with new and formidable structures of social hierarchy. It unquestionably did undermine the possibility for the kinds of personal independence that Jacksonians treasured. Their ability to use this perception to mobilize a massive and enduring political movement testifies to the power of the vision and the depth of its resonance with contemporary public experience.

America's corporate industrial economy was only in its infancy during Andrew Jackson's Presidency. Even by comparison to the "trusts" of the latter half of the nineteenth century, the "great moneyed corporations" that he fought were pathetically small. From a long historical perspective, it is clear that measures such as the vetoes of the Maysville Road and of the recharter of the Bank of the United States did little or nothing to slow their growth and proliferation. In his own day, however, Jackson's words and actions gave Americans who had reason to fear or resent the progress of the industrial and commercial economy a way to express their anger politically by voting for the President and his party. For Americans who thought otherwise, who thought that economic development was a form of moral and physical improvement essential to fulfilling the Republic's promise, Jackson's Presidency proved a lightning rod and a goad to organization. The two great political parties, Democrats and Whigs, who dominated American antebellum politics thus grew out of a contest over the relationship between the emerging capitalist economy and the traditions of republican liberty and equality.

National Parties
and Local Politics

AFTER ANDREW JACKSON stepped down from the Presidency, the state and national leaders who succeeded him could no longer rely on Old Hickory's commanding presence to give focus to the government or to balance the contending interests that sought to control it. Increasingly, they turned instead to political parties, the engines of support and opposition that grew up during Jackson's Presidency.

The development of party government was not a simple process. A significant antiparty sentiment had to be overcome, for early republican ideologues had frequently warned against the evils of political partisanship. Party leaders also had to learn a difficult political balancing act, weighing the needs of their parties for national structure and coordination against a concern for local autonomy and inspiration. The Whig and Democratic parties took shape in response to national events such as the Bank War and continued to address the largest political concerns of the federal government and the Presidency. A certain measure of centralization was necessary to make them work, but they drew strength from the loyalty of ordinary voters. They could attract such voter loyalty because party positions on national issues had a clear relevance to local events and to the problems of everyday life. Since local conditions varied everywhere, party-building also differed from place to place. It was a process that proceeded simultaneously—but at differing speeds and directions—at the national capital, in the states, and within local neighborhoods.

Before becoming President, even Andrew Jackson had discounted political partisanship. Though he always considered himself a strong Jeffersonian, he had called for reconciliation with selected Federalists in the years after 1815. Later experiences taught him differently. "No one can carry on this Govt. without support," he concluded after six years in office, "and the Head of it must rely for support on the party by whose suffrages he is elected." Convinced that the majority of the American voters shared his views and backed his measures, Jackson decided that successful opposition to him could arise only when those whom he once called "the predatory portion of the community" exploited trivial rivalries over personalities and local preferences to divide the majority and allow the election of candidates who were hostile to popular interests. The natural majority thus needed some institution by which it could find itself, learn its own mind, unite behind a single slate of candidates, and drive all "aristocratic" schemers to defeat. For Jackson that institution would be the Democratic-Republican Party that had been founded by Thomas Jefferson. "I have labored to reconstruct this great Party," he therefore wrote, "and to bring the popular power to bear with full influence upon the Government, by securing its permanent ascendancy."

Many other Americans were not as quick as Jackson and Van Buren to recognize the value of political parties. President Monroe had been acting in a well-established antiparty tradition when he tried to bring Federalists and Republicans together in the so-called Era of Good Feelings, and so had John Quincy Adams when he called upon Americans to uproot "the baneful weed of party strife." So far from regarding parties as the means of preserving liberty, traditional political thinkers had seen them as its enemies.

In 1828 the rival coalitions backing Adams and Jackson had worn the collective labels "National Republican" and "Democratic Republican," respectively, but in most localities the loosely knit alignments of that contest had scarcely comprised a party system. Most states gave a large majority to one candidate or another and voting turnout was small by later standards, suggesting that sectionalism and deference to traditional elites had as much to do with the outcome as party labels. Though the Jackson coalition was more willing to call itself a party than were the followers of President Adams, its members were still a motley and sprawling collection of diverse elements who agreed on little besides the personal attractions of Jackson himself.

Over the course of Jackson's two terms, the President's actions stripped his original supporters down to fighting strength and gave them a strong sense of group identity. The cumulative effect of the Maysville Road and Bank vetoes, the nullification struggle, and deposit removal was to alienate lukewarm supporters and to create among those who remained a rhetorical commitment in favor of legal equality for white men and against government aid to economic development. Perhaps most important, the emerging Democratic Party shared an emotional loyalty to Jackson and his legacy and a fervent desire, in the President's words, to give it "permanent ascendancy."

To give this body of like-minded supporters a practical structure, Jacksonians had embraced a number of techniques. A far-reaching network of state and county newspapers amplified the voice of the Washington *Globe* and transmitted news and party doctrine to followers at the local level. Patronage was distributed with an eye to rewarding loyalists and punishing dissidents who refused to support the party's principles or nominees. Perhaps most important, party conventions met regularly to choose candidates and to hammer out consistent platforms. Sometimes the delegates to county, district, and state conventions were elected by gatherings of party members lower down the hierarchy, and sometimes they were chosen less democratically, but in principle they were all pledged to support a convention's nominees, regardless of whether their own particular favorites won the party's approval. Jackson himself had endorsed party conventions as a means of enforcing unity and urged their extension into national politics. While once he had called for the abolition of the Electoral College and the direct election of the President, he came to put his faith in nominating conventions instead. "This is the only mode by which the people will be able long to retain in their own hands, the election of the President and Vice President," he insisted. A Democratic national convention accordingly gathered in 1831 to nominate Van Buren for Vice President and in 1835 to nominate him for President.

Van Buren's Whig opponents were slow to accept the need for

a national convention to establish party unity and discipline. Though the National Republicans had held a national convention in 1831, when Henry Clay was their unanimous choice, the infant Whig Party was not yet so unified as it approached the 1836 election. State and local gatherings brought three different Whig candidates into the field that year: General William Henry Harrison of Ohio in most of the North, Judge Hugh Lawson White of Tennessee in the South, and Senator Daniel Webster in his home state of Massachusetts. Though Webster was nationally famous, the other Whig candidates were local figures who claimed to offer the voters some improved aspect of Old Hickory himself, at least in relation to the supposed intriguer Van Buren. If the three Whig candidates had any national strategy at all in 1836, it was to throw the election once more to the House of Representatives, where factional intrigue might win victory for one of them as it had for John Quincy Adams. In fact, division only brought defeat in 1836, and the Whigs were later forced to adopt the party tools of the Democrats in order to hope for national victory.

For Whigs and Democrats alike, the creation of political parties was not limited to Washington and to the quadrennial task of choosing a President. The battles of party warfare were waged with votes, and votes were cast by ordinary Americans far from Washington who did not always approach the issues from the viewpoint of senators, congressmen, and Presidential appointees. Before the average voter could make clear sense of the finely printed charges and countercharges that crowded the narrow columns of his weekly country newspaper, he usually needed some means to relate the abstractions of far-off political debate to the texture of his own experience. Providing these connections was the task of the local corps of editors, office-seekers, and political activists who followed national events closely and developed their own firm loyalties to one party or another. Whether these local leaders believed sincerely in their party's platform or whether they were merely opportunists, they needed bonds between themselves and national leaders that could give them access to patronage and the prestige of a larger cause than personal ambition. They also needed to deliver votes. Bridging the gap between the local neighborhood and the distant affairs of the state and national capitals was a means to accomplish both objectives, and local activists applied themselves to it fiercely, each one struggling to show average voters that the sound and fury from distant places had immediate relevance to their own lives.

In some neighborhoods, the nationally significant issues of high finance had immediate resonance, as when some local corporation had aroused a controversy analogous to the Bank War. In other areas, activists had better luck with emotionally powerful collateral questions that were indirectly connected to the issues that dominated the national party platforms. In many parts of the North, for example, the dispute between Whigs and Democrats seemed to revolve around issues related to alcohol consumption, religion, and foreign immigration rather than banking or internal improvements. The prominence of these issues in local elections has persuaded some historians to discount the significance of economic controversy in the shaping of American antebellum politics, but this conclusion has probably been too hasty. The economic changes of the Jacksonian period affected different communities in different ways and the issues that provoked outrage in some places were meaningless in others. In the local areas that historians have studied carefully, arguments over so-called ethnocultural issues such as religion or alcohol turn out to be very closely related to the social and economic transformations that produced conflicts over banking and internal improvements in other places. With patience and a little digging, it becomes clear that most Jacksonian-era voters were wrestling with problems that stemmed from the same underlying sources, and that party identities and controversies were logical ways for political leaders and followers to address them.

To understand how the process of party formation worked, we must follow some local examples. No individual neighborhood was perfectly representative of its own state, much less the nation as a whole, so no example can illustrate all the ways that economic and cultural changes swept Jacksonian-era voters into the whirl of national politics. With this in mind, it is still very useful to study how local and national events could interact. We will look especially carefully at developments in the state of New York, not because New York was fully representative of all the others, but because events in the Empire State can illustrate with special clarity how national and local developments could interact. The story of party development in New York necessarily begins before the Jackson Presidency and extends beyond it, because the rhythm of state politics followed local circumstances as well as the pace of events in Washington.

The Mohawk River carves a fertile valley that leads from the Hudson River at Albany toward the Great Lakes to the west. Beyond it, the Genesee and a network of smaller rivers cut across a rich and extensive country well suited to agriculture and also blessed with falling water to power early industries. Long the target of ambitious projects of land speculation, western New York remained landlocked and underdeveloped until the Erie Canal pushed along its length to join the port of New York City with the waters of Lake Erie. Lying directly west of New England, the valleys and their surrounding hills were populated by pioneer emigrants from Massachusetts, Connecticut, and Vermont, who brought with them a still-powerful legacy of Puritan traditions, including an emphasis on the importance of conscience, piety, and personal and community improvement.

The Erie Canal was not complete until 1825, but as soon as its eastern portions were opened, these settlers responded quickly to their increased commercial opportunities. Farmers and their families gave up production of homespun cloth and brought in large crops of wheat for sale in urban markets. Water power stimulated a rapid move to industry in the towns along the canal: textiles in Utica, salt in Syracuse, shoes and flour milling in Rochester. Development brought more inhabitants, with villages turning into cities almost overnight. The five western counties along the canal grew 153 percent in the 1820s. In all probability, the economic effects of internal improvements and the Market Revolution were more dramatic in western New York than in any other region of rural America.

Under the pressure of market competition, the bonds between masters, journeymen, and apprentices tended to fragment in the towns along the Erie Canal as fast as or faster than elsewhere. Seeking to cut costs, manufacturers invested in laborsaving machinery or broke up complex manual processes into simple steps and relied on domestic outworkers to perform them. Either way, production tended to move out of the master's home and the workers tended to move with it, finding their own tenements in neighborhoods populated mostly by other wage earners. There they faced the possibility of remaining wage earners indefinitely, since their old skills were becoming irrelevant and they lacked the capital to succeed in business competition with their employers. Successful business owners, on the other hand, together with professionals and management-level employees, gained privacy in households composed exclusively of husbands, wives, and children, and lived beside neighbors who were increasingly likely to share the same income level and outlook on life.

The cultural consequences of economic change were likewise dramatic in this region. Though religious revivals were common throughout the North in this period, the social and cultural strains along the Erie Canal were particularly intense and fueled a uniquely fervent local tradition of evangelicalism. The fires of revivalism swept the area so frequently and so thoroughly that western New York became known as the "Burnt-Over District" and grew famous as a forge for perfectionist enthusiasms of all kinds, from abolitionism and feminism to spiritualism and Mormonism.

Revivalism in the Burnt-Over District was clearly related to the New England traditions of its inhabitants, but it also grew out of the social and economic transformations that early industrialization had brought to their lives. As studies by Mary P. Ryan and Paul E. Johnson have demonstrated, evangelical conversion did not occur randomly but according to a clear social logic. As home and work became physically separate, for example, middle- and upper-class households became the special sphere of mothers and children. Women in these circumstances found that evangelical values granted them greater independence and moral authority over their families and their personal lives, and they were accordingly the earliest converts to the evangelical movement. Among men, employers and entrepreneurs were anxious to reconcile their aggressive economic activities with the demands of conscience. They also longed to reassert a lost moral authority over their communities. Revivalists told these men that business achievement of the right kind was not an expression of mere greed. Instead, it could make a lasting contribution to the Kingdom of God if the businessman reformed his personal life and used his position to inspire others to reform theirs. Inspired in part by their wives, leading businessmen were accordingly prominent in the second wave of evangelical converts.

These businessmen faced a fundamental problem of social control. They had physically expelled their workers from their own households and had thus lost an important means of influencing their behavior. Still, they longed to exercise community moral leadership and particularly to prevent drunkenness and other misconduct that might encourage social disruption, crime, or inefficiency on the job. Coming to view rowdy or unproductive behavior as "sinful," converted employers reformed their own lives by cutting out alcohol, gambling, and frivolous amusements such as dancing and theatergoing. They also stopped the popular and long-established practice of treating employees and customers with strong drink. Off the job, they sought to control their workers' lives by seeking laws to restrict the consumption of alcohol and enforcing the quiet observance of the Sabbath in the working-class slums where their "hands" had come to live. They likewise rewarded churchgoing employees with steady work and the chance of promotion, so clerks, foremen, and young men on the way up were conspicuous in the third wave of evangelical converts.

For their part, workers still cherished the promises of liberty and equality extended by the American Revolution, though the new manufacturing economy made material equality with their employers practically impossible. They thus resisted any effort to make them give up their remaining rights to control their personal lives. In practice, this meant workers' rights to frequent the bars, theaters, circuses, and gambling halls that (according to one's point of view) either enlivened or debauched the low-rent districts of the new towns and cities. Even artisans who deplored the effects of alcoholism on families and individuals bridled at upper-class efforts to impose reform on their subordinates. In New York, moreover, male workers could vote, ever since rivalry between Bucktails and Clintonians had led both camps to go hunting for grateful followers by extending the suffrage to non–property holders. When canal-town wage earners were armed with the ballot, the teetotaling forces of order and sobriety could never get full cooperation from local politicians, and the bars stayed open. Nevertheless, conflicts over the legal regulation of drinking and public conduct on Sundays were central political issues in canal towns such as Rochester. In broad terms, in towns along the Erie Canal and elsewhere, the challenge that faced the Jacksonian middle and upper classes was to find some way of maintaining power and authority in the face of a restive and voting working class.

As important as revivalism and temperance would be to the development of politics in the Burnt-Over District, the earliest political shocks in the region came from a different but related quarter. One of the earliest and least-understood reform movements to emerge from this region was a remarkable campaign against the institution of Freemasonry. Superficially a nonreligious movement, Anti-Masonry shared many characteristics of the evangelical crusade against sin. Historian Kathleen Smith Kutolowski has found that its supporters were more likely to be evangelical converts than its opponents. The movement had a profound effect on the development of local and national politics in the Jacksonian era. In combination with revivalism itself, Anti-Masonry had a special importance in pulling together a mass-based political opposition to the Democratic Party. Though well endowed with bizarre aspects, the Anti-Masonic Party deserves a close examination.

The Masonic order was a private all-male association whose members swore to help one another and to uphold rational and secular moral values. Mysterious rituals and passwords, secret signs and handshakes, and solemn oaths to maintain the order's secrets supplemented Masonry's practical appeals and gave otherwise austere gentlemen a delicious sense of esoteric brotherhood and ersatz aristocracy. Originating in eighteenth-century England, modern Freemasonry spread rapidly through the early American Republic, and especially attracted the allegiance of ambitious politicians, businessmen, and professionals who appreciated the opportunity it presented for masculine conviviality and profitable personal contacts. George Washington, the Marquis de Lafayette, Henry Clay, and Andrew Jackson were all Masons, and as many as twenty thousand members, organized into some 450 lodges, followed their example in the towns and villages of New York by the middle of the 1820s. Though a certain resentment of the order was occasionally evident, no cornerstone-laying or important public celebration seemed complete without the presence of leading Masons performing arcane rituals in fanciful regalia.

This seemingly harmless fraternity showed an ugly aspect in May of 1826, when an itinerant stonemason named William Morgan threatened to publish a book revealing the order's secrets. An obscure drifter, Morgan had come to western New York to work on the Erie Canal and had briefly been affiliated with the Masons in Batavia while he worked there. Quarreling with his Masonic brethren, Morgan sought profit and revenge by writing a book to expose their secrets, but enraged Masons struck back by jailing him on a fraudulent charge of debt after failing to destroy his publisher's printing press. Winning release from prison, Morgan was immediately kidnapped and whisked away in a closed carriage despite his struggles and shouts of "Murder!" Subsequent investigation traced Morgan and his abductors as far as Fort Niagara, more than a hundred miles away, but no one ever saw the unfortunate stonemason again. In all likelihood, William Morgan was drowned by night in the Niagara River, "executed" by Masons for violating his solemn oaths of secrecy.

Morgan's disappearance alarmed his neighbors, but their worries turned to outrage when the authorities dragged their feet in the aftermath of his abduction. Masonic officials ridiculed the idea that crimes had been committed and suggested that Morgan had arranged his own disappearance as a publicity stunt. Grand juries assembled slowly, sheriffs procrastinated, prosecutors failed to question witnesses, judges allowed potential defendants to remain at large. Finally, some accused participants in the kidnapping were allowed to plead guilty to minor offenses and to evade serious punishment. Masons appeared to be the key actors in this striking display of judicial laxity. Moreover, when indignant citizens demanded a full investigation by the state, the Bucktail-dominated legislature trivialized their demands and refused to act. Organized and led by the Masonic fraternity itself, a vast conspiracy to obstruct justice had apparently protected the murderers of William Morgan.

Perhaps under ordinary circumstances the disappearance of a single friendless artisan, no matter how outrageous, would not have generated widespread furor. As subsequent events would demonstrate, however, economic and cultural tensions made western New Yorkers unusually sensitive in 1826. According to the resolutions of a growing number of protest meetings in the area, Masonry was unrepublican because its members considered themselves above the law. It was aristocratic because it was an exclusive fraternity whose members apparently swore to give one another preference in business, politics, and every other sphere of life. It was sacrilegious because Masons seemed to give lip service to Christianity while violating its substance. It was hostile to family values because it drew men away from their wives and children to all-male gatherings where alcohol flowed freely. In the emerging cultural environment of the Burnt-Over District, these violations of evangelical values seemed particularly offensive.

Perhaps most important, the competitive atmosphere of the new commercial economy made thousands uneasy that Masons were using secret and underhanded methods to help each other at everyone else's expense, thus gaining by stealthy collaboration the success others sought by strenuous personal efforts. Masonic boasting fed such fears; a widely reprinted speech by a Connecticut Mason in 1826 had asked "What is Masonry now?" and answered, thoughtlessly:

> IT IS POWERFUL. It comprises men of RANK, wealth, office and talent, in power and out of power . . . and it comprises . . . in large numbers, active men, united together . . . , so as to have the FORCE OF CONCERT, *throughout the civilized world!* They are distributed too, with the means of knowing one another, and the means of keeping secret, and the means of co-operating, in the DESK—in the LEGISLATIVE HALL—on the BENCH—in every GATHERING OF BUSINESS— in every PARTY OF PLEASURE—in every ENTERPRISE OF GOVERNMENT—in every DOMESTIC CIRCLE—in PEACE and in WAR— among ENEMIES and FRIENDS—in ONE PLACE as well as in another!

In the wake of Morgan's disappearance and the successful cover-up of his probable murder, such statements made the Masonic fraternity look more like a criminal conspiracy than a harmless voluntary association. As protests mounted and Masonic "stonewalling" persisted, Anti-Masonic gatherings in Batavia, Rochester, and neighboring communities began to announce that they would support no one for public office who would not fully renounce the institution of Freemasonry.

Some of these meetings were composed of women, who used the Masons' perceived defiance of evangelical domestic values as the occasion to make a rare public entry into politics. Two decades later, Elizabeth Cady Stanton, Lucretia Mott, and other evangelical women from the Burnt-Over District would assemble at Seneca Falls, New York, for the world's first women's rights convention. There they would make a revolutionary demand for the right to vote. Direct connections between Anti-Masonry and the emergence of modern feminism have yet to appear, but it is significant that a changing domestic environment and the religious initiative of Genesee Valley women led them to assert a public political role even as early as 1826.

The "blessed spirit" of Anti-Masonry grew so intense in the spring and summer of 1827 that ambitious organizers began to see its potential as the genesis of a political movement to rival the Albany Regency. The canal towns had always tended to favor Clintonians over Bucktails, since the canal was Clinton's brainchild. The Bucktails had scoffed at Anti-Masonic appeals, moreover, and they, too, constituted a kind of exclusive fraternity organized for mutual benefit. Led by Rochester editor Thurlow Weed, Monroe County Anti-Masons fielded a successful slate of legislative candidates in 1827 and called for the total destruction of the Masonic Order. In the campaigns that followed, Anti-Masons effectively combined the techniques of the religious revival with electioneering methods previously associated with Democratic Republicans: rallies, processions, partisan symbols, and fervent emotional appeals to rouse apathetic citizens to their danger. By combining populistic methods with an evangelical agenda, they were successful in driving established Masonic politicians from office and totally changing the tone of local politics. The new activists and officeholders were no longer the patriarchs of long-established upper-class families, but ambitious professionals who owed their positions to a democratic mass movement rather than to elitist connections and social clout. As such, they represented the future rather than the past.

As the election of 1828 approached, Anti-Masonic leader Thurlow Weed also moved to join forces with the campaign of President John Quincy Adams. It was a logical step, for Andrew Jackson was an unrepentant Mason, while Adams had never joined the order and even volunteered to reveal the mysteries of Phi Beta Kappa as his own contribution to the war against secret societies. More significantly, the President shared the same Yankee faith in self-improvement and internal improvements as the leading citizens along the canal. To Weed's chagrin, however, New York's leading National Republicans could not stomach the populistic fervor of the Anti-Masonic crusade and rejected his overtures. As a result, Martin Van Buren's Regency successfully delivered the Empire State to Andrew Jackson in 1828.

Unfazed by Adams's defeat, Anti-Masons extended their campaign to other states and launched an effort to organize a national
Anti-Masonic political party. Their movement quickly spread in
areas where Yankee inhabitants and evangelical values were prominent: Massachusetts, Pennsylvania, Vermont, Connecticut, Ohio,
the Michigan Territory, and elsewhere. In gubernatorial elections,
Anti-Masonic candidates quickly won 45 percent of the vote in
Pennsylvania, 48 percent in New York, and 35 percent in Vermont.
A national party convention was summoned for 1830. When it
assembled in Baltimore, the party nominated William Wirt of
Maryland for President and afterward campaigned for him in ten
states in the 1832 election. Wirt was the attorney for the Cherokee
Indians in their legal battle against deportation, and he symbolized
the Anti-Masons' identification with evangelical causes, though he
shared little of his supporters' animus against Freemasonry itself.
In the three-cornered contest between Jackson, Clay, and Wirt in
1832, the Anti-Masons seemed to attract anti-Jackson voters who
were repelled by Clay's licentious reputation, but their candidate
did not carry any state but Vermont.

Despite these initial successes, the Anti-Masons could not sustain themselves as a political movement. Wherever Anti-Masonry
flourished, Masons renounced their order in droves and left the
party with no further reason for existence. In western New York,
the crusade against Masonry divided the local elite, splitting
churches and families as well as town governments, while leaving
long-standing local controversies unresolved. According to Paul
E. Johnson's careful study of Rochester, New York, for example,
the Anti-Masonic town government was filled with new faces, but
still could not settle disputes between pious employers and roist-
ering workingmen armed with the vote. The Anti-Masonic explosion had cracked established political patterns, mobilized
previously apathetic voters, and generated partisan organizing, but
it left citizens unsatisfied who looked for a stable governing mechanism in local society and a permanent vehicle for evangelical
values in national politics.

These citizens finally found what they sought when the Whig
Party took shape in 1834. In all likelihood, the national confrontation between Andrew Jackson and the Bank of the United States
would have brought them together in any case, but Johnson has

shown how evangelical religion provided the cement that made Whiggery especially powerful in the Burnt-Over District. In 1831 a particularly effective revival campaign by evangelist Charles Grandison Finney doubled Rochester church membership in six months and healed old wounds among the town's established leaders. In the afterglow, Anti-Masons, ex-Masons, and ex-Bucktails found the charity to bury their differences. In the spring of 1834 representatives of these previously hostile political factions met to form the local branch of the Whig Party, pledging their mutual support for a fight against demon rum in Rochester, machine politics in Albany, and Jacksonian Democracy in Washington. This time, moreover, they were successful. Finney had converted large numbers of middle-level employees, who now joined the party of their employers and gave the forces of temperance and order an effective political majority at last. In the next election they captured the town and wrung it almost dry, at least temporarily. After years of stalemate, the revival and the Whig Party had taught local employers how to pursue their political objectives with democratic methods.

As it did elsewhere, the Bank War became the specific occasion for the formation of Whiggery in Rochester. The attractions of the party for the town's elite were obvious, for the pious and orderly businessmen of Rochester naturally sympathized with the policy of federally sponsored, systematic economic development. On the other side, Jackson attacked the Bank to defend personal liberty and an older pattern of economic relations. Workingmen who felt constrained by reforming busybodies and the long arm of the boss naturally rallied to his support.

At the same time, party choice was not a simple matter of economic reflex, for most voters were neither very rich nor very poor and did not divide themselves between the parties along strict lines of economic interest. Though most businessmen became Whigs and most laborers remained Democrats, there were some rich Democrats in western New York as well as many poor Whigs. Instead, the factor that most closely distinguished one party from another in Rochester and many other Northern towns was religion: the Whigs were the party of evangelical church members, while a greater proportion of Democrats belonged to nonevangelical sects or to no church at all. As the history of revivalism makes clear, however, church affiliation was itself a reflection of class standing and aspiration, so that cultural and economic concerns were closely intertwined in the creation of party loyalties.

The Whig Party in western New York was the child of Anti-Masonry as well as revivalism and class conflict, for it was the "blessed spirit" that had broken up older factional alignments and accustomed the Regency's foes to the popular methods that electoral success demanded. As a personal representative of the transition, Anti-Masonic organizer Thurlow Weed also stood at the head of the Whigs and went on to become one of the party's leading backroom powers nationally. The same pattern prevailed in other states as well, with most Anti-Masonic regions moving smoothly into the Whig column as the 1830s progressed.

Religious conviction and Anti-Masonic enthusiasm were not local substitutes for the national debate about economic development but lenses through which ordinary voters could perceive the issues of disputes such as the Bank War and consider their relevance to their own lives. Both locally as well as nationally, the Democrats saw themselves as the party of liberty, while Whigs claimed to be the party of improvement. Whether the subject was a bank, a road, or a school for the deaf, Whigs usually lined up in favor of a systematic program for social uplift, while Democrats worried that such projects might limit personal freedom or serve paternalistic purposes. Middle-class New Yorkers who embraced a faith in social and spiritual perfection found it just as logical to attack local saloons as to defend the Bank of the United States. By the same token, workingmen who resisted the bosses' efforts to tell them how to live and who saw a friendly drink with companions as an excellent way to slough off the regimentation of the mill could readily identify with a campaign to protect the Republic's liberty from banks and "rag money." The evangelical drive to dry up Rochester gave both sides an opportunity to see local and national issues with clarity before casting their votes. For each party, the association between national politics and local experience was so strong that one working-class woman in 1836 found it natural to answer a question about her husband's politics by replying, "Why he has always been Jackson and I don't think he has joined the Cold Water [i.e., the temperance movement]." Throughout the Burnt-Over District, evangelical majorities accepted the same logic, making the region one of Whiggery's most powerful national strongholds.

Far downstate from Rochester, the world of New York City presented a far different aspect from the revival-rocked countryside of the Burnt-Over District. The rapidly growing population of New York, already the nation's largest city, had passed 200,000 by 1830 and would quadruple in the next three decades. Trade was the first basis of the city's growth, for New York's excellent harbor had always made it ideal for importers and exporters, while the opening of the Erie Canal in 1825 had given it unsurpassed advantages over rivals such as Philadelphia, Boston, and Baltimore. The demands of commerce had also made New York a center for banking and insurance, with the leaders of Wall Street eager to displace Philadelphia as the capital of American finance. Finally, New York was a manufacturing city that produced ships, shoes, sugar, clothing, furniture, books, hardware, and a nearly infinite variety of other finished products. Mechanization and other changes in production methods had proceeded unevenly in these trades, so that some kinds of goods were being produced under factory conditions, while others were assembled by domestic outworkers in garret tenements, and still others were fashioned individually by the hands of skilled mechanics. New York was thus an immensely varied city, with a highly complex economy and a richly diverse population.

The city's merchants and bankers dominated commerce and finance and traditionally led city government as an act of *noblesse oblige*. Some of these men, like the fur magnate and real estate investor John Jacob Astor, had become fabulously wealthy as New York's commerce had expanded. At a less-elevated position, professionals, senior clerks, shopkeepers, and successful master craftsmen maintained respectable standards of living and constituted the city's middle classes. Other New Yorkers were wretchedly poor, dependent on relief from the city's almshouses and charitable societies in order to survive.

Perhaps the most rapidly changing group in New York was the men and women who worked in manufacturing. The same changes that transformed the work process in upstate Rochester had special force in Manhattan, as dozens of industries that had once relied on skilled artisans gave way to the "bastardization of craft," as

historian Sean Wilentz has called it, and the deteriorating relationship between journeymen and masters. Though small shops
remained common and factory-scale production was rare, traditional skills were losing their importance in the drive to produce
cheaply for mass markets. Successful masters prospered by these
developments and found themselves rising to the status of respected businessmen and manufacturers, though they sometimes
continued to call themselves by the ambiguous title of "mechanic."
Journeymen and small masters were less well served by change,
for the declining value of skill made it hard for men without capital
to rise in the hierarchy of the trade. Marginal craftsmen thus found
themselves toiling desperately just to stay in place. In response,
some journeymen formed labor unions to bargain with masters for
higher wages. Others formed an audience for radical protests
against the competitive economy and the accumulation of wealth
in private hands. Throughout the 1820s inflation and periodic reces-
sions increased the pressure on New York's artisanal community,
paving the way for a dramatic political movement on their behalf.

The artisans had a long history of active participation in city
politics. Defending a republican vision that stressed the centrality
of labor in the creation of the common good and the need for
mutual respect for the needs of all interests in society, masters and
journeymen joined together in craft associations to assert their
common role in public life. Organized as the Sons of Liberty,
artisans had led in the fight for American independence and, a
decade and a half later, in the campaign to ratify the U.S. Constitution. Angered by the elitism of New York's Federalist merchants, artisans later rallied to the cause of Thomas Jefferson and
made the city a Republican stronghold in the heyday of the first
party system. To do so, many took an active role in a fledgling
political organization, the Society of St. Tammany, where they
joined with politically committed or ambitious young men from
commerce or the professions to make New York City firmly Jeffersonian in the years preceding the War of 1812. Sometimes allied
with upstate Bucktails and sometimes rivaling them, Tammany's
leaders kept strong ties with the artisan community and paid careful
respect to the traditions of mutuality and republicanism that artisans defended.

Over the course of the 1820s, the increasing wealth of some
masters and the sense of exploitation among many journeymen

made repeated pledges of mutual interests within the trades seem hollow. In particular, the report that master craftsmen were about to increase the length of the working day from ten hours to eleven (with no increase in pay) aroused widespread anger and led to a protest meeting of five to six thousand workers in April 1829. Assembling in the artisan neighborhood of the Bowery, the workingmen resolved that "the Creator has made all equal" and that the promise of equality must be applied to economic life to be realistic. No one should be forced to become a wage earner "without receiving a guaranty that reasonable toil shall enable him to live as comfortably as others" and no one had the right to impose excessive hours of work on others. Though masters quickly disavowed any intention of increasing the workday, a Committee of Fifty kept meeting throughout the summer to devise further measures to protect struggling workers, while radical orators stirred Bowery audiences with calls for drastic social change. Scotswoman Frances Wright shocked middle-class observers with her denunciations of marriage, organized religion, and the privileges of wealth, while her companion Robert Dale Owen publicized demands for equal educational opportunity. Going much further, machinist, inventor, and self-taught intellectual Thomas Skidmore called for the equal division of all property as the only means of obliterating class distinctions. As changing social relationships closed off older opportunities, New York workingmen found themselves increasingly receptive to radical proposals for defending the promises of artisan republicanism.

In October the Committee of Fifty reconvened and presented its platform to a public meeting of five thousand workingmen. The document consisted of a radical preamble, probably written by Skidmore, which called for an eventual division of property to ensure genuine equality, and a more conventional set of interim demands for the abolition of private banking, chartered monopolies, imprisonment for debt, and other buttresses of privilege. Proclaiming that "past experience teaches that we have nothing to hope from the aristocratic orders of society and that our only course to pursue is, to send men of our own description, if we can, to the Legislature at Albany," the participants reassembled five days later to nominate a slate of Working Men's candidates for the upcoming elections. The nominations distressed Tammany, which normally counted on solid support from working-class wards, and also the city's business press, which denounced the leveling tendencies of universal suffrage. In the end, most of the Tammany candidates won as usual, but the Working Men elected one of their number to the state senate and won about a third of the total votes in the city. It was an impressive victory for a fledgling political movement.

Like the Anti-Masons, the Working Men failed to sustain them-selves as a permanent political force, though they brought lasting consequences to the emerging system of party politics. Ideological divisions within the group led to the expulsion of Skidmore and his radical followers, while a group of pro-tariff master mechanics quarreled with the supporters of Frances Wright and Robert Dale Owen over control of the organization's remnants. Disillusioned journeymen lost interest in the factional squabbling and the move-ment's energies dissipated, but New York's militant artisans did not give up their struggle for what they regarded as genuine re-publican equality.

Shifting from politics to organizing in the workplace, nine urban labor unions came together in 1833 to form the General Trades Union of the City of New York. Under its aegis, more than fifty unions and forty strikes were launched to protest wages and work-ing conditions in the years of skyrocketing inflation that marked the Jackson Presidency. By the time the trades union movement peaked in 1836, perhaps as many as one half to two thirds of the workers in the city were organized, a higher proportion than at any time in the nineteenth century.

The rapid development of New York's labor movement was hardly unique. Philadelphia mechanics had formed their own city-wide Mechanics Union of Trade Associations in 1827 and their own Working Men's Party in 1828, followed by the General Trades Union of the City and County of Philadelphia in 1834. At its height, the Philadelphia GTU embraced over fifty individual unions with a membership of ten thousand workers. Similar movements spread up and down the East Coast in the boom years of the 1830s, when journeymen everywhere felt squeezed by inflation and hardening class distinctions. The Working Men's Party of Boston took shape in 1830, while the more long-lived New England Association of Farmers, Mechanics, and Other Working Men first assembled in Providence in 1831 and pledged to defend the ten-hour day. Similar groups appeared in Newark and Trenton in New Jersey and in

Troy, Rochester, Buffalo, and about a dozen smaller towns in New York, as well as in scattered places in Ohio, Delaware, Connecticut, Massachusetts, New Hampshire, Maine, and Vermont.

Historians have disputed whether all of the members of these organizations were truly entitled to the name of "workingmen" or whether their movement can truly be regarded as an expression of wage earners' concerns. Some of the leaders or nominees of "Working Men's" political parties were no doubt sympathetic or opportunistic politicians, intellectuals, or professionals and not manual laborers themselves. Many were also straitened small masters who felt the sting of economic hardship and made common cause with journeymen even though they were also owners of capital and small-scale employers of labor. Given the rapidly changing nature of manufacturing in this era, and particularly the probability that a marginal master might quickly find himself back in the ranks of journeymen, it is probably best not to insist on an overly rigorous definition of "workingman" before passing judgment on the validity of these movements. The widespread character of their activities and the intensity of their calls for change adequately testify to the depth of feelings roused by the changing prospects for equality in Jacksonian cities, and to the genuine popular assumption that republican government was a legitimate avenue of defense.

In New York and elsewhere, the Jacksonian union movement fell victim to hard times. In February 1837 hungry men and women in Manhattan forsook the discipline of the strike and the picket line for the direct action of a flour riot. A month later, the Panic of 1837 hit the city and as many as one third of the city's wage earners quickly lost their jobs. Always difficult to sustain, workers' organizations fell apart in the ensuing depression, as former union members agreed to any terms to find or keep work. In the aftermath of the panic, moreover, professional politicians in each party sharpened their ideological programs and perfected their organizational apparatus until it became well-nigh impossible for a third-party effort by laborers or anyone else to gain a foothold. The two-party system was building its own monopoly of public discourse.

Despite its early failure, the union movement and the Working Men's Party had important implications for mainstream politics in New York. Like other state parties, New York Democrats were deeply split by the Bank War. Some leading members of the Albany Regency had a long and happy relationship with friendly banks and accepted the destruction of the B.U.S. as an opportunity for these state banks to escape from centralized control. More radical Democrats saw the fall of the Monster as the first step in a campaign against all banks and chartered monopolies. Spokesmen for the latter faction were quick to see parallels between workers' battles against "aristocratic" employers and the President's battle against "aristocratic" banks. Contesting conservative control of the party, these leaders did not hesitate to appeal to the bitter class resentments that the union and Working Men's movement had also tapped. "Power and wealth are continually stealing from the many to the few," warned the fiery Democratic editor William Leggett, likening the Bank War to the municipal struggles of New York's frustrated workingmen. "[Those who seek exclusive privileges] are emphatically the aristocracy; and . . . constitute the party which are now struggling against the democracy for the perpetuation of an odious and dangerous moneyed institution."

Supporters of the rival pro- and anti-Bank Democratic factions nearly came to blows at a famous meeting at Tammany Hall in October 1835. Pro-Bank Democrats controlled the podium and used this position to ram through their own slate of nominees for the next elections. Anti-Bank forces roared protests at the patently undemocratic proceeding, but opponents hastily adjourned the session and attempted to stifle further action by turning off the gaslights, plunging the hall into tumultuous darkness. Warned in advance of this time-honored trick at Tammany, dissidents had come prepared with pocketsful of the new, strike-anywhere "loco-foco" matches, with which they quickly lit candles, proceeding with the nomination of a rival, anti-Bank slate of candidates. Henceforth known as the Loco-Foco or Equal Rights Party, New York's hard-money Democrats used the ensuing elections to campaign against all forms of government monopoly and to attract working-class voters to this version of Democratic Party orthodoxy. Wary of political entanglements, the General Trades Union kept its distance from the Loco-Focos, but individual activists were closely involved in both movements.

As the two-party system took shape, Whigs sought to win the votes of wage earners by arguing that the interests of labor and capital were identical and that both needed tariff protection and a stable credit system to create the conditions in which both could prosper. These arguments were successful in some cases, and some of the more prosperous leaders of the early Working Men's movement later showed up on Whig tickets and platforms. Democrats fought back with themes plucked from Jacksonian rhetoric and the slogans of the Working Men's movement. According to popular party spokesmen, there was an endless war between capital and labor, the few and the many. Government aid to business was invariably designed to benefit the former at the expense of the latter; true equality demanded equal protection for all citizens and nothing more.

In the aftermath of Jackson's Presidency, when Vice President Martin Van Buren had succeeded to Old Hickory's mantle, New York and the rest of the United States were struck by economic reverses that reinforced the anti-monopoly appeal of the Loco-Foco Party. Though his own impulses were far from radical, President Van Buren felt compelled to embrace an anti-bank stance for the sake of party unity, thus lending legitimacy to the hard-money forces in his home state and opening the way for a re-unification of the New York Democracy. As they returned to Tammany in triumph, calling themselves "the fathers of the Church and even Mr. V.B. . . . only one of their recent converts," the Loco-Focos sought to keep their constituency and continued to make room in the party for egalitarian rhetoric and aspiring politicians from working-class backgrounds. Ely Moore, for example, labor's first representative in the U.S. Congress, had been president of the New York General Trades Union before he turned to Democratic Party politics. Later on, hard-drinking Democratic editor Michael Walsh served as a link between Bowery street gangs and fire companies and the more straitlaced disciples of the Democratic Party. Lambasting capital as "that all-grasping power which has been wrung, by fraud, avarice, and malice from the labor of this and all ages past," Walsh called himself the representative of "the honest hard-working young men who are dependent solely on the labor of their own hands for a subsistence." Unlike Thomas Skidmore and the earlier radicals, Walsh and his fellow Democrats of the 1840s and '50s had no idea of dismantling the structure of private property or the emerging relationship between capital and labor, but they drew on "Workie" themes and rhetoric to cement the loyalty of the Working Men's constituency to the Democratic

Party. To a large extent they succeeded, and New York City remained a Democratic citadel for most of the antebellum period.

On the whole, the ties between Democrats and labor grew
stronger in the 1840s, when the ethnic composition of the American
work force began to change dramatically. During that decade,
famine sent the first of many waves of penniless Irish immigrants
to seek refuge in America. The newcomers supported themselves
by the most grueling kinds of manual labor: digging canals, building
railroads, pushing bales and barrows on the docks. They also found
work in the early factories, where native American workers sometimes blamed the Irish for declining wage rates or deteriorating
working conditions. Overwhelmingly Roman Catholic in a pre-
dominantly Protestant culture, the Irish were also untouched by
the temperance movement, bitterly anti-English, and unwilling to
become the passive objects of evangelical reform. When they became eligible to vote, all these qualities inclined Irish immigrants
toward the Democrats, as the party that had already established
itself as friendly to labor, to individual liberty, and to cultural
diversity. As members of the party of middle-class respectability,
on the other hand, most Whigs tended to admire English Victorian
culture and to embrace the ideal of converting the world to Protestantism and the standards of evangelical propriety. Though some
Whigs, such as New York Governor William Seward, made
friendly overtures to the Irish, Whigs in general were less tolerant
than Democrats of the values and interests of the newcomers.

From time to time, Protestant resentment of Catholic immigration grew so fierce that hostility turned into violence. In 1834
Protestant rioters attacked and burned an Ursuline convent in
Charlestown, Massachusetts. Ten years later, rivalry between Irish
and native-born weavers led to four days of bloody rioting in the
manufacturing districts of Philadelphia. Native-born Americans
also launched several brief, third-party movements aimed at denying full political rights to foreign-born citizens or residents.
When these movements faltered, their supporters generally returned to the Whig Party coalition. When Whig politicians succeeded in winning the support of working-class voters, they
frequently did so by appealing to the native-born in open or subtle
opposition to Irish or German Catholics, invoking the values of
evangelicalism, temperance, or ethnic superiority in the process.

Ethnic rivalries thus made a significant contribution to the creation of political loyalties in the second party system.

Generally speaking, however, ethnocultural conflict was neither a prime mover of Jacksonian politics nor a unique political force that displaced class or workplace tensions as instigators of political change. Like Anti-Masons, who blamed their business difficulties on the machinations of a secret society, nativist workingmen who attacked the Irish or the Pope were using a convenient set of excuses to account for a pervasive national problem as it touched their own lives. Eagerly assisted by imaginative Whig organizers, both Anti-Masons and nativists came to see Democrats (rather than Masons or bosses or the market itself) as the source of all their troubles. In each case, religious commitments and upward aspirations made the Whig interpretation more attractive than its rivals, but religion and ethnicity had not substituted new motives for the voters' political activities. Indeed, ethnocultural tension only tended to reinforce the previously established patterns of Jacksonian politics. The original polarity between Democrats and Whigs, between the party of liberty and the party of improvement, which was hammered out first in the Bank War itself, only grew in the fires of ethnic and cultural conflict.

Events in other Northern states showed direct parallels with conditions in New York. Workingmen's parties and movements flared in many Eastern cities during the mid-1830s, and most of them yielded their followers to the Democratic Party. Anti-Masons were likewise active throughout New England and the western path of Yankee migration, and Anti-Masonic voters became eager Whigs in most constituencies. Districts that embraced the evangelical message of piety, sobriety, and hard work were likewise receptive to the gospel according to the Whig Party. In laboring communities, where wage-earning careers overlapped with Roman Catholic faith and the free use of alcohol, Democratic organizers had correspondingly greater success. In most cases, distinct community experiences in the Market Revolution underlay the unity of each party coalition and distinguished it from its opposition.

Southern party organizers also relied on local developments to convey the practical meaning of more distant political dramas. In North Carolina and Virginia, for example, local suspicion of Martin Van Buren encouraged some slaveholders to oppose the Magician as a Vice Presidential candidate in 1832 while remaining faithful to the Hero at the top of the ticket. Over the course of Jackson's second Administration, Whig activists used common concern over "executive usurpation" to link the planters who worried about government interference with slavery to those who fretted about government power over banking and currency. By 1836 many of the once-loyal Jacksonians of the Upper South who had questioned Van Buren's commitment to slavery were allied as Whigs with their former opponents of the National Republican Party.

Elsewhere in the South, sympathy for nullification drove many formerly Jacksonian planters to the Whigs, while Democrats won converts by appealing to up-country farmers who resisted the market economy and despised the power of plantation districts in matters of state politics. Georgia organizers exploited a long-standing factional dispute between the cotton and rice planters who had supported William H. Crawford for President in 1824 and up-country frontiersmen who were more sympathetic to Andrew Jackson. During the nullification crisis, the planter faction began to call itself the States Rights Party to express its solidarity with South Carolina, while the pro-Jackson yeomanry called themselves the Union Party. Under Van Buren, Georgia's States Rights Party joined the Whig coalition and vigorously championed state-supported railroad construction and private control of state banking, while the Union Party merged with the Democrats and resisted them. Party lines in Alabama and Mississippi likewise followed the contours of geography and commercial development, with plantation counties leaning toward the Whigs and Democrats predominating among the small farmers of the hill country.

In the Old Northwest, a tumultuous experience with unregulated, "wildcat" banks made state-level bank wars a prime arena for party formation. Whigs in Ohio and neighboring states endorsed proposals for "free banking" laws that gave the privileges of incorporation to any group of capitalists who applied for a charter and met certain broad requirements for corporate status. These laws laid the basis for modern state provisions for incorporation. Democrats, by contrast, were divided between "soft" factions who were willing to charter state banks on a case-by-case basis and "hards" who sought to abolish all banks and expel paper currency from circulation. In every state, party battles between Whigs and Democrats took a slightly different form, but consistent lines of argument kept the party system intact and brought home the personal meaning of Washington's distant struggles.

As party organizers continued their work in the states, events in the distant capital did not stand still. Following his successful election campaign, President Van Buren faced a serious financial panic that strained his personal and political resources to the limit, exposing the limits of his own abilities even as it strengthened the hold of party commitments in Congress and the electorate. Seizing their chance in the election of 1840, Whigs sought to solidify their cohesiveness as a party and to carry the techniques of election-eering pageantry even further than the Democrats had ever done. Though they won the election of 1840 for General William Henry Harrison, Whigs missed the chance to redirect the goals of the federal government to conform with their long-held objectives. Instead, they were ultimately left with John Tyler, a President who refused to follow the party's agenda and failed to establish his own. The Van Buren, Harrison, and Tyler Presidencies each added new dimensions to the emerging pattern of party government and showed ever more clearly how Presidential leadership and party regularity had become jointly indispensable to successful American government.

— 7 —

Van Buren, Harrison, and Tyler

IN CERTAIN RESPECTS, Martin Van Buren made an unlikely successor to Andrew Jackson. Physically, the pair of them made an excellent target for caricaturists, for the Vice President was short and getting stouter whereas the President was tall and thin. Jackson, moreover, was headstrong and inclined to extremes, while Van Buren was a cautious compromiser. Jackson was also famous for his simple and forthright declarations of principle, while Van Buren had a reputation for evasiveness and intrigue. Most notably in the case of the Bank War, Van Buren had demurred or urged more caution on many of the chief policy decisions of Jackson's Administration. Even their nicknames bespoke the difference between unbending rectitude and supple maneuver: the Hero versus the Little Magician, Old Hickory versus the Slippery Elm. On one all-important subject, however, Jackson and Van Buren stood especially close, and that was the importance of a strong Democratic Party.

Partisan commitments came naturally to Martin Van Buren. He had learned his earliest political lessons as a foot soldier for Thomas Jefferson in the election of 1800, and his experience with Federalist rivals had taught him that republicanism thrived best when party lines were strong. Van Buren then spent most of his early manhood using patronage and caucus discipline to shape the Bucktail faction of New York Republicans into a reliable party machine. He originally came to Washington as a critic of President Monroe's policy of amalgamating Federalists and Republicans, and he first supported Jackson for President as a means to reunite North and South in a revived Jeffersonian Republican Party. It was thus entirely fitting that his Presidential Administration should have seen the emergence of a full-fledged national party system.

Over the course of his Presidency, however, Van Buren demonstrated that partisanship was not enough. Conventions, caucuses, party newspapers, and patronage networks could provide the muscle to be elected and to muster support for a President's program, but these devices could not create goals or a vision for an Administration. A superb party organizer, Van Buren gave few signs that he knew what he wanted to do in the Presidency once he achieved it. Quickly confronted by a serious financial panic, Van Buren did not know how to respond. His party became a machine without a steering mechanism, a task force without a task. Not surprisingly, he was defeated overwhelmingly for reelection in 1840.

As Andrew Jackson's designated successor, Martin Van Buren was nominated for the Presidency without controversy by a Democratic national convention that met in Baltimore. The same body also bowed to the wishes of Jackson and the Kitchen Cabinet and selected Congressman Richard Mentor Johnson of Kentucky as its nominee for Vice President. Johnson was a faithful Jacksonian in Congress and a frontier Indian fighter who boasted of killing the Shawnee chief Tecumseh. Though the choice of Van Buren was a foregone conclusion, the selection of Johnson caused trouble, for the Kentuckian had scandalized respectable opinion by his radical statements in favor of equal rights and, even worse, by his open liaison with a slave woman and his efforts to have their daughters accepted as social equals in white society. Johnson was popular in the West, however, as well as among Eastern workingmen, and the whip of party discipline went to work on his behalf. Virginia Democrats refused to endorse him, but the other states fell into line. In the new vision of republican politics, unity would be seen as essential to victory.

Slow to grasp this insight, three Whig candidates opposed Van Buren in 1836: Daniel Webster in Massachusetts, William Henry Harrison in the rest of the North, and Hugh Lawson White in the South. Like Jackson, Harrison was a frontier military hero. His most famous encounter was the defeat of Tecumseh's Shawnee confederation at the Battle of Tippecanoe in 1811, but he had also won the Battle of the Thames, an important victory in the War of 1812. Since then Harrison had served in the U.S. House of Representatives and the Senate and briefly as U.S. minister to Colombia. When Andrew Jackson removed him from that post for interfering in local politics, Harrison retired to his large farm at the North Bend of the Ohio River and supplemented his slender income by serving as clerk of the Court of Common Pleas in Hamilton County, Ohio.

It was a respectable career, though hardly distinguished, yet Whig politicos saw great promise in the old soldier's record. The validity of Harrison's military accomplishments was disputed and somewhat faded in any case, but his military record could be presented as a Whiggish counterpart to Andrew Jackson's more famous victories. Though "Old Tippecanoe" lived in a free state, his father had signed the Declaration of Independence for Virginia. Best of all, he supported most of Henry Clay's economic program without suffering from the Kentuckian's numerous personal liabilities. Though Clay would have liked the nomination, practical political managers in the key states of New York and Pennsylvania recognized Harrison's potential as an uncontroversial public favorite and pointed out the importance of attracting new groups such as the Anti-Masons into the Whig coalition. Clay was a Mason, while Harrison was not, and such considerations of "availability" were essential to party victory in the new political landscape.

Hugh Lawson White was actually an old friend of President Jackson's and claimed to be a loyal Jacksonian still, who only regretted that the wily Van Buren had schemed his way into the old man's confidence. White objected to the supposedly vulgar demagoguery and partisanship of the "New York school of politics" and also questioned the New Yorker's reliability on the slavery question. Though White claimed adherence to original Jackson principles, his Tennessee backers had long been restive under the President's anti-bank and antidevelopment policies. Using the pretext of Van Buren's ascendency, these leaders (whom historian Charles Grier Sellers, Jr., has called "Jackson men with feet of Clay") used White's candidacy to organize a Southern anti-Democratic coalition that could reconcile the followers of Clay and Calhoun. Different as they were in some respects, the two camps shared a common interest in regional economic development and the preservation of slavery, and the Southern Whig Party would become their common political home for the next two decades.

In the campaign that followed the nominations, party organization was a major issue. Whigs deplored the tests of group loyalty, the spirit of impersonal discipline, and the tactics of spoilsmanship that party politics entailed. Preferring the guidance of private conscience to the dictates of mass organization, Whigs recalled George Washington's farewell strictures against partisanship and insisted that party government was synonymous with corruption. "When *party* is the watchword and the ensign of those who fight for the spoils," declared Senator John Bell of Tennessee, one of White's principal backers, "those who would guard the public liberty and our free institutions from pollution and overthrow must range themselves under a different standard." A Harrison convention in Ohio likewise proclaimed that its candidate would be "President of *the Nation*, and not of a *party*—and make the offices what the Constitution designed them to be, *agencies for the benefit of the people, and not bribes with which to purchase votes*." Often avowing respect for Jackson personally, Whigs voiced regret that human frailty and partisan blindness had led the Old Hero into the clutches of the Little Magician and his habits of partisan manipulation.

Democrats countered antiparty arguments as Jackson and Van Buren had—by invoking the example of Thomas Jefferson, by warning of the dangers of disunity, and by suggesting the treacherous alternatives to party unity. Most of the long "Statement" issued in the name of the Democratic national convention in 1835 was a stalwart defense of partisanship. The authors scoffed at Whig criticism that their convention was "intended alone to preserve the power of party and perpetuate party principles." They admitted that partisanship could be carried to negative extremes but declared frankly that differences of interest and opinion in a free country would inevitably give rise to parties and that the public interest actually benefited from vigorous party competition. Parties served as watchdogs of the honesty and efficiency of public servants and could arrest abuses of power by irresponsible officeholders. Above all, parties made it possible for the single individual with honest convictions to obtain some influence in government. Alone, such a person could do nothing, but in combination with others he might have a substantial impact. Even if the individuals in a party were forced to give up certain minor political goals of their own in order to reach a common agreement, these concessions would not signify a disgraceful lapse of principle. Instead, it "would not only be inexcusable, but highly criminal," for good citizens to allow the cause of liberty to be defeated simply "because, in pride of opinion, they would not [make a] sacrifice, on a question of mere expediency." Accordingly, the address concluded, "when parties act on honorable principles, there is no danger from their existence." Instead of holding aloof from partisanship, it was the duty of all good citizens to identify the party that was truly devoted to the preservation of liberty and the Constitution and to give it their fullest support.

The Democrats' appeal also pointed out that no Whig candidate could win a popular majority, so that victory could come to one of them only if the election were thrown into the House of Representatives. Every good Jacksonian remembered the disastrous "corrupt bargain" that had ensued the last time such a thing had happened. They also recalled the danger of sectional cleavage that Van Buren himself had raised nine years earlier, when he called for a party alliance between "the planters of the South and the plain Republicans of the North." By nominating Harrison in the North and White in the South, the Democrats claimed, the Whigs were pandering to sectional prejudice and would undermine the Union, but "true Republicans can never lend their aid and influence in creating geographical parties." Insisting that the slavery question had no legitimate place in national politics, the Democrats condemned abolitionists and sought to reassure anxious Southerners of Van Buren's safety on the slavery question. They also denounced the Bank of the United States, but made no effort to address future problems of the country. Like their Whig opponents, they treated the election as a referendum on Jackson's Presidency.

The growth of the abolition movement in the North and, above all, the Southern response to it lent substance to Democratic fears of sectional politics. In 1831 William Lloyd Garrison of Boston had begun publishing *The Liberator*, an abolitionist paper that surpassed all predecessors in the vehemence of its demands for "immediate emancipation." The same year, Nat Turner's bloody rebellion broke out in Virginia, and proslavery spokesmen needed no evidence to convince them that the two events were connected.

In 1833 Garrison and his supporters founded the American Anti-Slavery Society, and began to bombard Congress with petitions to abolish slavery in the District of Columbia. In 1835 they dispatched a huge shipment of antislavery tracts to Charleston, South Carolina, ostensibly hoping to win white converts in the citadel of slavery, but Carolinians accused them of reckless efforts to incite another slave revolt.

Southerners replied to abolitionists with furious rebuttals and attacks on free speech itself. After a long and bitter debate, the House of Representatives imposed a "gag rule" on petitions relating to slavery, ordering all of them tabled without being read or referred to committee, thus seeking to prevent reformers from addressing Congress on this subject or giving sympathetic congressmen an opportunity to put antislavery speeches on the public record. In Charleston the postmaster allowed a mob to invade the sanctity of the mails and burn the abolitionist literature before it was delivered, while Postmaster General Amos Kendall declared that the federal mails would be closed to "incendiary" materials forbidden by state law. Almost unanimously, the Jacksonian political coalition sought to defend slavery against abolitionist attack.

Still alarmed, Southern political leaders demanded further proslavery pledges from their Northern allies, pledges that most Democrats were happy to provide. Leaders swore that Northern Democrats had no interest in abolition and pointed for proof to the numerous mobs in their section who had set upon abolition meetings and printing presses to stamp out all advocacy of emancipation or racial equality. Southerners remained suspicious, however, and began a series of ever more stringent demands that national and local political candidates be absolutely reliable in their loyalty to white liberty and black slavery.

Southern Whig leaders did not neglect the opportunity that anxiety over slavery had given them. Throughout the South, voters in the plantation districts—who had the greatest stake in slavery—saw the need as well for a sound currency and a smoothly operating credit system. They also tended to bridle at the signs of executive usurpation, party discipline, and rhetorical incitement of the poor against the rich. They were naturally drawn to the Whig candidacy of Judge Hugh Lawson White, but their "aristocratic" agenda had little appeal among ordinary Southern yeomen. The issue that did draw planters and plain folk together was the safety of slavery,

and "White men" used the Judge's name and the Vice President's
New York origins to play on racial fears in counterpoint.

Their message was very simple. In the words of a Virginia editor,
"vote for a Northern President from a free state, and when the
test comes, he will support the abolitionists." Quite apart from
the specific actions that an antislavery President might take to
endanger the South, Southern Whigs implied that the character of
the President gave tone to the whole of American society. Without
a slaveholder in the White House, they suggested, whose family
would be safe from the assassin's midnight ax? "Our domestic
institutions are threatened with annihilation!" shrieked the leading
press of Whig Georgia, and where was Van Buren? "He is not of
us," answered the Whig candidate for governor of North Carolina.
"He is a Northern man in soul, in principle, and in action. . . .
He is an Abolitionist." The well-publicized existence of Richard
M. Johnson's mulatto family was also the subject of extensive
scurrilous commentary, despite the fact that many planters maintained similar relationships behind a veil of semisecrecy.

Van Buren vainly protested his fealty to slavery. "Since I was
a boy I have been stigmatized as the apologist of Southern institutions," he complained to a correspondent, "and now forsooth
you good people will have it . . . that I am an abolitionist." Democrats mounted elaborate and well-documented defenses of their
candidate's respect for Southern white sensibilities, but they were
not completely successful. Whigs made great gains throughout the
South, especially in the plantation districts of most states, and
established themselves as a serious opposition force in Jackson's
former stronghold. Fundamentally, Southern Whigs and Southern
Democrats were divided over the same issues that divided the
parties in other sections—internal improvements, the Bank War,
executive usurpation, even the tariff—while both were equally dedicated to the preservation of slavery. Nevertheless, racial appeals
made invaluable Whig propaganda in the formative election of
1836.

In the end, Van Buren captured 170 electoral votes, while his
combined opponents garnered only 124. He made especially dramatic advances in New England, capturing Maine, New Hampshire, Rhode Island, and Connecticut in the region that had given
only one electoral vote to Andrew Jackson eight years earlier. In
the popular vote, however, Van Buren barely squeaked by with a

razor-thin majority of 50.2 percent; Whig candidates had done well almost everywhere. Under the banner of Hugh Lawson White, Whig gains had been especially impressive in the South Atlantic states, where the Democratic share of the popular vote dropped from 83.2 percent in 1832 to 52.7 percent in 1836. Much to Jackson's chagrin, White even carried their common home state of Tennessee. In the slave states as a whole, the two-thirds Democratic majority of 1832 dwindled to exactly one half of the popular vote four years later. As a result, the two parties had become almost evenly matched throughout the country, with no party having more than a 54.0 percent majority in any one section. Despite internal divisions, the Whigs had become an effective opposition party, and two-party competition would become a permanent fixture of the nation's public life.

Van Buren took office in a ceremony that was as much a tribute to his departing predecessor as it was to the new President himself. "For once," as Thomas Hart Benton remarked later, "the rising was eclipsed by the setting sun." The genial New Yorker did not show any displeasure, knowing how much his own popularity derived from Jackson's blessing. Indeed, he did what he could to encourage the sense that his Presidency would be a prolongation of Jackson's. His inaugural address echoed many of the themes of Jackson's Farewell Address, but without the General's fiery style. He also kept most of Jackson's Cabinet secretaries in office, replacing only outgoing Secretary of War Lewis Cass of Michigan with South Carolina Unionist Joel R. Poinsett.

The balmy weather of Van Buren's Inauguration Day belied the stormy times that lay ahead. The speculative boom that had dominated the last years of Jackson's Presidency was cresting rapidly. In particular, the Bank of England became alarmed in early 1837 by the rapid expansion of loans to America and by an outflow of gold. To check these developments, it abruptly restricted credit to firms doing business with the United States, and British cotton buyers had to reduce their purchases of America's leading export. Coincidentally, a poor harvest had driven up the price of food in Britain and hungry workers were buying less cotton clothing as they struggled to pay for bread. When British demand for American cotton fell, its price did also, and suddenly American merchants who had gambled on a steady or rising price felt the powerful threat of bankruptcy.

Failures began in New Orleans as early as March 1837, the same month that Martin Van Buren took office as President. Distress hit the mercantile houses of New York and Philadelphia by the end of the month, and the pressure spread to banks as paper promises lost their value and noteholders called for specie. On May 9 New York banks lost a reported $652,000 in hard currency, and they suspended specie payments the next day. As soon as they heard the news, banks all over the country did likewise, and gold and silver virtually vanished from circulation overnight.

Unlike the brief recession of 1834, triggered by Nicholas Biddle's actions in the Bank War, the effects of the Panic of 1837 did not rapidly disappear. Quite suddenly, prices for most American staples declined and business activity stagnated in all the major cities. Internal improvements and other major construction projects came to a halt and workers lost their jobs. The textile and shoe manufacturing centers of New England also reported a general suspension of business and widespread unemployment. In many cases, production picked up again after prices fell far enough, but the brief suspension of specie payments in 1838 did not last. The ensuing Panic of 1839 was even more devastating than its predecessor. Along with many other banks and businesses, Nicholas Biddle's Bank of the United States of Pennsylvania closed its doors forever, and nine states defaulted on their bonds. Losses were especially heavy on the southwestern cotton frontier, where land speculation and the expectation of constantly rising prices had burdened many planters with debts they could no longer hope to repay. Flight was the solution for many slaveholders, as they bundled their human property off to Texas and abandoned their once overpriced acreage to the weeds and the bill collectors. Though American farmers and artisans kept up production for domestic use, the commercial and export-oriented sectors of the economy suffered widespread bankruptcy and unemployment well into the 1840s.

Though the immediate causes of the panic lay abroad, Whigs and Democrats were quick to blame each other for the crisis. According to President Van Buren, the catastrophe was grim retribution for past sins. The President blamed "overaction in all the departments of business," but especially the rapid expansion of bank credit and excessive borrowing to finance speculation in the public lands. Behind his technical explanations, the President pointed to moral causes—what he called "the rapid growth among all classes, and especially in our great commercial towns, of luxurious habits founded too often on merely fancied wealth, and detrimental alike to the industry, the resources, and the morals of our people." In other words, the problem was a loss of public virtue, and the solution was a chastened rejection of paper wealth, credit buying, and the luxurious consumption encouraged by the banks and bank notes so much admired by Whigs. Above all, declared Van Buren, the solution was not to vest more power in the general government. "All communities are apt to look to government for too much," he intoned, firmly closing the door on government intervention to relieve the commercial economy or restore confidence in the straitened credit system.

Van Buren's political opponents quickly took the opposite tack. Whigs blamed the panic on Democratic attacks on the credit system, including the destruction of the B.U.S. and the efforts to establish an all-specie currency. According to them, these measures had undermined business confidence and brought on the collapse of credit. The Specie Circular of 1836 took especially heavy criticism as an obstacle to the smooth operation of banking and credit, and Van Buren faced heavy pressure to rescind it. In the words of a New York businessmen's gathering, the "widespread disaster [could be] ascribed to the interference of the general government with the commercial and business operations of the country; its intermeddling with the currency; its destruction of the national bank; its attempt to substitute a metallic for a credit currency; and finally, to the issuing . . . of . . . the 'specie circular.' "

The Specie Circular had mandated a small but potentially destabilizing transfer of bullion from Eastern cities to Western banks, depriving Eastern markets of hard currency at a moment of peak demand. One historian has called it the "jeweled pivot" on which the financial events of 1837 turned, while some dispute its importance. The Specie Circular had certainly acquired a powerful symbolic significance as a sign of the government's fundamental hostility to credit and paper money and thus made a substantial psychological impact on the nation's trading communities.

Staying on the course set by Jackson, Van Buren decided to leave the Specie Circular in place for the present, but the bank suspension forced him to issue more than calls for national repentance. Various pieces of hard-money legislation forbade the government to accept the notes of non-specie-paying banks, or to use such notes to pay its own debts, or to deposit its funds in a suspended bank. Intended to protect a sound currency by punishing suspending banks, these laws now made it virtually illegal for the government to spend, receive, or deposit any money at all. A variety of makeshifts and sleights of hand were available to keep the government operating in the short term, but a permanent solution was clearly necessary. Though he hated to give Whig orators a platform to gloat over the failures of Democratic economic reforms, Van Buren had no choice but to call a special session of Congress in September to deal with the emergency.

When Congress assembled in the fall of 1837, Van Buren proposed to remedy the government's unhappy relationship with banks by severing it. Ever since the suspension began, the land offices and customhouses of the government had kept the money they collected in their own vaults. Instead of working out a new relationship with the state banks or capitulating to the calls for a new federal bank, Van Buren suggested that the government make this ad hoc practice official policy by continuing to hold and disburse its own money without the use of any bank at all. Likewise, he wanted the government to accept nothing but specie or the notes of specie-paying banks in payment of public obligations. Like the old B.U.S., the Treasury would immediately demand specie for these notes and thus take over some of the regulatory functions of Biddle's old "Monster." In sum, Van Buren asked for a nearly complete divorce between the government and the banks, so that the government would not be caught with worthless paper or without full access to its funds in the event of another suspension. Commentators were quick to label this idea the "Subtreasury" or the "Independent Treasury."

Congress agreed to certain measures for immediate relief, but balked at the Independent Treasury. Though Van Buren thought of the measure as a moderate proposal that would allow the government and the banks to go their separate ways in peace, hard-money radicals crowed that confidence in the banks would disappear when the government seemed to brand them officially as unsafe repositories for the public funds. Stripped of government support, the hated institutions would surely crumble. Accepting the same logic, Whigs and conservative Democrats refused to have anything to do with Van Buren's idea and called for renewed use of the state banks, despite the suspension of specie payments.

Congress thus adjourned without taking action on the President's proposal for reform of the banking and currency system.

Another President might have accepted defeat and changed course, but Van Buren persisted. Unwilling to embrace a bold Loco-Foco program to press beyond banking and currency reform to a full-scale attack on "monopoly," he also feared the political consequences of abandoning the hallowed anti-bank formulas of Andrew Jackson. After the special session of the Twenty-fifth Congress, he continued to call for the Independent Treasury, until the battle for it had consumed the bulk of his Presidency. Not until July 4, 1840, when the shock of a second specie suspension had hit the country, was Van Buren able to sign the bill he asked for three years earlier. Undisturbed by the opposition to the Independent Treasury, Van Buren left the hard work of enacting his proposal to his followers in Congress and seemed to concentrate instead on the pleasures of being President. Shaping his measures for short-term political effect, he clung to orthodox Jacksonian policies without the energy or imagination to make them take hold.

The details of the grueling political slugfest that resulted from Van Buren's proposal to divorce the government and the banks are perhaps less significant than the fact that his Administration was taken up by a prolonged national debate about government policy on banking and currency. On one side, the Whigs and their allies among "Conservatives," as pro-bank Democrats were called, battled tirelessly for the "credit system," a network of paper obligations and impersonal market mechanisms underpinning America's transition to a rapidly growing, market-dominated economy and society. In the words of New York Conservative Nathaniel P. Tallmadge, the "credit system is the distinguishing feature between despotism and liberty; it is the offspring of free institutions: it is found to exist, and its influence is felt, in proportion to the freedom enjoyed by any people." Tallmadge explicitly compared the paper-money system to the technological achievements of the Transportation Revolution and asked, "Shall we attempt to overthrow, subvert and destroy a system which has produced all these blessings?" Whigs and Conservatives thought the answer was obvious.

Whigs were especially insistent that the government deposit its funds in banks, so lenders could use them as the backing for further loans to private customers. Rather than lying idle in vaults, the public money should be put to work for public purposes, by indirectly financing more development in a capital-starved economy. On the other side, orthodox Democrats railed endlessly against the "money power" and its threat to the Republic, demanding a return to slow, stable development and the preservation of egalitarian political and economic relations among white men. Rather than feed more reckless development, the government should guard the public treasure against the greed of more financial monsters. In the course of this debate, the last major defection from the Jacksonians took place as Conservatives such as Tallmadge and Virginia's William C. Rives failed to return to the orthodox Democratic fold.

Lacking strength at the top, Van Buren's Administration drifted into ineffectiveness. In Florida, the Seminole Indians fought against removal to the West and pinned down seven of the Army's fourteen regiments as they launched guerrilla attacks from their hiding places in the swamps. A border clash with Canada ended peacefully, but much of the credit went to Whig General Winfield Scott. Responding to military failure, Secretary of War Joel R. Poinsett devised a plan to put the several state militias under national control, but did not stop to ponder the political consequences. Far too centralized for the diffuse American society of the 1830s, Poinsett's plan was hastily withdrawn when critics charged that the combination of the Independent Treasury and the "standing army" would give Van Buren an irresistible power from the "union of the purse and the sword." Disavowals came too late. The Administration managed to appear both weak and power-hungry at the same time, giving Whigs grounds for optimism as 1840 approached.

Bright Whig prospects were seriously threatened by internal disunity. The party had gathered adherents gradually, as each major development of Jacksonian policy alienated a different bloc of former Democrats. The result was a highly diverse, even contradictory, coalition that seemed to have difficulty agreeing on anything except its own ambition to replace the Democrats in office. Millard Fillmore, then a young Whig activist from upstate New York, put the problem neatly:

Into what crucible can we throw this heterogeneous mass of old national republicans, and revolting Jackson men; Masons and anti-Masons; Abolitionists, and pro-Slavery men; Bank men & anti-Bank men with all the lesser fragments that have been, from time to time, thrown off from the great political wheel in its violent revolutions, so as to melt them down into one mass of pure Whigs of undoubted good metal?

Ever since 1834 the main crucible of Whig unity had been the feverish fear of "executive usurpation," but opposition to the Jacksonians' alleged abuse of power had not prevented Van Buren's election in 1836. In 1840 Whigs would need something more substantial than that. At the very least, they would need single candidates for President and Vice President who could win the support of all factions in the party and appeal successfully to a broad spectrum of voters. As Whig journalist Richard Hildreth put it, writing in the Boston *Atlas*, "What avail all other qualifications under Heaven if the candidate be not popular?"

At least as much as a popular candidate, the Whigs needed popular ideas. They had to decide what they believed in as a party and persuade other Americans to join them. Anything less would reinforce their status as a potpourri of elitist malcontents, lacking any legitimate claims on the electorate as a whole. Fortunately for Whig prospects, the superficial diversity of their party membership masked an underlying unity. Despite their many differences, Whig bankers and planters, reformers and opportunists all shared many elements of a common vision of an American future. To present themselves as a credible and effective alternative to the Democrats, their greatest task was to make this vision attractive to a majority of ordinary voters.

The fundamental political goals of many Whigs included both the prosperity they expected from a commercialized economy and the spread of the evangelical virtues they associated with economic progress: hard work, temperance, frugality, domesticity, literacy, benevolence, gentility, and a desire for self-improvement. In their minds, policies such as the tariff, the B.U.S., and federal support for internal improvements or moral reform were both valuable in themselves and means to these ends. To their distress, however, the nation's highest political leaders had long insisted that Whig ideals were both wrong-headed and destructive. According to Jacksonians, the man who pinned his hopes on bank credit or paper money or publicly funded internal improvements lacked the independence necessary for a virtuous republican citizen. A slave to the caprice of markets and moneylenders, he had traded his manhood for "rag currency," but would lose even this mess of pottage whenever his creditors chose to cook up a panic. Though Whigs insisted that their vision of the future would improve life for everyone, Jacksonians so far had persuaded a majority of voters that no one would truly benefit from Whig plans but merchants and bankers and paper-money con men—a new aristocracy of "associated wealth."

Despite the apparent weakness of Martin Van Buren, therefore, most Whig leaders seem to have realized that the powerful grip of Jacksonian ideology would be their most formidable obstacle in 1840. Though they still held high hopes for their traditional program, they saw little chance of success until voters had come to see an expansive capitalist economy as both personally beneficial and consistent with republican traditions. To make this case, Whigs needed to shake their image as the party of financial aristocrats and create a vision of democratic capitalism, in which every American, no matter how humble, could work hard, get ahead, improve his family's welfare, and still maintain the advantages of the Revolutionary past. Putting the party's thinking in cynical terms, one Kentucky Whig assured Congressman John Pope that he would back no more programs that lacked a popular appeal. *"I have no faith, said he, in this democracy, but it is the road to success.* I tell you I have no faith in it, but . . . *no fellow shall out democrat me."* Speaking more idealistically, William Henry Harrison hoped that Americans would come to believe that democracy and the credit system were not only compatible, but "the only means, under Heaven, by which a poor industrious man may become a rich man without bowing to colossal wealth." The songs and slogans of the 1840 Whig campaign were a largely successful effort to bring this message home to a majority of American voters.

Searching for a candidate to convey their convictions, Whig leaders thought first of Henry Clay. Witty, charming, eloquent, with a long record of congressional leadership, the Kentuckian was a favorite with the party faithful and still sought the Presidency with consuming ambition. The father of the American System continued to attract Americans who were hungry for development, and Southern Whigs seemed more willing to accept its risks from the hands of a fellow slaveholder. Van Buren assumed unquestioningly that Clay would be his opponent and complacently looked forward to a campaign based on his renewed appeal for a Bank of the United States.

Neither Clay nor Van Buren had fully realized, however, that a new generation of unsentimental party managers had taken over Whig machinery in many states, men whose practical calculations gave more weight to victory than to romantic reruns with "Harry of the West." Thurlow Weed of New York typified the new breed: a cigar-chomping editor who had launched the Anti-Masonic movement into politics, the rumpled, slouch-hatted manager had never sought public office for himself, but he reveled in his mastery of the fine details of party management and political stratagem. Masterminding the New York gubernatorial campaign of his friend and ally William Seward, Weed had captured the Empire State from Van Buren's Regency in 1838 and was determined to do likewise on a national scale in 1840. Sizing up Clay's chances, Weed saw a slaveholder, a Mason, and a close friend of the B.U.S. These traits were all political liabilities at New York's grass roots, and the Whigs could not win if they failed to carry the nation's most populous state. Speaking bluntly, Weed told Clay he was "unavailable" (i.e., unelectable) and set about finding another standard-bearer for the 1840 ticket.

Two of the Whigs' three champions from 1836 were still active possibilities. General William Henry Harrison had demonstrated solid vote-getting potential throughout the North, although Southerners suspected him of abolitionist leanings. Old Tippecanoe could reassure these doubters that the federal government had no power to interfere with slavery, however, and his popularity remained high. Daniel Webster also remained interested in the race, but party professionals discounted his chances, even in Massachusetts. Facing the inevitable, Webster bowed out in favor of Harrison and absented himself from the nomination struggle by embarking on a voyage to England. After his ancient rival Clay had been eliminated, Webster returned and campaigned actively for his party's ticket.

Another alternative was Major General Winfield Scott, the army commander who had soothed tensions along the Canadian frontier when British efforts to quell a period of political unrest there led to outbreaks of border conflict in 1838 and 1839. He thus enjoyed Northern support, especially in New York, but his Virginia origins gave him credibility in the South. Such characteristics had once been very slender qualifications for the Presidency, but Andrew Jackson had shown that a successful general with unknown views on civilian issues could mount a formidable candidacy. As one New York activist explained, "Scott's name will bring out the hurra boys." Anticipating the campaign strategy that would later pay off for Harrison, he added that "the General's lips must be hermetically sealed, and our shouts and hurra's must be long and loud."

Determined to field a single Presidential candidate in 1840, the Whigs called a convention to sort out the claims of competing contenders. They gathered at Harrisburg, Pennsylvania, on December 4, 1839, and soon deadlocked, with Clay winning 103 votes on the first ballot and Harrison and Scott trailing with 91 and 57, respectively. Balloting continued without much change until Harrison supporter Thaddeus Stevens of Pennsylvania executed a decisive "dirty trick" that finished Scott's candidacy. Strolling past the Virginia delegation, Stevens casually dropped a letter from the General expressing an indiscreet hostility to slavery. Like several other Southern delegations, Virginia had been voting for Clay while endorsing Scott as their second choice, but the "intercepted" message changed their minds. Suddenly fearing that continued deadlock would bring forward the "abolitionist" Scott as a compromise candidate, Virginians deserted him and precipitated a rush to Harrison. When Thurlow Weed then delivered the votes of New York to the Ohioan, the final vote stood at 148 for Harrison, 90 for Clay, and 16 for Scott. Determined to avoid further controversy, the delegates then adjourned quickly without adopting a platform. Pragmatists reasoned that ideological floor fights would do no one any good, and demonstrated clearly how power over Presidential campaigning had shifted from legislative caucuses and local gatherings to the smoke-filled rooms of national conventions.

Clay was briefly bitter in defeat, but he had written a letter prior to the convention endorsing whomever the party might choose. Bruised feelings began to heal when this statement was read from the podium, but Clay's supporters nevertheless declined the opportunity to put one of their number on the ticket as Vice Presidential nominee. The place went instead to Senator John Tyler of Virginia, a personal friend of Clay's who shared almost none of the Kentuckian's views. In effect, Tyler was even more of an Old Republican than Andrew Jackson and had split with the Administration on the issue of executive usurpation. His selection as Vice

Presidential nominee gave sectional and ideological balance to the ticket, but little else; in the words of New York aristocrat Philip Hone, the combination of "Tippecanoe and Tyler too" had "rhyme, but no reason in it." Whig professionals would come to regret this drawback, but they ignored it for the present, preferring to capitalize on the rhymes and even to set them to music.

Superb imagery for the most effective campaign jingles appeared in the aftermath of the Whig national convention, inadvertently supplied by a flippant Democratic newspaper. Expressing his dismay at Harrison's nomination, a frustrated Clay supporter told a reporter that "Old Tippecanoe" ought to decline in Clay's favor, and wondered aloud how the General might be persuaded to step aside. Inserted into his story, the reporter's jocular reply soon became much more newsworthy than the rest of the interview: "Give him a barrel of hard cider, and settle a pension of two thousand a year on him," the Democrat gibed, "and my word for it, he will sit out the remainder of his days in his log cabin . . . and study moral philosophy."

The journalist's wisecrack was intended to rub salt into the wounds of Henry Clay's outmaneuvered followers, as well as to ridicule the pretensions of Ohio's favorite son. Belying the Whig reputation for elitism, Harrison was famous for his easy, unpretentious manners and folksy amiability, but Democrats discounted him as an office-seeking hack who could be easily bought off with a sinecure. In mocking Old Tippecanoe, however, the journalist had also disparaged the lives of thousands of rural families who still lived in log houses and drank home-fermented beverages, not to mention the nostalgia of thousands of others who already saw the passing of the frontier as a sign of moral and political decay. In reality, William Henry Harrison did not live in a log cabin, and he probably drank very little hard cider, but no matter. The characteristic dwelling and beverage of the frontier were both glorified by Whig papers and celebrated from uncounted platforms and parade grounds until they came to symbolize the new popular appeal of the Whig Party. Using the reporter's gaffe to paint Democrats as elitists, Whigs described themselves as the genuine party of the people. Offering a newly democratized version of their older economic platform, Whigs fought the Presidential election of 1840 singing and marching behind the symbols of log cabins and hard cider.

The tone was set early by a mammoth convention of Whig young men, summoned to Baltimore to "ratify" the Harrison nomination and to drown out the Democratic national convention, which was meeting in the same city at the same time. Songs, parades, floats, banners, and speeches filled the local racetrack night and day, all designed to convey the Whig message in the simplest and most powerful way possible. At least some Whigs bemoaned the use of such tactics. "I regret the necessity, real or imagined," wrote Henry Clay, "of appealing to the feelings and passions of our Country-men, rather than to their reasons and their judgments." Clay's scruples were not allowed to interfere with success, however, and the Log Cabin Campaign roared into high gear.

Picking up on well-established themes, Whig rallies in the campaign attracted thousands with a combination of raucous pageantry and stirring rhetoric. Log cabins sprouted everywhere to serve as local headquarters and the sites of neighborhood campaign rallies. Replying to Senator Benton's boast that he had "set the ball in motion" in favor of the expunging resolution, Whigs built enormous buckskin balls and rolled them from rally to rally. When audiences tired of oratory at such gatherings, party managers beguiled them with music, and glee clubs and sing-along sessions became essential features of party gatherings. So did vast quantities of hard cider, as Whigs revived their stalled political prospects with mug after mug of the sparkling beverage. Special newspapers appeared, often following the example of the *Log Cabin*, a campaign sheet edited by New York journalist Horace Greeley. Recruited by Weed and Seward, Greeley filled his columns with reprinted speeches, anecdotes, and electioneering verses set to popular melodies. Mixing entertainment with serious political argument, Whigs were determined to reach the ordinary voter at last.

Whig image-makers began as the Jacksonians had in 1828, by portraying their frontier general as the model of martial virtue while condemning his opponent as a decadent aristocrat. According to one popular ditty,

> *The knapsack pillow'd Harry's head*
> *The hard ground eas'd his toils;*
> *While Martin on his downy bed*
> *Could dream of naught but spoils.*

Borrowing a trick from Democratic celebrations of the Battle of New Orleans, Whigs timed their mass rallies to coincide with anniversaries of Harrison's encounters with the enemy in the War of 1812. Breaking with tradition, Harrison himself joined these celebrations and became the first Presidential nominee to take to the campaign trail on his own behalf. Over and over, the candidate heard himself compared to Cincinnatus, the victorious Roman general who modestly preferred farming to politics, but yielded to popular demand and resumed power when the Republic stood in danger.

Steady denunciation of "Martin Van Ruin" also played a central role in Whig campaign rhetoric. The President had always been something of a dandy, sporting yellow silk waistcoats, delicate doeskin gloves, and similar finery. He had also put on substantial weight since his dapper days in the New York Senate. Whig spokesmen embroidered on these details to portray Van Buren as a profligate who rioted in luxury, perfuming his profuse side-whiskers with "Double Extract of Queen Victoria," while poor men suffered from the cruel effects of a financial panic brought on by the misuse of Presidential power.

The most devastating attack came from Representative Charles Ogle of Pennsylvania, who regaled Congress for three days in April with charges that Van Buren had refitted the White House as a "PALACE *as splendid as that of the Caesars and as richly adorned as the proudest Asiatic mansion.*" According to Ogle, while American workingmen struggled for bread and the hero of Tippecanoe watched sadly from his log cabin, President Van Buren had been squandering the people's money at the rate of more than seventy dollars a minute. Among other frippery, Ogle charged, the money had gone for "*massive gold plate and French sterling silver services,*" Royal Wilton carpets, nine-foot plate glass mirrors, and even a Presidential bathtub! To crown it all, he announced breathlessly, the White House gardens had actually been relandscaped to add several "clever sized hills . . . , every pair of which . . . was designed to resemble . . . AN AMAZON'S BOSOM, with a miniature knoll or hillock on its apex, to denote the n-pple."

Disgusted Democratic editors branded Ogle's performance an "OMNIBUS OF LIES," and tried to point out that Van Buren had actually spent less on the White House than any previous President.

Regardless of the facts, Ogle's tirade still made exquisite propaganda, and copies soon flooded the mails in doubtful districts. Local speakers took up the same themes and it was soon well established in the minds of many voters that Van Buren, the humble tavern keeper's son who never went to college, was actually a dissipated aristocrat, while Harrison, a West Point graduate and the scion of Virginia's plantation gentry, was a poverty-stricken pioneer. The politics of "image-making" had never been more effective.

Democrats protested that the Whig campaign was meaningless, a rigmarole, but the songs and slogans were effective because they were actually quite meaningful to their audiences. Arguments for traditional Whig policies still appeared within the electioneering pageantry. Harrison himself prepared the way for a new version of the Bank of the United States, for example, by suggesting that he might agree to one if congressional leaders demanded it. "With my mother's milk did I suck in the principles on which the Declaration of Independence was founded," Harrison assured the cheering crowd, and adroitly framed the possibility of a new bank as a matter of principled submission to the popular will.

Other party campaigners continued to emphasize a standard Whig view of the good society and the means to achieve it. Like many others, one typical speaker to the Whig young men's convention in Baltimore blamed hard times on Democratic efforts to pit the poor against the rich. "By incessant and unrelenting assaults upon capital, good faith, and enterprise," Judge Hanson charged, they have "disunited the interest, and thereby torn asunder the good feelings which bind men to each other." Contrasting Whig views of prosperous social unity with Jacksonian divisiveness, Hanson appealed directly to the commercial leanings of farmers and artisans who had tasted the benefits of the new market economy and wanted more. In accordance with Democratic policy, he charged, "all surplus produce is to rot in the granary of the farmer for the want of markets furnished by the employment of artisans and laborers, fisheries, factories, work-shops, roads and canals. The condition of the country is to be improved by arresting all improvement; debts are to be paid by the annihilation of property." Echoing a similar theme, William C. Preston of South Carolina promised a Philadelphia audience that when Harrison was elected, "we should then see the whole country rise, and expand, and teem with prosperity. Industry would find encouragement and protection, the shackles would be removed from commerce, confidence would be restored, and no man would have cause to fear any fatal blow to his prospects from the government." In effect, Whigs were defending a version of what today is called the "trickle-down" theory of prosperity: promoting the interests of businessmen promotes the interests of all classes by restoring "confidence," leading investors to expand their activities, creating new jobs and new opportunities for the poor.

In contrast to Democratic acknowledgments of social conflict, Whigs continued to evoke an organic notion of society in which potential adversaries—employers and workers, merchants and farmers, rich and poor—were bound harmoniously together by reciprocal ties of trust and dependency. At a typical Whig rally, one reporter claimed, "all classes and conditions in life, learned and unlearned, rich and poor, gentle and simple, seemed to remember for once that their interests were the same." As befitted the spokesmen for a new, aggressively capitalist culture, however, Whigs did not rely on sentiment alone to bind their society together. Refurbishing an ancient political metaphor, Daniel Webster likewise reminded listeners in Saratoga, New York, that "the analogy between the human system and the social and political system is complete." The Massachusetts orator added a new twist, however, when he identified the circulating fluid that sustained his organic society. "What the life-blood is to the former circulation," he explained, "money, currency, is to the latter; and if that be disordered or corrupted, paralysis must fall on the system." He then proceeded to show in conventional Whig fashion how the ills of the body politic could be traced to the Democratic experiments with hard currency.

Appeals to a unified but hierarchical vision of society also lay behind Whig invocations of the eighteenth-century republican legacy. Unlike previous generations of conservatives, Whigs did not expect every man to remain forever in the social place defined for him by birth. They celebrated the benefits of social mobility and saw its rewards going naturally to the hardworking and virtuous. Seeing themselves as perfect examples of this process at work, however, prominent Whigs tended to feel entitled to recognition as the natural leaders of society and government. In this sense, they saw themselves as the legitimate successors of earlier gen-

erations of benevolent community leaders and longed for the deferential acceptance of their position by a grateful mass of voters.
In their view, however, Jackson's theory of the President as the
direct representative of the people and the political party as the
vehicle of the people's will undercut the proper role of local elites.
Under Jackson, unknown party hacks had usurped the leadership
of individual communities, using the rhetoric of class conflict to
whip up meetings, rallies, and resolutions that could be presented
in the papers as partisan evidence of the people's will. Whigs
therefore struggled mightily to portray Jacksonian notions of democratic and partisan politics as profoundly unrepublican and to
restore themselves as the proper successors of the Revolutionary
generation.

In his own campaign speeches, Harrison sought to establish his
republican credentials and to refute the charge of Federalism by
continually invoking the names of Jefferson, Madison, Monroe,
and a panoply of other Democratic-Republican and Antifederalist
heroes. He also sought to reestablish the legitimacy of community
leaders who still dominated the legislative assemblies of state and
nation. "The [legislative] representatives of the people were once
the source of power," he reminded his audiences, but Jackson had
ridden roughshod over Congress even as he trumpeted republican
slogans. Despite Jackson's claims to defend the Republic, asserted
Harrison, *"The Government is now a practical Monarchy!"* and he
fervently promised that "I will use all the power and influence
vested in the office of President of the Union to abridge the power
and influence of the National Executive." Emphasizing this commitment, he also pledged to serve for one term only, to take no
part in the choice of his successor, to stay out of the legislative
process, and to do his best to put down "the violence of party
spirit," which he called "a serious mischief to the political welfare
of the country."

Just as the Whig economic program looked to a new world of
production and exchange, Whig republicanism embodied a transformed cultural tradition, with significant new elements that had
not appeared in the eighteenth-century version. Neither a patriar-
chal squire nor a deferential yeoman, the ideal Whig voter was a
sober and hardworking husband and father, energetic and consci-
entious on the job, attentive to the needs of his family, and receptive to the sanctifying power of faith. He thus paid at least

token allegiance to domestic and evangelical ideals. Paradoxically, moreover, the Whigs fought to establish their vision of a properly hierarchical society by using fervently egalitarian rhetoric. No matter how much leading Whigs may have longed for a vanished deference, their campaign style embraced all the various forms of democratic political culture. These cultural innovations had already supported Whig growth in local elections and they likewise played a conspicuous role in the Presidential election of 1840.

The apparent contradiction between the Whigs' desire to replace Democratic spoilsmen with established community leaders and their fervent embrace of egalitarian rhetoric stemmed from their changing conception of social order. Recognizing that a fluid marketplace society could not depend on a rigid, inherited hierarchy, Whigs sought a meritocracy in which economic, political, and cultural leaders won their places by the exercise of hard work, self-improvement, and self-control. Though they championed the opportunities of the marketplace as the ideal vehicles for self-improvement, they looked to family and faith for the moral inspiration that would lift the pursuit of wealth above the sordid level of mere greed. Just as Whigs flourished new egalitarian symbols in their electoral campaign in 1840, they also harnessed new ideals of gender and religion to their cause.

According to one of the earliest historians of Harrison's election, 1840 "was remarkable as the first campaign in which the women generally engaged, and, by their smiles and songs and encouragement, promoted the election." As this comment implied, however, the role of Whig women was to support their menfolk's efforts from the sidelines, not to campaign vocally or to agitate for the right to vote themselves. Female participation in the campaign was nevertheless significant in establishing Harrison as the candidate who best embodied the attractions—for both men and women—of the burgeoning cult of domesticity.

According to most accounts, "the ladies" were a prominent part of Whig parades and rallies. Cheering, waving handkerchiefs, presenting banners and bouquets, women conveyed the impression that Harrison was the candidate best suited to defend home, family, and fireside. Men who wished to be good providers and thus to deserve the emotional support of a loyal, loving wife could best demonstrate their devotion by voting the Whig ticket. "I call upon you, men, to shield the fairest flower that blooms," cried former

Mississippi Congressman Seargent S. Prentiss, "by staying the hand and resisting the blow that would destroy its sweetness and beauty. You should feel every honorable sensation . . . as a man—as a Whig—to exert yourselves in protecting all of womankind." Pointing to Democrats as purveyors of an entirely different code of masculine conduct, Whig spokesmen denounced Vice President Johnson's mulatto mistress, hinted that Martin Van Buren fathered illegitimate children, and connected their rivals with Fanny Wright, the female partisan of New York's radical workingmen who scorned a submissive role for women and denounced conventional marriage.

While carefully observing the proprieties regarding their public roles, Whig women endorsed the same views. Lucy Kenney became one of the first American women to write campaign literature, when she published a pamphlet for Harrison under her own name. At an all-female political meeting in rural Ohio, Whig matrons raised cups of tea in repeated toasts to "Old Tippecanoe," pledging that "he who protected the Widow and Orphan in 1813, will not be by them forsaken in 1840." Underscoring the same point, editors ran repeated stories of Whig Lysistratas who exerted their moral authority over men by boldly using sex as a political bargaining chip. In genteel terms, that is, marriageable Whig women were allegedly refusing all suitors unless they agreed to vote "for the Protector of the Western home, the Log-Cabin candidate." By adopting such appeals, Whigs clearly hoped to attract male voters who had in some way accepted the cult of domesticity and the trade-offs it implied: workplace diligence and sexual fidelity from husbands in exchange for loyal emotional support at home; moral authority for wives in exchange for steadfast adherence to the restrictive principles of "true womanhood."

Not surprisingly, Whigs who linked their party with the cult of domesticity likewise tied it to the cause of evangelical religion. Though Whigs were emphatically the party of economic development, they were also the champions of what they saw as social order and sound morality. Like the early Whigs of New York's Burnt-Over District, other Northern Whigs worried that economic progress not sanctified by religious dedication might lead to an orgy of greed, debauchery, and sin, all failings they associated with unregenerate Democrats. The rising level of business activity and evangelical concern collided most obviously over the issue of sabbath observance, with ministers calling for the suspension of Post Office business on Sundays while unconverted businessmen insisted on the uninterrupted flow of remittances, merchandise, and market information. Evangelicals were likewise distressed by slavery, by intemperance, by the widespread tolerance of dueling, and by Jackson's harsh treatment of the Southern Indians, many of whom were evangelical converts. More generally, Whiggish ministers deplored what historian Richard Carwardine has summarized as " 'licentiousness'—swearing, drinking, gambling, whoring, theatre-going—and a disrespect for the law which . . . resulted in the violent rampaging of mobs." Identifying Harrison as the candidate to oppose these trends, politicians and evangelical ministers joined in an effort to promote Whiggery as the party of genuine Christianity.

Harrison himself thus won praise as "a sincere Christian," "a good Sunday school . . . church going man," "one who highly respects religion." Whig publicists emphasized the honesty, morality, and humanitarianism of the Farmer of the North Bend, while Van Buren was repeatedly denounced for his love of luxury, his tolerance of financial impropriety, and his complicity in the embezzlement of Jacksonian spoilsman Samuel Swartwout. Henry Clay tied evangelical concerns over business and political morality to the old republican concerns for virtue, and thousands of lesser imitators followed his example. "A REPUBLIC CAN ONLY EXIST UPON THE FOUNDATION OF VIRTUE AND GOOD MORALS," Clay thundered, and mentioned the repudiation of debts by depression-stricken states and private borrowers as a prime example of national sin. Though Harrison, like Jackson, first came to prominence as a conqueror of Indians, his dealings with defeated native Americans were praised as benevolent and just, while Van Buren was denounced for the brutality of Indian removal and especially for the Army's use of bloodhounds to track fugitive Seminoles in Florida. Vice President Johnson likewise took criticism for his 1829 report to Congress defending the transportation of mail on Sunday as required by the separation of church and state. Most fundamentally, Whigs linked Democrats to every variety of subversive doctrine in religion, family life, and class relations. As Whig editor Horace Greeley put it, "wherever you find a bitter, blasphemous Atheist and enemy of Marriage, Morality, and Social Order, there you may be certain of one vote for Van Buren."

Whig appeals to the domestic and evangelical values of some voters coexisted a bit uneasily with the lavish consumption of hard cider among others. Democrats tried hard to capitalize on this seeming inconsistency, but their fulminations against "swigs" did not get them very far. Until rather recently, cider or fermented apple juice had been the most popular family beverage in the rural North. It was almost always homemade and so commonplace that it rarely came on the market for sale. Early temperance advocates had condoned the drink and preferred it to distilled spirits such as whiskey and rum. Ironically, W. J. Rorabaugh, a careful student of American alcohol consumption, has found that its use had fallen drastically in the decades just before 1840 and would practically cease thereafter. For the men who drank it in the log cabin campaign, hard cider was thus an old-fashioned beverage that recalled the warmth and good cheer of rural families and communities in the days before the expansion of the market economy. Hardly a meaningless symbol, cider made an overt appeal to domesticity and pioneering enterprise—particularly when drunk as part of a toast to protective tariffs or a sound credit system. Both the log cabin and the cider barrel were thus fitting embodiments of the Whig vision of an American capitalism that was not only economically productive, but also democratic and compatible with the best of America's past. It also contained a good measure of alcohol— fully enough to enliven the dullest rally. The success of the log cabin and hard cider symbolism thus testified to the strength of Whig party principles and to the truth of General Harrison's declaration to a Dayton rally: though he would not make partisan pledges, he was indeed a partisan candidate. As Harrison had put it, the Whigs' "selection of him is proof enough that he will carry out the doctrines of his party."

Completely unprepared for the Whig campaign attack, the Democrats of 1840 seemed baffled by the question of how to respond. "We could meet the Whigs on the field of argument and beat them without effort," claimed the New York *Evening Post*, "but when they lay down the weapons of argument and attack us with musical notes, what can we do?" For many Democrats, the answer was to struggle doggedly to shift the terms of controversy back to familiar terrain: the threat of aristocracy, consolidation, Federalism, abolition, and the Monster Bank. According to the Washington *Globe*, "The question to be decided at the next Presidential election" was simple: "SHALL THIS BE A GOVERNMENT OF THE BANKS OR OF THE PEOPLE?" With Senator Felix Grundy of Tennessee, Democrats insisted that the real issue was "that man is fit for self-government, and by the aid of Almighty God, the people shall and will rule." While Whig young men marched noisily outside, Grundy reminded the Democratic national convention in Baltimore, "we are the friends and advocates of equal rights—we want no adventitious aid, either from exclusive privileges or banking corporations." Unlike the Whigs, Democrats did not hesitate to spell out their principles in a nine-point party platform. Embracing strict construction of the Constitution, their resolutions rejected a national system of internal improvements, a protective tariff, collection or distribution of surplus revenue, a national bank, and Whig proposals to assume the state debts. Abolitionist efforts to interfere with slavery and nativist demands to limit the political rights of foreigners drew condemnation. Above all, the Democrats declared "the separation of the moneys of the government from banking institutions, is indispensable for the safety of the funds of the government, and the rights of the people."

Old Hickory himself emerged from retirement at the Hermitage to reinvigorate these slogans, and Postmaster General Amos Kendall led a massive organizing effort to enlist committees, circulate newspapers, raise liberty poles, and generally counteract the Whig assault. Turning Whig claims for domesticity on their head, Democrats presented themselves in effect as the party of "true manhood," mocking the sixty-seven-year-old Harrison as a superannuated and effeminate "Granny" or "petticoat general" whose military laurels were suspect and who could not be trusted to answer his own mail. Scrambling to neutralize the journalistic taunt that had made log cabins and hard cider the symbols of the Whig campaign, they ridiculed the fiction that the affluent General Harrison inhabited a log cabin and identified themselves as the true party of farmers and workingmen. Still convinced that they constituted a natural majority of the citizens, Democrats found it hard to believe they could ever lose an honest election, and warned one another repeatedly that their most serious enemy was vote fraud. Their efforts would succeed in bringing out a much larger Democratic electorate than in 1836, but they failed to change the structure of the campaign itself.

Democrats found themselves hamstrung by the credibility of

Whig accusations. To voters who were feeling the pinch of hard times, one popular Whig slogan had instant appeal: "Matty's policy, 12½ cts. a day and French soup, Our policy, 2 dols. a day and Roast Beef." On evangelical issues, Democrats could not deny that Jacksonians such as Richard M. Johnson had championed the separation of church and state and rejected most efforts to impose sabbath observance on both state and national governments. Fanny Wright's lover and radical associate Robert Dale Owen, moreover, was a Van Buren candidate for the Electoral College in New York, put on the ticket in a conscious effort to appeal to radicalized workingmen. Van Buren's Administration was likewise vulnerable on a long list of equally damaging charges ranging from the "standing army" proposal by Secretary of War Joel Poinsett, to corruption by spoilsmen, to failure in the Seminole War. Under the circumstances, it is perhaps surprising that the Democrats did as well as they did.

When the ballots were counted, Harrison had carried nineteen states out of twenty-six, with 52.9 percent of the popular vote. His margin in the Electoral College was a smashing 234 to Van Buren's 60. The biggest news of the election, however, was the massive increase in turnout. Political scientist Walter Dean Burnham estimates that fully 80.2 percent of eligible voters cast a Presidential ballot in 1840, though turnout in the elections of 1828, 1832, and 1836 had only reached an average of 56.9 percent. Whigs and Democrats both benefited from this upsurge, for Martin Van Buren actually won 367,000 more votes in 1840 than he had in 1836. But it was the Whigs who had outdone themselves. By presenting their traditional program in a popular format, party managers had gathered over half a million new voters to the Whig ticket and raised their party, for the present at least, from minority to majority status. Despite their disavowals of Jacksonian-style partisanship, moreover, Whigs had learned that party organization could succeed where principled individualism could not. The combination of discipline and hoopla had paid off, and no future campaign could afford to do without them. "They have at last learned from defeat the art of victory," mourned the *Democratic Review*. "We have taught them how to conquer us!"

Despite their skill at learning Democratic lessons, unfortunately, the Whigs' triumph in 1840 was quite literally short-lived. William Henry Harrison took the oath of office on March 4, 1841, and delivered the longest inaugural address in U.S. history, standing outside the Capitol without an overcoat. As in the campaign itself, he denounced the excessive power of the executive, promised to defer to Congress, and pledged to serve but a single term. Thereafter, apparently still seeking to dispel doubts about his physical vigor, the aging President disdained suitable clothing and protection as he braved Washington's raw March weather and plunged into an exhausting round of official entertaining and discussions with clamorous office-seekers. The strain proved too great. William Henry Harrison was dead of pneumonia at the end of a month and John Tyler of Virginia became the first Vice President to succeed to the Presidency upon the death of the incumbent.

Tyler's experience in the Presidency was particularly difficult, and his difficulties illustrated how thoroughly the development of a party system had changed the process of government. Even his official status was challenged by some observers, who questioned the constitutionality of his claim to the *office* of President as well as to its "powers and duties," though most contemporaries (as well as subsequent generations) accepted the logic of Tyler's precedent-setting assertion. More serious problems arose from Tyler's status as a party leader. If Van Buren had proved that no President could succeed on the basis of party strength alone, Tyler showed that convictions alone were also insufficient. Without the support of a strong political party, all future Presidents would be helpless. The reverse was also true. Whig control of Congress was meaningless so long as President Tyler was committed to blocking the Whig program. The net result of the Tyler Presidency was political deadlock.

Though Tyler had been the Whig nominee for Vice President, his faith in the Old Republican, states'-rights school of politics put him at odds with the overwhelming majority of his party. William Henry Harrison had won the White House after pledging to subordinate himself to Whig party barons in Congress, men who favored protective tariffs, distribution of the proceeds of public land sales, and a national bank. Whigs had also trumpeted the need for a President to follow the advice of his "constitutional advisers" in the Cabinet. Seeking stability in the moment of transition, Tyler had asked Harrison's Cabinet nominees to retain their posts, and they had agreed. As a result, President Tyler now faced a Cabinet led by Daniel Webster as Secretary of State and a Congress dominated by Henry Clay. Could he swallow his constitutional scruples and govern according to Harrison's partisan mandate? Could he regain the support of the Jacksonians, whom he had earlier spurned, and govern the nation with their support? Or could he find enough independent supporters to do without the help of either party? Though Tyler clearly favored the latter course, it turned out that the answer to each of the three questions was a resounding no.

Like Harrison before him, Tyler soon found that Senator Henry Clay had never fully accepted the fact that his bid for the Presidency had been unsuccessful. Bridling at the Kentuckian's overbearing manner, even the pliant Harrison had once been forced to exclaim, "You forget, Mr. Clay, that I am the President." With Harrison dead, Clay now regarded himself as an unrivaled party leader with a clear mandate to implement the Whig party program. Soon after Congress met at the end of May, Clay submitted resolutions in the Senate outlining his intention to abolish the Independent Treasury, to replace it with a national bank, to increase the tariff, and to provide for the distribution of the proceeds of the public lands. This program put him on a collision course with President Tyler.

The severest conflict erupted over the question of a bank. At Clay's request, Secretary of the Treasury Thomas Ewing submitted a plan for a "Bank and Fiscal Agent" incorporated in the District of Columbia, with power to establish branches in the states with their consent. This bill was tailored to meet the President's constitutional principles, but Clay thought it weak and replaced it with a bill to charter a new and powerful bank very similar to the one destroyed by Andrew Jackson. When this bill emerged from Congress, Tyler vetoed it as unconstitutional. Trying again, congressional Whigs passed a second measure, which lacked the features in Clay's bill that Tyler had found objectionable. To the party's consternation, Tyler vetoed this bill as well, leading all the members of his Cabinet to resign in protest, except for Webster, who found himself in a delicate negotiation with Great Britain. Shortly afterward, congressional Whigs passed resolutions that effectively expelled the President from his own party.

Undaunted, John Tyler sought to govern without regard to party lines. He formed a new Cabinet from the "corporal's guard" of politicians who continued to support him and launched a Presidency dedicated to territorial expansion and states' rights. The

Administration won a major diplomatic success when Secretary of State Daniel Webster settled a long-standing boundary dispute between Maine and British-held Canada, but Tyler set his sights on the more difficult task of annexing the Republic of Texas to the United States. Once a province of Mexico, Texas had been settled by American slaveholders seeking new territory for King Cotton. When Mexico launched an antislavery crackdown, Anglo-American settlers proclaimed their independence in 1836 and defeated Mexican efforts to subdue them. Many Texans and Americans were eager to unify the two republics, and when Daniel Webster finally resigned as Tyler's Secretary of State, his successor quickly negotiated a treaty of annexation. Opponents pointed out that Mexico had never recognized the independence of its former province and would fight to prevent its absorption by the United States. The acquisition of Texas would also lead to the creation of one or more new slave states, a disquieting prospect to abolitionists and to ordinary Northern voters who resented the power of the South in Congress. Whigs seized upon Texas as a partisan issue and successfully blocked the ratification of the treaty of annexation. The Texas question thus loomed as a prominent sectional and partisan issue in the election of 1844. Though President Tyler launched an independent effort to win election in his own right, the existing parties mostly ignored him. They prepared instead for a campaign that would pit Henry Clay of the Whigs against a Democratic opponent who almost everyone assumed would be Martin Van Buren.

As it turned out, the nomination slipped through Van Buren's fingers when the ex-President took an unpopular stand on the Texas issue. Still seeking to unify the "planters of the South and the plain Republicans of the North," Van Buren preferred to keep divisive sectional issues out of politics and to wage campaigns over party matters that transcended sectional divisions. When Van Buren and Clay both came out against immediate annexation, Clay was able to retain his popularity among Whigs, but Van Buren lost heavily among Southern Democrats. When the Democratic national convention assembled, the New Yorker could not muster the necessary two-thirds majority, and the nomination went to a loyal Jacksonian understrapper, former Governor James K. Polk of Tennessee. Running on an expansionist platform calling for "the reoccupation of Oregon and the reannexation of Texas," Polk gained a narrow victory in 1844 and once more snatched the Presidency from a frustrated Henry Clay.

In the final hours of the Tyler Administration, Democrats secured Texas by the constitutionally doubtful expedient of a joint congressional resolution. Their actions gladdened the heart of a dying Andrew Jackson, who finally succumbed to his ancient wounds and illnesses in 1845. As Whigs had predicted, however, annexation led to war with Mexico under Polk and territorial expansion to the Pacific Coast. A quarrel over whether slavery should be permitted in this new territory ultimately tore the Jacksonian party system apart and precipitated the Civil War.

In the 1840s and early 1850s, however, the party system seemed strong and political breakdown was hard to foresee. Like most elections since Jackson's day, the Presidential elections of 1848 and 1852 revolved around the rivalry between the Democratic and Whig parties. So did most of the state and local contests of the period. Most states were almost evenly divided between the two parties, and party members in one state usually preferred to act in concert with fellow partisans from distant states than cooperate with members of the opposing party closer to home. As Martin Van Buren had foreseen, these habits tended to bolster national unity and diminish sectional rivalry. In particular, most Southern voters and politicians rejected the efforts of John C. Calhoun and his followers to unite them in a single force for the protection of slavery and sectional interests. Northern voters likewise resisted antislavery appeals to unite against the "slave power," and clung instead to party loyalties forged in the older battle over the "money power." Momentarily, at least, the structure of American politics had stabilized.

The Second American
Party System

PREPARING for the election of 1840, Whig publicist Calvin Colton wrote a series of essays over the signature "Junius" which became famous as statements of Whig party principles and which were later republished in book form as *The Junius Tracts*. In them, Colton made an admission that many of his fellow partisans were reluctant to make. "The two great parties of this country," he remarked, "will always remain nearly equal to match each other, and every few years there must be a change." Colton thus conceded what Democratic activists had long maintained: that a political party system must exist in America and that each party must acknowledge its opponent's legitimacy and its right to take power when elected. Though some Whigs would always have a preference for "no party" government and some Democrats would always assume that no party but their own could ever represent the "real people," Colton's admission was a sign that the political changes of the Jacksonian era were achieving a broad level of acceptance among voters and leaders alike.

The routine pattern of rivalry between Democrats and Whigs that emerged under Andrew Jackson and his successors is often called the second American party system. The name calls attention to the idea that the rivalry of the parties was more than an unrelated string of independent elections and distinguishes it from the earlier rivalry between Hamiltonian Federalists and Jeffersonian Republicans. During the life of the second American party system, most voters affiliated with one party or the other and kept a loyalty to it for as long as the system itself existed. Depending on which party held the local majority, the results of most elections could be safely predicted in advance. Politicians and party activists also seemed to accept a similar set of assumptions about what was important in politics and how political goals should be pursued. The second party system thus constituted a distinct episode in the evolution of American political culture, with important differences between the periods that preceded and followed it.

The second party system remained the dominant force in American politics from the Administration of Andrew Jackson to the middle of the 1850s. For most of this period, Democrats held the upper hand in Presidential elections, winning six of the eight contests from 1828 through 1856. Whigs had better luck in state and congressional elections, however, and the Jacksonians could never take their dominance for granted. This was particularly true after the middle of Andrew Jackson's second term, when Jackson's opposition began to coalesce, to broaden its base, and to assume a permanent party identity. This movement accelerated under the influence of the Panics of 1837 and 1839, bringing the party system to something like maturity in 1840. Sixteen years later, the second party system had already disappeared in some areas and was rapidly breaking apart in most others. Its duration was therefore short, but the second party system was important because it set up the conditions that would lead to the Civil War and because it remained the model for American political practice thereafter.

A startling increase in political participation was one of the most distinctive features of the second party system. By the time of Jackson's first election in 1828, most states had removed most significant property requirements for voting by white men, but property and tax-paying limitations were still serious in Rhode Island, Virginia, and Louisiana, and South Carolina's electoral votes were still determined by its legislature. Despite this wide availability of the franchise, however, only about one quarter of adult white males cast a ballot in the Presidential election of 1824. Four years later, participation reached 56.3 percent in the exciting Adams-Jackson contest of 1828. Turnout stayed about the same for the elections of 1832 and 1836, but surged up to 78.0 percent in 1840 and remained near the same high level for the rest of the antebellum period.

Within most states, moreover, the largest spurt in voter turnout can be linked to the earliest organization of popular political parties, and not simply to the charismatic appeal of Andrew Jackson himself. The statistics seem to show that Jacksonian party organizations were able to arouse high levels of enthusiasm among voters and to bring them to the polls in much higher proportions than was typical in the early nineteenth century or throughout the twentieth.

Increased turnout combined with the events of Jackson's Presidency to erode state and sectional-based politics. During the 1820s, most states cast a lopsided vote for a single candidate, but state races grew more competitive as many more voters decided to participate. Under Jackson, moreover, the Democratic Party grew stronger where it once had been weak and weakened where it once was strong. As the parties became more closely matched at the grass roots, the contest for President became a central recurrent ritual in almost every community. By the same token, prominent state leaders could no longer take their fiefdoms for granted and could not throw the weight of a united state electorate to whomever they chose. To maintain control in most states, they needed a clean bill of party health, and that required cooperation with fellow partisans from other states. The politics of sectionalism was accordingly weakened.

Voters who were mobilized by the second party system chose a party loyalty early and tended to stick with it, usually voting the same way, year after year, in local, state, and federal elections. If they ever felt dissatisfied with their party's nominee, most voters seem to have preferred not to vote at all, rather than vote for the candidate of the opposing party. In quantitative terms, William G. Shade has shown that the Pearson correlation coefficient between the 1828 vote for Andrew Jackson and his support four years later stands at more than +.90; correlations between the Democratic returns for President from 1840 and 1852 range between +.70 and +.80, and state-level contests showed an equally high level of party loyalty.* In such circumstances, politicians usu-

---

* Statisticians use "Pearson correlation coefficients" to measure the relationship between two sets of data, such as the election returns of two different years. The coefficient varies from +1.0 (which indicates a perfect positive relationship) to 0 (which indicates no relationship at all) to −1.0 (which indicates a perfect negative relationship). A correlation of +.90 thus shows that Andrew Jackson's 1832 vote in most states was almost exactly proportional to his vote there in 1828.

ally did not try to convert members of the opposition to their own cause. Instead of seeking to sway the undecided, candidates made speeches and shook hands to keep up the enthusiasm of their own party followers, while managers made every effort to identify party members and to get them to the polls without fail.

These tactics required elaborate measures of local organization. Committees of neighborhood activists kept close contact with individual voters, reinforcing their loyalty with campaign literature and bringing them faithfully to the polls. Coordinating these efforts, an elaborate hierarchy of county, district, and state conventions took shape, each one charged with selecting nominees for the appropriate set of elections, choosing delegates to the next highest round of party gatherings, and adopting resolutions of sentiment on particular public issues. Conventions theoretically bound all participants to support the eventual nominee, and party insiders sought to control conventions' outcomes by prearrangements, but they could not guarantee success and had to pay careful attention when insurgent local conventions gave notice that leaders were drifting out of touch with active public opinion at the grass roots. To complement this system of conventions, Democrats took the lead in establishing permanent central committees at both the state and national levels, to coordinate party activity during election campaigns and periods when conventions could not meet.

Consistent party voting spread from general elections into Congress. After 1835, 90 percent of all Democrats in the U.S. House of Representatives voted the same way in about two thirds of all roll-call votes, and their Whig colleagues reached a similar level of cohesion by the early 1840s. For the life of the second party system, most congressmen continued to worship at the "shrine of party" and voted on party rather than sectional lines. Over the same period, congressional committee assignments fell under partisan control and the contest for Speaker of the House of Representatives settled into a straightforward test of party strength. By the mid- to late 1830s, similar levels of party discipline had also appeared in most state legislatures.

The contrast between Whig and Democratic behavior clearly grew out of conflicting economic and sectional goals, as Whigs advocated the rapid transformation of America's economy and Democrats tended to resist it. But did the Whigs and Democrats really represent different classes or interests? Did they draw their votes and leadership from contrasting segments of society, or were party choices based on more intangible factors? Is it possible, as some historians have argued, that party rivalry was based on nothing more than personal ambition for public office, and that differences in party rhetoric were mere "claptrap" masking a fundamental consensus on matters of public policy?

Historians have had difficulty settling these questions precisely. From time to time, scholars have attempted to locate the core Jacksonian constituency among frontiersmen, or small farmers, or urban workers, or slaveowners, or upwardly mobile businessmen, only to have these generalizations upset by the citation of contrary examples. Certainly the Jacksonian party won some support from all these groups, but so did the Whigs. In most places, no one recorded the political preferences of average citizens, and the states that did so can be rightfully regarded as exceptional; no definitive national comparison of the income, wealth, occupation, or education of Whigs and Democrats can ever be made. Even if the data were available, moreover, it is doubtful that any mathematical calculation could entirely explain the origins of party preferences, for numbers alone do not reveal what the parties meant to their adherents. Like their modern counterparts, Jacksonian voters based their political choices on values and attitudes that they shared with others in a living community only partly defined by concrete matters such as wealth or birthplace. Rigid formulas to explain party choices will never be fully reliable, but a few general themes stand out from the local studies that have been made.

First, most political leaders were wealthier and better educated than the average citizen, from the highest levels of the federal government down to the lowest county or ward committee. Then as now, a certain level of income and leisure was necessary to give a potential activist the opportunity to pursue political influence, and up to a point, the more powerful the position, the more wealth and leisure were needed to pursue it. Political success brought tangible rewards, moreover, since the best positions were well paid compared to the incomes of average Americans. Most United States senators were thus wealthier than most ward committeemen. In this sense, like modern political parties, neither party in Jacksonian America was strictly representative of the common man.

Once allowances are made for the privileged status of officeholders in general, however, some clear differences between the parties are apparent. Many of the most detailed studies have been undertaken for the Southern states, and the authors generally find that Whig officeholders were wealthier than their Democratic counterparts. In 1850, for example, Whig legislators in Georgia, Florida, Alabama, North Carolina, Kentucky, and Tennessee owned more valuable land than the Democrats, though the reverse was true in Virginia, Mississippi, and Arkansas. In most of these states, the same pattern held in the distribution of slave property. If Whigs were not entirely a "broadcloth and silk stocking party" in the Old South, their strength did seem to lie in those districts which chose the wealthier representatives.

It also seems clear that the nation's very wealthiest urban leaders were overwhelmingly Whig. To be precise, two studies of New Yorkers and Bostonians worth more than $100,000 in the 1840s found that 84.3 percent of the former and 89.0 percent of the latter were Whigs. These results are hardly surprising; given the very vocal differences between the parties on the subject of great wealth, it would be remarkable if rich men did not prefer the Whig Party. The studies are significant, however, because they indicate that influential contemporaries did not regard the parties' rhetoric as meaningless.

Finally, both parties were fairly evenly matched among rank-and-file voters. It could hardly be otherwise, since neither party could hope to find a voting majority based exclusively on the very rich or the very poor. Even so, quantitative studies have tended to show that Whigs had a greater advantage among market-directed or urban-oriented voters, while Democrats had the edge in communities of isolated farmers or permanent wage earners. In North Carolina, voters in county seats were much more likely to prefer Whigs than their neighbors in rural precincts. In Boston, all neighborhoods of the city were Whig, but poor wards had a much higher proportion of Democrats than the average ward. When most of the Whig voters of Rochester signed a pro-bank petition in 1834, 81 percent of mill owners rallied to the cause, but only 10 percent of the day laborers. These data are not conclusive, but they are highly suggestive. The conclusion of an exhaustive study of Alabama politics by Professor Thomas B. Alexander and his students would probably apply to most of the nation's rural areas: "In the counties with the more advanced stages of general economic development, with the greater cash cropping and the greater commercial contacts with the outside world, in short, in the counties more nearly in the main stream of the national and world economy, Whig party appeals were more effective. And these appeals were more effective to [*sic*] all types of voters regardless of individual economic status." Conversely, Democrats were more popular in regions where the inroads of the Market Revolution were more limited, and more dreaded, than in more commercialized areas. In big cities and other areas where the power of commerce was already supreme, Democrats were more popular among those who resented the effects of change, most notably workingmen who were losing the chance for a shop of their own as market pressures tightened on their ranks.

In addition, ethnocultural tension also affected the choices of Jacksonian voters, but it did not supplant such questions as "equal rights" or the Bank War, issues actually at the forefront of Jacksonian party discourse. Among all groups, the issues of cultural difference and class conflict were too deeply intertwined for us to say that religion or ethnicity by itself was more important than other matters.

Differences in party ideology ran parallel to differences in social profile. Whigs and Democrats both drew heavily on republican traditions and both worried about the balance between liberty and power, but they diverged profoundly over the specific powers they feared and the liberties they sought to protect. For the Washington *Globe*, the main issue of the election of 1840 continued to be "SHALL THIS BE A GOVERNMENT OF THE BANKS OR OF THE PEOPLE?" and Democrats continued to believe that liberty was in greatest danger from the power of what they often called "associated wealth." For the triumphant Harrison, however, the election had pitted "the spirit of liberty" against the "the spirit of party," and for his fellow Whigs the greatest danger to individual freedom remained the folly, the passions, and the ignorance of human masses, especially when aroused by demagogues and spoilsmen.

Starting with a common ideological tradition, the two parties had selected and embellished contrasting strands of republican doctrine as they confronted the social and political implications of economic change. For Democrats, a republic was not possible without a virtuous and independent citizenry, and political independence could not exist without a basis in economic independence. Clearly harking back to Jefferson's vision of a self-sufficient yeomanry, Democratic radical Orestes Brownson articulated an implicit ideal of Democratic theory and policy when he called for a society where "instead of one man's working for another and receiving wages therefor, all men will be independent proprietors, working on their own capitals, on their own farms, or in their own shops." Like the Working Men's theorist Thomas Skidmore, Brownson demanded the abolition of inheritance and the redistribution of wealth, radical notions that mainstream Democrats totally rejected even when they shared his fundamental ideals. For party editor Francis P. Blair, for example, the key issue was not the ownership of capital but whether a worker could govern his own life. He therefore honored, in his words,

> the healthy mechanic or artisan, who works for himself at his own shop, or if he goes abroad, returns home to his meals every day, and sleeps under his own roof every night; whose earnings are regulated by the wants of the community at large, not by the discretion of a pernicious master; whose hours of labor depend on universal custom; who, when the sun goes down, is a freeman until he rises again; who can eat his meals in comfort, and sleep as long as nature requires.

Whether they toiled on farms or in workshops, such independent citizens comprised "the producing classes," "the great body of the people," "the bone and sinew of the country" whom Andrew Jackson invoked again and again as the wellspring of public virtue and the greatest guardians and beneficiaries of republicanism.

Jacksonians tended to view history as an eternal struggle between the many and the few, between the liberty of the virtuous and productive majority and the power of a wicked and greedy minority that sought to exploit them. The American Revolution had given the majority the power to protect itself, but the rapid growth of an advanced capitalist society seemed to put the Revolution's triumphs at risk. By creating new and formidable concentrations of wealth and reducing unlucky citizens to a permanently unequal status, the Market Revolution posed a profound threat to the Republic. In the words of a New Jersey orator, "If there is any danger to be feared in a republican government, it is the danger of associated wealth, with special privileges and without personal liability. It is the aristocracy of wealth we have to fear; and that is the only aristocracy from which danger is to be apprehended."

The solution, Democrats insisted tirelessly, must begin with "Equal Rights," and they made this slogan a constant byword of their discourse. At the height of the Bank War, Andrew Jackson himself had called "equality among the people in the rights conferred by the Government" "the great radical principle of freedom," and his supporters were quick to agree. A popular song among Democratic shoe workers, for example, wove the idea of equality among punning references to the tools of the shoemaker's trade in order to declare the basis for their nascent labor union.

> Now EQUAL RIGHTS *the motto*
> Wax *your* threads *as true* souls *ought to;*
> *Though the run-*round *bosses bristle,*
> *We'll raise a* peg*, and let them whistle.*
> *Stick to the* last*, brave cordwainers!*
> *In the end you'll* awl *be gainers!*

The theme of equal rights likewise appeared as a standard feature of ordinary Democratic campaign platforms. As New York delegates put it in 1840, "True Democracy . . . looks upon men as equals, entitled to equal influence in public affairs, and to equal protection in their private walks."

Perhaps the most dedicated proponent of Democratic equality was William Leggett, the Loco-Foco editor of the New York *Evening Post*. Leggett carried the principle of equality much further than most other Democrats, but his basic views were widely shared and President Van Buren recognized him with party patronage. Arguing in a series of stinging editorials in the middle 1830s, Leggett declared that "the fundamental principle of all governments is the protection of person and property from foreign and domestic enemies; in other words, to defend the weak against the strong." Leggett's sentence may appear illogical to twentieth-century readers, for later reformers who wished to protect the weak have attempted to redistribute property rather than simply protect it and have championed special government programs to benefit particular groups: Social Security for the aged, welfare for the poor, affirmative action for minorities, and so on. Leggett and his fellow Jacksonians envisioned no such programs, however. When they thought about unequal laws, they remembered the large body of Whiggish provisions to encourage new forms of economic activity: protective tariffs, corporate charters, subsidies to internal-improvements companies, and a long list of special privileges for the bankers who issued the nation's currency. They therefore tended to agree with Leggett that "the sole reliance of the laboring classes is the great principle of *equal rights*," and they relied on legal equality to protect the poor against economic oppression.

The Democratic doctrine of equal rights had a special meaning in the slaveholding South. "Equal rights" there implied "states' rights," or the equal rights of slaveholders to preserve their local institutions. As the Democratic national platform of 1844 put it, "every citizen *and every section of the country* [italics added] has a right to demand and insist upon an equality of rights and privileges." Though Jackson had insisted on federal supremacy in the nullification crisis, he had backed down on the substance of the tariff question, indicating that the federal government would not force-feed a Northern industrial economy at Southern expense. In the name of states' rights, Jacksonians had also allowed Southerners to persecute the Indians and rob the mails of abolitionist literature. Using the states'-rights formula to maintain a carefully neutral position on slavery, Democrats preserved their party as an intersectional alliance. For the remainder of the antebellum period, the national Democratic Party remained far more protective of Southern autonomy than any of its competitors.

"Limited government" was a natural Democratic corollary to the ideas of states' rights and civic equality. If vigorous government activity was usually harmful, Democrats reasoned, it was best for government to do as little as possible. "The world is governed too much" became the motto of the Washington *Globe*, and Jacksonians coined the slogan "That government is best which governs least." As Democrats saw it, activist government appealed to selfishness by offering financial rewards to favored classes and individuals, and thus corrupted the Republic by inspiring a scramble for public plunder. To preempt such selfish attacks, Jackson warned, government must "confine itself to equal protection, and, as Heaven does its rain, shower its favors alike on the high and the low, the rich and the poor." As he acknowledged, this policy would leave certain inequalities in place, for "equality of talents, of education, or of wealth cannot be produced by human institutions." Even so, limited government was better than the alternative.

The Democrats' commitment to equal rights and limited government buttressed their support for popular democracy, always understood to mean rule by the majority of free white men. If citizens' rights were to be equal, all must have an equal vote, and public questions should be settled by the public voice. Old Hickory had glorified "the will of the people" even before the machinations of Adams and Clay stripped him of his Presidential victory in 1824 and 1825. Thereafter, as historian Robert Remini has emphasized, he called for the direct election of senators, judges, and the President, rotation in office, and the right of voters to instruct their representatives in Congress. Nor did this interest in democracy stop with President Jackson. In 1837 John L. O'Sullivan, who edited the party intellectual journal *The Democratic Review*, defined his magazine's central task as "the advocacy of that high and holy *democratic principle* [and] the vindication of that principle from the charges daily brought against it." In the states, Democrats usually took the lead in expanding the right to vote, in making legislatures more responsive to majority views, in expanding the number of elective offices, in offering binding instructions to members of Congress, and in submitting controversial laws to the tests of popular referendums.

Jacksonian Democrats likewise championed U.S. territorial expansion. Long before he became President, Jackson had taken the law into his own hands to promote the acquisition of Florida, and his fellow Democrats worked tirelessly for the annexation of Texas and Oregon. Democratic President James K. Polk had the strong support of his party when he pushed for war with Mexico, hoping to gain California, Utah, and New Mexico in the process. When American armies succeeded in the invasion of Mexico itself, some Democrats even called for the conquest and absorption of "all Mexico," only to relent when they realized how many millions of Indians and mixed-blooded Hispanic people would thus be added to the national population. Coining the phrase that summed up the policy of national territorial expansion, editor John L. O'Sullivan used *The Democratic Review* to proclaim America's "manifest destiny to overspread and to possess the whole of the continent which Providence has given us for the development of the great experiment of liberty."

Territorial ambitions were closely tied to Democrats' worries about economic change. During the Hayne-Webster debates, South Carolina's Senator Hayne revived an old canard that New England sought to impoverish ordinary yeomen by depriving them of the chance to move West, and thereby forcing them to accept low-paying jobs in the early factory system. Fearing a somewhat different fate, slaveholding Democrats worried that a shortage of new slave territory might hem in the plantation system, leaving the slave states outnumbered in Congress and surrounded by hostile societies devoted to free labor. Hoping to allay these anxieties, Democrats favored cheap land prices and settlers' preemption privileges. These policies would offer a second chance to hard-pressed farmers and planters from the seaboard states, they reasoned, and Eastern employers would keep wages high in order to retain their labor force. The doctrines of Manifest Destiny were usually expressed in ringing tones of spread-eagle nationalism, but the aggressive slogans masked a defensive inspiration.

The Democrats' commitment to equality for whites led them to welcome foreign immigrants to America and to champion the cause of foreign republican revolutions. The Democratic platform of 1840 cited "the liberal principles embodied by Jefferson in the Declaration of Independence" to denounce "every attempt to abridge the present privilege of becoming citizens, and the owners of soil among us." The same plank appeared verbatim in every subsequent Democratic platform through 1856. In frontier states such as Michigan, moreover, Democratic legislators were willing to extend voting rights to all white male "residents" whether or not they were fully naturalized U.S. citizens, while Whigs were far more reluctant to enfranchise immigrant newcomers. Neither party was initially exempt from nativist prejudice, but the Whig embrace of the evangelical reform agenda frequently put them at odds with working-class, Catholic, and foreign-born voters, while the Democratic defense of liberty made room for widely divergent private behavior. As foreign immigration swelled in the 1840s, class and cultural issues intersected and German and Irish newcomers found readier acceptance in Democratic ranks and became a mainstay of party strength throughout the North.

If insistence on white male equality made Democrats receptive to the immigrant, it likewise hardened their attitudes to Americans of other races. Racism and support for slavery were thus logical aspects of Democratic Party ideology. The same national platforms that defended the rights of white immigrants denounced abolitionism by name and insisted "that Congress has no power, under the constitution, to interfere with or control the domestic institutions of the several States." Speaking for the Jackson Administration, Attorney General Roger Brooke Taney declared that free blacks were "a separate and degraded people" who could never be recognized as citizens of the United States. Twenty-five years later, Chief Justice Taney repeated this opinion in his decision on the famous Dred Scott case. Southern Democrats tended to agree with John C. Calhoun that slavery was a "positive good" rather than a necessary evil, while Northern Democrats asserted their own full equality by repeatedly attacking the claims of blacks. Northern Democratic legislators took the lead in narrowing or abolishing the few political rights still held by free blacks. Even when they showed no sympathy for slavery per se, Northern Democrats usually opposed abolitionism on the grounds that emancipation would send waves of freed blacks northward to compete with working-class whites. At the popular level, Democratic activists and local leaders kept close ties to the emerging tradition of blackface minstrel shows, in which white actors lampooned blacks and entertained all-male, urban audiences with racist songs and comedy. Even when Pennsylvania Democrat David Wilmot broke loose from Southern leadership in 1847 and demanded the exclusion of slavery from the territories gained from Mexico, he did so in the name of white supremacy. "I plead the cause and the rights of white free men," he declared to the House of Representatives. "I would preserve to free white labor a fair country, a rich inheritance, where the sons of toil, of my own race and color, can live without the disgrace which association with negro slavery brings upon free labor." For the rest of the antebellum period, Wilmot's brand of "antislavery" was as far as most Northern Democrats could go.

Beginning with the same body of republican tradition as the Democrats, the Whigs chose to emphasize different themes within it and offered a dramatically different assessment of economic changes promised by the Market Revolution. As early as 1824, Henry Clay had put market principles at the core of his social values, and proclaimed that "the greatest want of civilized society is a market for the sale and exchange of the surplus of the produce

. . . of its members." Subsequent Whigs fully shared his enthusiasm for civilization and commerce. John Quincy Adams had expressed a similar vision in his first annual message, declaring that "liberty is power," rejoicing that "the spirit of improvement is abroad upon the earth," and warning Congress not to be "palsied by the will of our constituents." Daniel Webster would endow these values with a thrilling patriotic cast as he hymned the twin glories of the Union and the protective tariff. Southern Whigs shared this vision when they fought for internal improvements to transport the products of their plantations, for banks to finance their trade, for distribution of the proceeds of public lands to pay for state investments and for public education. Whig farmers and mechanics of the free states joined the same circle when they accepted the importance of urban markets and the value of tariff protection. By their own lights, the Whigs could claim with justice to have something for everybody.

Throughout the period of their existence, Whigs insisted on the importance of economic progress through diversity, in which varied interests grew more specialized and more prosperous by exchanging their respective products and talents through the marketplace. Like Daniel Webster, Henry Clay drew easily on an organic model of society and denied "any real incompatibility between the interests of Agriculture, Commerce and Manufactures. . . . A conflict between them would be just as unnatural and absurd, as between members of the human body." But if the body was to be a model for society, some members must command the head while others performed the inferior tasks of bone and muscle. A leading Tennessee Whig thus protested the "fatal tendency" of Democrats "to array the ignorant against the intelligent, the poor against the rich, the wicked against the pious, the vulgar against the decent, the worthless against the worthy, and thieves against honest men." From time to time, Whig extremists denounced what they saw as the ruinous consequences of universal suffrage. More commonly, they stressed the compatibility of all classes and interests and explained how "the producing classes" included lawyers, bankers, and merchants as well as laborers, artisans, and farmers. Whigs thus insisted that the capitalists of America had risen to wealth by their own merits and not by special privileges, and promised that every frugal and hardworking citizen could follow them. Avoiding flat denials of republican equality, the Whigs implied clearly that political leadership was best left to those who had already achieved economic success. As historian John Ashworth has put it, they "maintained an almost deafening silence on the entire subject of political democracy."

Given the scarcity of capital in America and the nation's vulnerable position in relation to better-established English manufacturers, Whigs were quick to sense that their vision of economic progress would depend on government encouragement. Clay's American System was a complex, interlocking program for economic development that neatly tied protective tariffs to distribution, federal subsidy of internal improvements, and a powerful national bank, all of which required active management by the national government. Following their notions of improvement, Whigs likewise lent active government support to a wide range of useful or benevolent private enterprises: banks; corporations; transportation projects; public hospitals; prisons; institutions for the blind, the deaf, and the insane; public schools; and temperance crusades. Inspired by evangelical piety, they gave generously to and served actively in missionary societies, reform associations, temperance unions, and, significantly, antislavery societies. If "the spirit of improvement [was] abroad upon the earth," as John Quincy Adams declared, Whigs were in its forefront.

The Whig preoccupation with "improvement" left the party with little enthusiasm for territorial expansion. Unlike most Democrats, Whigs longed to replace the primitive subsistence economy with refined patterns of moral and technological development. In their eyes, the acquisition of new unsettled territory was more likely to dilute or attenuate the forces of order and civilization and to slow down national progress. In the 1844 Presidential election, front-runners Martin Van Buren and Henry Clay both came out against the immediate annexation of Texas. Van Buren's stand cost him the Democratic nomination, while Clay retained the favor of the Whigs. During the Mexican War that followed, even Southern Whigs denounced the Democrats' hunger for more territory, correctly predicting that expansion would precipitate a fatal struggle over slavery. When Democrats shouted "Manifest Destiny," Whigs replied with Daniel Webster, "You have a Sparta, embellish it!"

Whigs were likewise reluctant to enfranchise large numbers of foreign immigrants, particularly those who did not subscribe to middle-class standards of respectability. Though Whig employers were eager to obtain the cheap labor that the newcomers provided, they preferred to withhold full acceptance, including the right to vote, from prospective citizens who showed insufficient faith in hard work, self-improvement, thrift, sobriety, punctuality, and evangelical piety. Some Whigs, notably New York Governor William Seward, made strenuous efforts to appeal to immigrant voters and to meet their legitimate needs. More commonly, Whigs tended to reject those whom North Carolina Senator Willie P. Mangum called "the bandit of the Apennines, the mercenary Swiss, the hungry loafer of the cities of the Old World, the offal of the disgorged jails, penitentiaries, and houses of correction of foreign countries." Though nativism and anti-Catholicism appeared occasionally in both parties, they were far more prevalent among Whigs than Democrats.

If Whigs were unwilling to grant full rights to "unqualified" immigrants, their acceptance of human inequality made them more willing than Democrats to accord partial rights to blacks and Indians. Instead of treating manhood and full citizenship as indivisible, Whigs could envision a gradation of rights and responsibilities ranging from one end of the social scale to the other. Edward Everett thus maintained that "the wholly untutored white man is little better than the wholly untutored red man," while the Whig editor of the *American Review* declared that "free institutions are not proper to the *white* man, but the courageous, upright and moral man." Democrats tended to oppose any suffrage rights for nonwhites, but even Southern Whigs could occasionally support the right to vote for free blacks who could pass requirements such as a property test. Though Southern Whigs were just as protective of the rights of slaveholders as Democrats were, Northern party members were more receptive to abolitionism than their Democratic neighbors. The Liberty and Free Soil parties found Whig areas such as the Burnt-Over District congenial territory for hunting votes, while Democratic mobs were quick to stone, tar-and-feather, or even murder antislavery spokesmen.

How did the Whigs reconcile their unease with white equality and democracy in an America ruled by white male suffrage and the rhetoric of majority rule? In part, the Whigs failed to reconcile these conflicting pressures and thus lagged behind Democrats in their ability to forge a party organization and win public office. As the campaign of 1840 showed, however, Whigs could democratize their doctrine by promising ordinary voters a wider diffusion of prosperity as a result of Whig measures such as the tariff or a sound credit system. In democratic Whig parlance, the true aristocrats were the spoilsmen who would monopolize the privileges of office for themselves and their corrupted henchmen, not the entrepreneurs who opened the benefits of the Market Revolution to everyone. Jacksonians might charge repeatedly that the Whig program sacrificed liberty for elusive wealth, but Whigs could argue in reply that the combination of liberty with poverty was meaningless, that a poor nation could not be truly free any more than a poor man could. A progressive, commercial civilization offered true liberty to Americans, Whigs argued, by freeing men from ignorance, isolation, and primitive frontier conditions. Learning to minimize the elitist implications of their doctrines, Whigs could present an attractive political program that won majority support in many states and districts, and occasionally in Presidential elections.

Despite their ideological divergence, moderate Whig and Democratic spokesmen shared a pragmatic commitment to compromise and negotiation within the framework of the existing laws and Constitution. The decentralized nature of American government left Whigs to pursue a program of subsidized economic development in the states they controlled, while Democrats insisted on *laissez-faire* policies in Washington. Partisans of both sides could thus be somewhat satisfied in the midst of the most heated disagreements. Democratic attacks on "monopoly" never went so far as to authorize a full-scale class war on concentrated capital, moreover, and even the Bank veto ruled out more radical measures to implement its principles or attack existing grants of privilege. No matter how much they suffered at the polls or muttered darkly of revolution, no dire emergency ever tempted senior Whigs to discuss extralegal measures to defend their favored interests, as the nullificationists did. Outside the ranks of a few ideologues, moreover, many Democratic politicians saw the practical advantages of Whiggish forms of progress and were prepared to welcome them if particular interests got no undue privileges from the state. Over time, moreover, Whigs as well as Democrats developed a facility for working with the party tools of electoral politics, effectively using mass appeals to win their objectives by democratic means. Whig and Democratic Americans used the second party system to thrash out basic disagreements over economic change, but there was never any question of taking that fight outside the realm of conventional politics.

How much Whigs and Democrats agreed with one another is clearer when we look at the experience of John C. Calhoun, the one major player in the arena of antebellum politics who did not accept the basic party principles of the contest. Calhoun's base was in South Carolina, the one state of the Old South that lacked a significant nonplantation section and a politically powerful bloc of white nonslaveholders. Unlike their other Southern colleagues, planter-politicians of South Carolina had no experience with political trade-offs or the balance of contending interests. They shared the same opinions and material concerns, even the same family connections. They expected to run South Carolina exactly as they chose, and most of the time they did so, rarely stooping to the vulgar arts of democratic electioneering or bowing to the demands of contending interests. Carrying the same attitudes to national politics, they never seriously conceded that the benefits of the federal Union might require from them any substantial sacrifices in return. Instead, they tended to regard compromise as total defeat, a degrading affront unacceptable to men of honor and principle.

A product of his state's political culture and a spokesman for its elite, John C. Calhoun shared its repugnance for democratic politics and majority rule. He particularly resented compromises that might imperil "liberty," especially the liberty of white Southerners to enslave blacks. His efforts to defend slavery from the slightest challenge appeared in the nullification movement, in the drive to ban abolitionist petitions from Congress, and in the effort to acquire Texas. Throughout this long fight, Calhoun's chief enemy was not abolitionism itself but "corruption," a word he tended to use for any sacrifice of principle for the sake of some immediate practical advantage. It was "corruption" that would lead Southerners to lower their guard and abandon vital principles on which the defense of slavery depended, so Calhoun opposed it everywhere. He worried that the "corrupt bargain" between Adams and Clay would destroy liberty, and turned to Jackson as the only alternative. When Van Buren bested him in the factional rivalry of Jackson's early Presidency, Calhoun worried some more, and soon decided that even under Jackson, "a corrupt system to be founded on the abuse of the power and patronage of the government" would again put liberty in danger. Holding himself aloof from both political parties, Calhoun urged his fellow Southerners to shun the corruption of the party system and stand together as a united sectional interest in defense of slavery.

Calhoun's concerns about corruption blended easily with his doubts about democracy. While Democrats boasted loudly about the glories of majority rule, Calhoun's "Exposition and Protest" against the tariff had declared that "constitutional government and the government of a majority are utterly incompatible." Near the end of his life, he expanded on these observations in two lengthy treatises of political theory, the *Disquisition on Government* and the *Discourse on the Constitution and Government of the United States*, each warning against the tendency of numerical majorities in popular governments to plunder minorities and the tendencies of majorities to use corrupt methods to buy off opposition and maintain themselves in power. The *Disquisition* is famous for its suggestion that nothing but a "concurrent majority," based on the consent of all major interest groups in society, could protect liberty from the plundering tendency of a merely numerical majority. Among other things, the *Discourse* proposed to implement such a concurrent majority by establishing a dual Presidency, one each for the slave states and the free states, each with a veto over the actions of the other. Throughout these writings, and indeed throughout his career, Calhoun revealed an urgent need, as the *Disquisition* put it, to "[assign] to power and liberty their proper spheres."

In the light of early American thinking about republicanism, there was nothing unusual about Calhoun's fears about compromise, corruption, or partisanship. The political experience of the Jacksonian era, however, had brought Democratic politicians to a forthright endorsement of party measures and even persuaded most Whigs that the new tools of organization could actually remedy the problems that Calhoun still blamed them for. For him, parties could arise only from a selfish passion to possess the spoils of office and could be productive solely of corruption. The compromises necessary to keep a party together could only whittle away the principles necessary to defend minority rights. In practical terms, the compromises made by Southerners to maintain the existence of either national party would eventually give the nonslaveholding majority power to interfere with the liberty of the slaveholding minority. Drawing doleful lessons from the history of republics, Calhoun warned that the corruption growing from majority rule and party government could bring down the government. "Rome sank," he reminded his readers, "as must every community under similar circumstances, beneath the strong grasp, the despotic rule of the chieftain of the successful party;—the sad, but only alternative which remained to prevent universal violence, confusion and anarchy."

Calhoun fought partisanship by attempting to detach Southern leaders from the grip of Democrats and Whigs and unite them in a solid phalanx for the defense of slavery and other sectional interests. "Putting aside all minor divisions," he repeated tirelessly, "the South should unite as one man." It was for this reason that Calhoun had joined the Jacksonian coalition and initially sought to control it. Foiled by Van Buren's political skill and by Jackson's own independence, he assumed control of the nullification movement, hoping to shore up his position in South Carolina even while inspiring a sectionwide stand against the tariff. Defeated again, Calhoun watched bitterly as other Southern politicians divided the South into rival camps of Whigs and Democrats. Cooperating first with one, then with the other, Calhoun was happy with neither. He accepted the post of Secretary of State from the nonpartisan Tyler Administration and used it to pursue Texas and defend the Lone Star Republic against the abolitionist hopes of Great Britain, but he could not make this position into the stepping-stone to the Presidency that it had once been. Though South Carolina leaders kept aloof from the second party system, Calhoun was unable to detach more than a handful of other sectional leaders from the "shrine of party." While Calhoun sought a proper balance between power and liberty and further protection for his section's interests in impractical schemes such as the proposal for a dual Presidency, his Whig and Democratic colleagues were as yet content with the mechanisms of the party system itself. For a time, at least, serious Americans preferred an earnest debate over economic development to a pitched battle over slavery.

Eventually, the sectional confrontation that Calhoun longed for did disrupt the party forged by his ancient enemies Jackson and Van Buren. During the 1850s, Whigs and Democrats moved to compromise their differences over economic development, but the question of slavery's fate in the federal territories became so divisive that the Jacksonian party system disappeared. Though John C. Calhoun did not live to see the secession of the Southern states in the winter of 1860–61, the outbreak of the Civil War did vindicate his analysis of the underlying power of sectional tensions in antebellum politics.

Calhoun's prescience cannot detract from his antagonists of the Jacksonian era who put partisanship before sectional controversy. The leaders and voters who created the second party system faced a critical turning point in American social and political development that demanded political choices. Would the government promote the Market Revolution by a nationally coordinated policy of support? Would it tolerate piecemeal encouragement or resistance by the states? Or would it starve development by a policy of purposive inaction? Moreover, as economic changes created new social classes and new dependence upon the power of an impersonal market, would American political culture endorse the erection of new forms of social and political domination, or would leaders and citizens devise new forms of republican civic equality?

Wrestling with these questions, Americans of the Jacksonian era thrashed out settlements that left enduring consequences. The Market Revolution proceeded, but without the orderliness or the official sanction to favoritism that a national planning policy might have given it. In principle, civic equality became even more important than before and remained as an unfulfilled legacy to be claimed and disputed by succeeding generations of Americans. In the process, habits of partisan politics were established that have weakened in the twentieth century but never entirely disappeared.

Using the rhetoric of republicanism to justify their actions, Democrats and Whigs had altered many aspects of the tradition almost beyond recognition. Most obviously, eighteenth-century republicans had viewed the "common good" as solid and unitary and regarded political partisanship as evidence of corruption. By the 1850s American political activists took competing public interests for granted and accepted political parties as indispensable. If certain aspects of party politics still troubled sensitive citizens, most realized that such practices as party patronage systems or strict party discipline could be used for good purposes as well as bad. In the process of creating a party system, moreover, Americans had also overturned an older set of power relationships in society.

The traditional authorities of master and squire had given way to the more fluid power exercised by employers, ward bosses, and the marketplace itself. These shifts in turn had made it easier to broaden the circle of political rights, break down restraints of the popular will, and legitimize the power of the majority. Without disturbing the sanctity of private property, Americans had also jettisoned the notion that liberty depended on a formal balance between the power of property and the power of numbers.

Above all, the Jacksonians' celebration of the rights of the common man had encouraged the belief that individual self-improvement was the supreme goal of American society. It had become the government's highest duty to smooth the way for this process, by providing the tools for improvement—education and transportation facilities, for example—or simply by getting out of the way. If we can believe their own statements, neither the Whigs nor the Democrats had intended such an individualistic outcome. Each party had spoken instead for its own vision of a larger American community. Nevertheless, the changes in the republican tradition encouraged by the Whigs and Democrats had brought Americans closer to a "liberal" view of society and government by the end of the Jacksonian era.

Even so, the transition was still incomplete. No matter how much the United States had changed in the Age of Jackson, a look at political history and party rhetoric reveals that innovation had been carried out under the auspices of diverse themes in traditional republican values. When he killed the Monster Bank, for example, Jackson had acted in the name of an older economy of small producers, not for a wide-open system of unhindered capitalist development. For their part, the Whigs' nostalgia for older patterns of deference shows clearly that their eyes, too, were firmly fixed on the past, even as they laid the groundwork for a future industrial economy.

While they learned the trade of broker-politician, moreover, party operators learned increasingly that one set of interest conflicts could not be bartered or compromised successfully. Slavery and free-labor advocates could not split the differences between them; they were obliged to see their interests in essentially republican terms, as matters of life or death, of indivisible public good that demanded a total solution. More and more insistently, the slavery question called Americans to make an absolute commitment for the defense of liberty against power, variously defined as the "Slave Power" in the North or as the menace of "Black Republicanism" in the South. The transition from republican to liberal politics could never be complete while this issue remained unsettled.

Republican rhetoric has never disappeared from American politics. It has survived with special vitality among those who raise voices of protest, who wish to rally the "people" in self-defense against oppressive powers that afflict them. Jacksonian rhetoric was especially characteristic of the Populist movement of the late nineteenth century and in innumerable episodes of community protest in the twentieth, from incidents of labor insurgency to more "conservative" movements such as tax revolts or opposition to "forced busing." Language that pitted liberty and virtue against power and corruption was likewise prevalent in the Watergate scandal, as Americans rediscovered republican reflexes that many had forgotten. The Jacksonian role in preserving these instincts has clearly been pivotal.

The legacy of Jacksonian politics has thus proved far more durable than its specific institutions. Americans have continued to worry about the balance between liberty and power, generally preferring a balance that has tilted toward liberty. Even when party loyalties seem to wane among the voters, government without a two-party system seems inconceivable. For better or worse, support for the institutions of a centrally managed economy died with the Monster Bank, and confidence in an efficient, independent, and nonpartisan civil service never fully recovered from "rotation in office." Today, conservatives oppose the inhibiting restraints of "big government," while liberals favor government actions to restrain "monopolies" that threaten individual liberty: racial or gender discrimination, environmental polluters, or big business itself. Both sides are faithful to certain strands of the Jacksonian republican legacy. Both sides also seek to appeal directly to the "people" over the "interests" who bind their will, whether these are defined as labor unions or corporate lobbyists, meddlesome bureaucrats or fraudulent defense contractors. Equality and democracy are likewise enduring slogans, while corruption and abuse of power are still favorite political enemies. If Andrew Jackson could never restore the old Republic, he succeeded remarkably in shaping the changing Republic that followed him.

Essay on Sources

American historians have repeatedly sifted the surviving evidence of "Jacksonian democracy," hoping to find there some clue to the essence of American democracy in general. Printed literature on the subject is therefore vast, as scholars have interpreted and reinterpreted what they have found. I have learned an enormous amount from my predecessors in this field and I encourage every interested reader to do likewise. The following is an abbreviated list of works that I have found most useful in preparing this book.

General Sources

Interested readers may begin with one or more very useful bibliographies and historiographical essays. I have relied extensively on Robert V. Remini and Edwin A. Miles, comps., *The Era of Good Feelings and the Age of Jackson, 1816–1841* (Arlington Heights, Ill., 1979). An incisive critique of recent literature appears in Sean Wilentz, "On Class and Politics in Jacksonian America," *Reviews in American History* 10 (1982), 43–63, while the bibliographical essay in Edward Pessen's *Jacksonian America* (Homewood, Ill., 1978) is the most comprehensive of its genre.

The first interpreters of Jacksonian America were the foreign visitors who streamed across the Atlantic to report on the young Republic for a curious European audience. The preeminent commentator was Alexis de Tocqueville, whose *Democracy in America*, J. P. Mayer, ed.; 2 vols. (New York, 1966) is still carefully gleaned for insights on the character and destiny of the United States. Of Tocqueville's fellow tourists, I have especially benefited from Michel Chevalier, *Society, Manners, and Politics in the United States*

(Boston, 1839); Harriet Martineau, *Society in America*, 3 vols. (London, 1838); Basil Hall, *Travels in North America, in the Years 1827 and 1828*, 3 vols. (Edinburgh, 1928); Frances M. Trollope, *Domestic Manners of the Americans* (New York, 1949); and Thomas Hamilton, *Men and Manners in America*, 2 vols. (Philadelphia, 1833).

The most widely known survey of Jacksonian America is Arthur M. Schlesinger, Jr.'s *The Age of Jackson* (New York, 1945). Schlesinger attracted a large public following, but a generation of historians rebuked him for portraying Old Hickory as a harbinger of Franklin D. Roosevelt and the New Deal. In the 1950s, "consensus" historians preferred to think of Jacksonians as entrepreneurs or "expectant capitalists" who fought monopoly to advance their own fortunes. The classic expression of their views is the chapter on Jackson in Richard Hofstadter, *The American Political Tradition* (New York, 1948). Writing from the same "entrepreneurialist" perspective, Glyndon G. Van Deusen prepared a popular survey of the period, *The Jacksonian Era, 1828–1848* (New York, 1959). More recently, Robert H. Wiebe has offered an ambitious and admirable analysis in *The Opening of American Society: From the Constitution to the Eve of Disunion* (New York, 1984). Finally, through the generosity of Charles Sellers, I was able to examine the manuscript of his forthcoming volume in the Oxford History of the United States series, after my own work had gone to press. To be titled *The Market Revolution, 1815–1848*, Sellers's work promises to be an outstanding synthesis of the culture and politics of antebellum America.

For more direct access to the world of Jacksonian public life, students should turn to the published collections of private papers left by leading politicians of the era. For my purposes, the most valuable of these has been John Spencer Bassett, ed., *Correspondence of Andrew Jackson*, 7 vols. (Washington, D.C., 1926–35). A complete edition of the Jackson papers has also begun to appear; see Sam B. Smith et al., eds., *The Papers of Andrew Jackson*, 2 vols. to date (Knoxville, Tenn., 1980–). For the texts of official pronouncements by Jackson and other Presidents, I have relied on James D. Richardson, comp., *A Compilation of the Messages and Papers of the Presidents*, 10 vols. (Washington, D.C., 1896–98).

Among Jackson's major adversaries, Clay, Webster, and Calhoun are all honored by ongoing publications series of their private and public correspondence. See James F. Hopkins et al., eds., *The Papers of Henry Clay*, 8 vols. to date (Lexington, Ky., 1959–); Charles M. Wiltse et al., eds., *The Papers of Daniel Webster*, 15 vols. in 3 series to date (Hanover, N.H., 1974–); and Robert L. Meriwether et al., eds., *The Papers of John C. Calhoun*, 18 vols. to date (Columbia, S.C., 1959–). These men were also the subjects of earlier collections of letters and speeches which must be consulted for the texts that incompleted modern series have not yet republished. See Calvin Colton, ed., *The Works of Henry Clay*, 6 vols. (New

York, 1857); J. W. McIntyre, ed., *The Writings and Speeches of Daniel Webster*, 18 vols. (Boston, 1903); and Richard K. Crallé, ed., *Works of John C. Calhoun*, 6 vols. (New York, 1853–55). The reader should also sample Charles Francis Adams, ed., *Memoirs of John Quincy Adams, Comprising Portions of His Diary from 1795 to 1848*, 12 vols. (Philadelphia, 1874–77).

The papers of Jackson's leading supporters are less well served than those of his opponents, but see Thomas Hart Benton, *Thirty Years View*, 2 vols. (New York, 1854), and Herbert Weaver et al., eds., *Correspondence of James K. Polk*, 7 vols. to date (Nashville, 1969–   ). Rambling but invaluable, John C. Fitzpatrick, ed., "The Autobiography of Martin Van Buren," appears in Vol. II of the *Annual Report of the American Historical Association for the Year 1918* (Washington, D.C., 1920).

A number of fine biographies also cover the lives of the leading antebellum politicians. The most important of these are not only detailed accounts of their subjects' careers, but indispensable sources for the period as a whole. I have benefited immeasurably from the fine scholarship and vivid prose of Robert V. Remini's *Andrew Jackson and the Course of American Empire, 1767–1821* (New York, 1977); *Andrew Jackson and the Course of American Freedom, 1822–1833* (New York, 1981); and *Andrew Jackson and the Course of American Democracy, 1833–1845* (New York, 1984). Jackson's immediate predecessor is the subject of two magisterial volumes by Samuel Flagg Bemis, *John Quincy Adams and the Foundations of American Foreign Policy* (New York, 1949) and *John Quincy Adams and the Union* (New York, 1956). Old Hickory's nimble understudy has also received considerable scholarly study in recent years. See Donald B. Cole, *Martin Van Buren and the American Political System* (Princeton, N.J., 1984), and John Niven, *Martin Van Buren: The Romantic Age of American Politics* (New York, 1983).

The three great opponents of Jackson who never won the Presidency themselves are the subjects of Merrill Peterson, *The Great Triumvirate: Webster, Clay, and Calhoun* (New York, 1987). Each one is also the subject of several independent biographies. For the most recent, see Irving H. Bartlett, *Daniel Webster* (New York, 1978); Maurice G. Baxter, *One and Inseparable: Daniel Webster and the Union* (Cambridge, Mass., 1984); Glyndon G. Van Deusen, *The Life of Henry Clay* (Boston, 1937); Charles M. Wiltse, *John C. Calhoun*, 3 vols. (Indianapolis, 1944–51); and John Niven, *John C. Calhoun and the Price of Union* (Baton Rouge, La., 1988). Equally valuable as a general source for the period is William Nisbet Chambers, *Old Bullion Benton: Senator from the New West* (Boston, 1956).

The Great Body of the People

Basic overviews of the antebellum economy appear in Douglass C. North, *The Economic Growth of the United States, 1790–1860* (Englewood Cliffs, N.J., 1961), and Stuart Bruchey, *The Roots of American Economic Growth, 1607–1861* (New York, 1965), while the transforming impact of new transportation technology appears in George Rogers Taylor, *The Transportation Revolution, 1815–1860* (New York, 1951). Thomas C. Cochran treats the early factory system and its ancillary activities in *Frontiers of Change: Early Industrialism in America* (New York, 1981), while Edward Pessen has described how economic change led to greater inequality in "The Egalitarian Myth and American Social Reality," *American Historical Review* 76 (1971), 989–1034, and in *Riches, Class, and Power Before the Civil War* (Lexington, Mass., 1973).

The notion of a "Market Revolution" that included greater changes than simply the development of new forms of transportation has been central to my understanding of material pressures operating on Jacksonian Americans. Christopher Clark sketched a basis for this concept in "The Household Economy, Market Exchange, and the Rise of Capitalism in the Connecticut Valley, 1800–1860," *Journal of Social History* 13 (1979), 169–90. Supporting information appeared in Percy Wells Bidwell, "Rural Economy in New England at the Beginning of the Nineteenth Century," *Transactions of the Connecticut Academy of Arts and Sciences* 20 (1916), 241–399, and Percy W. Bidwell and John I. Falconer, *History of Agriculture in the Northern United States, 1620–1860* (Washington, D.C., 1925). Robert A. Gross, "Culture and Cultivation," *Journal of American History* 69 (1982), 42–61, and Clarence H. Danhof, *Change in Agriculture* (Cambridge, Mass., 1969), both provide fascinating accounts of the impact of new conditions on Northern rural life.

In the South, market-oriented agriculture was the foremost business of the slave plantation. Lewis C. Gray, *History of Agriculture in the Southern United States to 1860*, 2 vols. (Washington, D.C., 1933) is a fundamental source on this institution, while the literature on slavery itself is now enormous. For thorough yet contrasting accounts, readers may begin with Kenneth M. Stampp, *The Peculiar Institution* (New York, 1956), and Eugene D. Genovese, *Roll, Jordan, Roll* (New York, 1976). Malcolm J. Rohrbough describes the expanding cotton frontier in *The Land Office Business* (New York, 1968). For the differences between Southern plantations and small farms, see Morton Rothstein, "The Antebellum South as a Dual Economy," *Agricultural History* 41 (1967), 373–82; Gavin Wright, *The Political Economy of the Cotton South* (New York, 1978); and the pathbreaking work of Steven Hahn, especially *The Roots of Southern Populism* (New York, 1983). The political relationship between slaveholders and nonslaveholders is the subject of Harry L. Watson, "Conflict and Collaboration: Yeomen, Slaveholders, and Politics in the Antebellum South," *Social History* 10 (1985), 273–98.

An exciting group of labor historians has explored the transition from artisanal to mass-market production in Jacksonian towns and cities, and the resistance of artisans to their resulting loss of status and independence. See David Montgomery, "The Working Classes of the Pre-Industrial American City, 1780–1830," *Labor History* 9 (1968), 3–22; Alan Dawley, *Class and Community: The Industrial Revolution in Lynn* (Cambridge, Mass., 1976); Bruce Laurie, *Working People of Philadelphia* (Philadelphia, 1980); and especially Sean Wilentz, *Chants Democratic: New York City and the Rise of the American Working Class, 1788–1850* (New York, 1984). Thoughtful community studies that examine the rise of factories in the countryside include Anthony F. C. Wallace, *Rockdale* (New York, 1978); Jonathan Prude, *The Coming of the Industrial Order* (Cambridge, 1983); and Thomas Dublin, *Women at Work* (New York, 1979).

The clearest explanation of early-nineteenth-century banking and currency problems appears in Peter Temin, *The Jacksonian Economy* (New York, 1969). Neither Ralph C. H. Catterall, *The Second Bank of the United States* (Chicago, 1902), nor Murray Rothbard, *The Panic of 1819* (New York, 1962), is likely to be superseded. For the South, see Larry Schweikert, *Banking in the American South from the Age of Jackson to Reconstruction* (Baton Rouge, La., 1987). Finally, Morton Horwitz, *The Transformation of American Law, 1780–1860* (Cambridge, Mass., 1977), is a key work for understanding the legal response to the Market Revolution.

Republican Theory and Practice

Intellectual historians have revolutionized the study of American political thought in recent years by elucidating the concept of "republicanism." The best introductions to their writings are two review essays by Robert E. Shalhope: "Toward a Republican Synthesis: The Emergence of an Understanding of Republicanism in American Historiography," *William and Mary Quarterly*, 3rd ser., 29 (1972), 49–80, and "Republicanism and Early American Historiography," *William and Mary Quarterly*, 3rd ser., 39 (April 1982), 334–56. For dissenting views that stress the early importance of American liberalism, see Louis Hartz, *The Liberal Tradition in America* (New York, 1955), and the work of Joyce Appleby, especially *Capitalism and a New Social Order* (New York, 1984).

Changes in the practice of republican government are described in Chilton Williamson, *American Suffrage from Property to Democracy, 1760–1860* (Princeton, N.J., 1960), and Rowland Berthoff, "Independence and Attachment, Virtue and Interest," in Richard Bushman et al., eds., *Uprooted Americans* (Boston, 1979), 97–124. Fletcher M. Green, *Constitutional Development in the South Atlantic States, 1776–1860* (Chapel Hill, N.C., 1930), is an invaluable survey. There is regrettably no equivalent for the Northern and Western states, but Merrill D. Peterson has brought together a revealing set of debates in *Democracy, Liberty, and Property* (Indianapolis, 1966). For the influence of racial and gender stereotypes on republican thinking, see George M. Fredrickson, *The Black Image in the White Mind* (New York, 1971); Ronald T. Takaki, *Iron Cages* (New York, 1979); Reginald Horsman, *Race and Manifest Destiny* (Cambridge, Mass., 1981); Leon Litwack, *North of Slavery* (Chicago, 1961); and Barbara Welter, *Dimity Convictions* (Athens, Ohio, 1976). Reform movements and the evangelical revival are discussed in John L. Thomas, "Romantic Reform in America, 1815–1860," *American Quarterly* 17 (1965), 654–81; Ronald G. Walters, *American Reformers, 1815–1860* (New York, 1978); and Donald G. Mathews, *Religion in the Old South* (Chicago, 1977).

The debate over the place of political parties in a republic appears in Michael Wallace, "Changing Concepts of Party in the United States: New York, 1815–1825," *American Historical Review* 74 (1968), 453–91; Richard Hofstadter, *The Idea of a Party System* (Berkeley, Calif., 1972); and Ralph Ketcham, *Presidents Above Party* (Chapel Hill, N.C., 1984). Ronald P. Formisano describes the long persistence of antiparty ideology in "Political Character, Antipartyism, and the Second Party System," *American Quarterly* (1969), 683–709; "Deferential-Participant Politics," *American Political Science Review* 68 (1974), 473–87; and *The Transformation of Political Culture* (New York, 1983). Norman K. Risjord has described the dissenters from changing republican policies in *The Old Republicans* (New York, 1965), while Glover Moore recounts the crisis that most alarmed these Southerners in *The Missouri Controversy, 1819–1821* (Lexington, Ky., 1953). Richard H. Brown examines the consequences of the Missouri crisis in "The Missouri Crisis, Slavery, and the Politics of Jacksonianism," *South Atlantic Quarterly* 65 (1966), 55–72.

A Corrupt Bargain

The best overview of politics from the War of 1812 through the Monroe Administration is George Dangerfield, *The Era of Good Feelings* (London, 1953). Detailed accounts of Presidential politics of the 1820s appear in the previously cited biographies of the major participants, while William G. Morgan sorts out conflicting charges of corruption in "John Quincy Adams versus Andrew Jackson," *Tennessee Historical Quarterly* 26 (1967), 43–58. For the Adams Administration, see Mary W. M. Hargreaves, *The Presidency of John Quincy Adams* (Lawrence, Kans., 1985). Two works by Robert V. Remini are central to the rise of the Jackson movement: *Martin Van Buren and the Making of the Democratic Party* (New York, 1959) and *The Election of Andrew Jackson* (New York, 1963). John William Ward explores the basis for Andrew Jackson's popular appeal in *Andrew Jackson: Symbol for an Age* (New York, 1962). For all Presidential elections in this period, the essays, documents, and voting returns collected in Arthur M. Schlesinger, Jr., and Fred J. Israel, eds., *History of American Presidential Elections: 1789–1968*, 3 vols. (New York, 1971), are likewise indispensable.

"Our Federal Union. It Must Be Preserved"

Andrew Jackson's White House years are the focus of a fine study by Richard B. Latner, *The Presidency of Andrew Jackson* (Athens, Ga., 1979). Among Jackson's biographers, Remini puts special emphasis on the reform aspects of Jackson's appointment policies, including rotation in office. Leonard D. White wrote the standard account of antebellum government operations in *The Jacksonians* (New York, 1954), while Sidney H. Aronson compared the backgrounds of Jackson's appointees to those of previous Presidents in *Status and Kinship in the Higher Civil Service* (Cambridge, Mass., 1964). Readers with an interest in foreign policy should consult John M. Belohlavek, *Let the Eagle Soar* (Lincoln, Neb., 1985).

Jackson's Indian policy has received increased attention in recent years. Ronald N. Satz, *American Indian Policy in the Jacksonian Era* (Lincoln, Neb., 1975), is a comprehensive survey, while *Fathers and Children* by Michael Paul Rogin (New York, 1975) is a brilliantly suggestive analysis that finally exceeds what the evidence will bear. Francis Paul Prucha defends the removal policy in "Andrew Jackson's Indian Policy: A Reassessment," *Journal of American History* 56 (1969), 527–39, as does Robert V. Remini, though with greater even-handedness. See his *The Legacy of Andrew Jackson* (Baton Rouge, La., 1988). For the Indians themselves, see Ralph S. Cotterill, *The Southern Indians* (Norman, Okla., 1954); Grant Forman, *Indian Removal* (Norman, Okla., 1953); William G. McLoughlin, *Cherokee Renascence in the New Republic* (Princeton, N.J., 1986); and Michael D. Green, *The Politics of Indian Removal* (Lincoln, Neb., 1982).

The nullification episode is the subject of two excellent monographs: William W. Freehling, *Prelude to Civil War* (New York, 1966), and Richard E. Ellis, *The Union at Risk* (New York, 1987). Several scholars have tackled the unique political culture of South Carolina; the most comprehensive analysis can be drawn from Kenneth S. Greenberg, *Masters and Statesmen* (Baltimore, 1985). The resolution of the controversy is the subject of Merrill D. Peterson, *Olive Branch and Sword* (Baton Rouge, La., 1981). For insight on a problem with relevance to both Indian removal and nullification, see Daniel Feller, *The Public Lands in Jacksonian Politics* (Madison, Wis., 1984).

Killing the Monster

Carter Goodrich discusses the Maysville veto and the policy of state assistance to the transportation revolution in *Government Promotion of American Canals and Railroads, 1800–1890* (New York, 1960). For Jackson's response, see Carlton Jackson, "The Internal Improvement Vetoes of Andrew Jackson," *Tennessee Historical Quarterly* 25 (1966), 261–79, in addition to the biographies and monographs already cited.

The Bank War has attracted the attention of numerous scholars. Bray Hammond examined it from an entrepreneurial perspective in his monumental *Banks and Politics from the Revolution to the Civil War* (Princeton, N.J., 1957). By contrast, Robert V. Remini's *Andrew Jackson and the Bank War* (New York, 1967) pointed to the Bank's threat to democratic government. Jean Alexander Wilburn described the B.U.S. itself in *Biddle's Bank: The Crucial Years* (New York, 1967), and John J. McFaul treated the reaction of state banks in *The Politics of Jacksonian Finance* (Ithaca, N.Y., 1972). Peter Temin's *The Jacksonian Economy* (already cited) minimized the economic impact of the Bank War, but Richard H. Timberlake, Jr., "The Specie Circular and Distribution of the Surplus," *Journal of Political Economy* 68 (1980), 109–17, suggests that the Specie Circular may indeed have touched off the Panic of 1837.

National Parties and Local Politics

State-level studies of Jacksonian politics are voluminous; readers should consult specialized bibliographies for states not covered in detail here. For western New York, however, Whitney R. Cross, *The Burned-Over District* (Ithaca, N.Y., 1950), is crucial, as are Paul E. Johnson, *A Shopkeeper's Millennium* (New York, 1978), and Mary P. Ryan, *Cradle of the Middle Class* (Cambridge, England, and New York, 1981). For Anti-Masonry, see Michael F. Holt, "The Anti-Masonic and Know Nothing Parties," in Arthur M. Schlesinger, Jr., ed., *History of U.S. Political Parties*, 4 vols. (New York, 1973), I, 629–36, and the articles of Kathleen Smith Kutolowski: "Antimasonry Reexamined," *Journal of American History* 71 (1984), 269–93; "Freemasonry and Community in the Early Republic," *American Quarterly* 34 (Winter 1982), 543–61; and (coauthored with Ronald P. Formisano) "Antimasonry and Masonry: The Genesis of Protest, 1826–1827," *American Quarterly* 39 (1977), 139–65. Paul Goodman's *Towards a Christian Republic*

(New York, 1988) is an excellent study of the "blessed spirit" in New England.

Sean Wilentz's previously cited *Chants Democratic* is the outstanding study of working-class politics and culture in Jacksonian New York City. Other important works include Amy Bridges, *A City in the Republic* (New York, 1984); Walter Hugins, *Jacksonian Democracy and the Working Class* (Stanford, Calif., 1960); Edward Pessen, *Most Uncommon Jacksonians* (New York, 1967); and Jerome Mushkat, *Tammany* (Syracuse, N.Y., 1971).

Several studies of states not discussed in detail here were nevertheless important inspirations for this book. Foremost among these are W. Mills Thornton III, *Politics and Power in a Slave Society: Alabama, 1800–1860* (Baton Rouge, La., 1978), and James Rogers Sharp, *Jacksonians versus the Banks* (New York, 1970). Marc W. Kruman, *Parties and Politics in North Carolina, 1836–1865* (Baton Rouge, La., 1983), is likewise a key state study. A subtle and perceptive analysis of individual voter preferences appears in Paul Goodman, "The Social Basis of New England Politics in Jacksonian America," *Journal of the Early Republic* 6 (Spring 1986), 23–56. Shifting political alignments in Jackson's home state (and among his earliest backers) appear in Charles Grier Sellers, Jr., "Banking and Politics in Jackson's Tennessee, 1817–1827," *Mississippi Valley Historical Review* 41 (1954), 61–84, and, by the same author, "Jackson Men with Feet of Clay," *American Historical Review* 62 (1957), 537–51. For my own exploration of social tension and political change in a local setting, see Harry L. Watson, *Jacksonian Politics and Community Conflict* (Baton Rouge, La., 1981).

Van Buren, Harrison, and Tyler

In addition to the full-scale biographies already cited, there are two modern studies of Van Buren's term as President: Major L. Wilson, *The Presidency of Martin Van Buren* (Lawrence, Kans., 1984), and James C. Curtis, *The Fox at Bay* (Lexington, Ky., 1970). Economic difficulties are treated in Reginald C. McGrane, *The Panic of 1837* (Chicago, 1924), while the growing importance of the slavery issue appears in William J. Cooper, Jr., *The South and the Politics of Slavery, 1828–1856* (Baton Rouge, La., 1978).

William Henry Harrison is the subject of *Old Tippecanoe* by Freeman Cleaves (New York, 1939). His successful quest for the Presidency is covered by Robert Gray Gunderson in *The Log Cabin Campaign* (Lexington, Ky., 1957). Other important treatments of this crucial election are William Nisbet Chambers, "The Election of 1840," in the previously cited Schlesinger and Israel, eds., *History of American Presidential Elections*, I, 643–744; Michael F. Holt, "The Election of 1840, Voter Mobilization, and the Emergence of Jacksonian Voting Behavior," in William J. Cooper, Jr., et al., eds., *A*

Master's Due (Baton Rouge, La., 1985), 16–58; and Richard Carwardine, "Evangelicals, Whigs, and the Election of William Henry Harrison," *Journal of American Studies* 17 (1983), 47–75. A. B. Norton, comp., *The Great Revolution of 1840* (Mount Vernon, Ohio, 1888), is a superb collection of Whig campaign oratory. W. J. Rorabaugh traces the history of hard cider in *The Alcoholic Republic* (New York, 1979). For the Tyler Administration, readers should consult Oliver Perry Chitwood, *John Tyler: Champion of the Old South* (New York, 1939). Clay's defiance of Tyler and efforts to govern despite White House opposition are the subjects of George Rawlins Poage, *Henry Clay and the Whig Party* (Chapel Hill, N.C., 1936). William R. Brock exposes the weakness of late Jacksonian politics in *Parties and Political Conscience* (Millwood, N.Y., 1979).

The Second American Party System

The concept of a series of American "party systems" appears in William Nisbet Chambers and Walter Dean Burnham, eds., *The American Party Systems* (New York, 1967). Applying the term to Jacksonian politics, Richard P. McCormick's *The Second American Party System* (Chapel Hill, N.C., 1966) is an exhaustive state-by-state catalogue of political organizing efforts. McCormick also showed the important role of party organizations in boosting voter turnout in "New Perspectives on Jacksonian Politics," *American Historical Review* 65 (1960), 288–301, an insight followed up by William Nisbet Chambers and Phillip C. Davis, "Party, Competition, and Mass Participation," in Joel H. Silbey et al., eds., *The History of American Electoral Behavior* (Princeton, N.J., 1978). The most comprehensive survey of the second party system's basic structures is now William G. Shade, "Political Pluralism and Party Development," in Paul Kleppner et al., eds., *The Evolution of American Electoral Systems* (Westport, Conn., 1981), 77–112.

Partisan behavior in Congress is the subject of Thomas B. Alexander, *Sectional Stress and Party Strength* (Nashville, Tenn., 1967), and Joel H. Silbey, *The Shrine of Party* (Pittsburgh, 1967). Herbert Ershkowitz and William G. Shade reported similar findings at the state level in "Consensus or Conflict? Political Behavior in State Legislatures During the Jacksonian Era," *Journal of American History* 58 (1971), 591–621. Edward Pessen documents the superior wealth of urban political leaders in "Who Governed the Nation's Cities in the 'Era of the Common Man'?", *Political Science Quarterly* 87 (1972), 591–614, while two books by Ralph A. Wooster make the same case for the South: *The People in Power* (Knoxville, Tenn., 1969) and *Politicians, Planters, and Plain Folk* (Knoxville, Tenn., 1975). The connection between Whiggery and urban wealth is documented by Frank Otto Gattell, "Money and Party in Jacksonian America, *Political Science Quarterly*

82 (1967), 235–52, and Robert Rich, "A Wilderness of Whigs," *Journal of Social History* 4 (1971), 263–76. Richard P. McCormick demonstrated that the two parties could not have drawn exclusively from one economic class or another in "Suffrage Classes and Party Alignments," *Mississippi Valley Historical Review* 46 (1959), 397–410, but Thomas B. Alexander and his students showed a broader relationship between market involvement and party choice in "The Basis of Alabama's Ante-Bellum Two-party System," *The Alabama Review*, 19 (1966), 243–76.

Lee Benson introduced the "ethnocultural" analysis of Jacksonian politics in *The Concept of Jacksonian Democracy* (Princeton, N.J., 1961). His student Ronald P. Formisano amplified it in *The Birth of Mass Political Parties* (Princeton, N.J., 1971), and Robert Kelley has offered a general survey in *The Cultural Pattern of American Politics* (New York, 1979). For a balanced critique, see Richard L. McCormick, "Ethno-Cultural Interpretations of Nineteenth-Century American Voting Behavior," *Political Science Quarterly* 89 (1974), 351–77.

John Ashworth has written an excellent analysis of opposing party beliefs in *"Agrarians and Aristocrats"* (London, 1983), while Lawrence Kohl probes the psychological dimension of party convictions in *The Politics of Individualism* (New York, 1989). Further valuable studies of political thought include Rush Welter, *The Mind of America, 1830–1860* (New York, 1975), and Major L. Wilson, *Space, Time, and Freedom* (Westport, Conn., 1974). Whig party beliefs are described in Glyndon G. Van Deusen, "Some Aspects of Whig Thought and Theory in the Jacksonian Period," *American Historical Review* 63 (1958), 305–33; Daniel Walker Howe, *The Political Culture of the American Whigs* (Chicago, 1979); and Thomas Brown, *Politics and Statesmanship* (New York, 1985). For the Democrats, see Marvin Meyers, *The Jacksonian Persuasion* (Stanford, Calif., 1957), and Jean H. Baker, *Affairs of Party* (Ithaca, N.Y., 1983).

William W. Freehling explains the contrast between Calhoun and the Jacksonian political mainstream in "Spoilsmen and Interests in the Thought and Career of John C. Calhoun," *Journal of American History* 52 (1965), 25–42. Richard L. McCormick discusses the parties' embrace of "pork barrel" politics in "The Party Period and Public Policy," *Journal of American History* 66 (1979), 279–98, while Michael F. Holt explores the aftermath of Jacksonian politics in *The Political Crisis of the 1850s* (New York, 1978).

Index